IS AMERICA D

C000151607

15/14

IS AMERICA DIFFERENT?

A New Look at
American Exceptionalism

Edited by

BYRON E. SHAFER

CLARENDON PRESS · OXFORD
1991

Oxford University Press, Walton Street, Oxford OX2 6DP
Oxford New York Toronto
Delhi Bombay Calcutta Madras Karachi
Petaling Jaya Singapore Hong Kong Tokyo
Nairobi Dar es salaam Cape Town
Melbourne Auckland
and associated companies in
Berlin Ibadan

Oxford is a trade mark of Oxford University Press

Published in the United States
by Oxford University Press New York

British Library Cataloguing in Publicaton Data
Data available
ISBN 0–19–827734–2

Library of Congress Cataloging-in-Publication Data
Is America different?: a new look at American exceptionalism/edited
by Byron E. Shafer.
p. cm.
Includes bibliographical references and index.
1. National characteristics, American. 2. United States-Civilization.
I. Shafer, Byron E.
E169.1.I79 1991 973—dc20 90-19691
ISBN 0–19–827734–2

Typeset by Spantech Publishers Pvt Ltd, New Delhi 110060
Printed in Great Britain by
Bookcraft (Bath) Ltd, Midsomer Norton, Avon

Preface

'American exceptionalism', summarized, is the notion that the United States was created differently, developed differently, and thus has to be *understood* differently—essentially on its own terms and within its own context. 'Exceptionalism' has, in truth, joined that handful of concepts which attempt to characterize a society as a whole, and this fact alone surely gives arguments involving the concept—arguments over the essential elements of distinctiveness in Japanese society, or French society, or that of any other chosen country—a certain intellectual intensity. Yet in the beginning, there was *American* exceptionalism, and because the notion crystallized there first, and especially because the phenomena connected with it offered an apparently inescapable challenge to broad descriptions of societal developments elsewhere, it has been the American version which has proved most able to stimulate continuing debate.

As is often the case, the notions underlying a putative American exceptionalism—a sense of critical distinctiveness in political, economic, religious, or cultural life—predated the creation of a summarizing term.[1] Nevertheless, when that term was ultimately created, to assemble and highlight the existing alleged elements of the American difference, its creation appeared only to fuel the argument—from the convinced and the sceptical, the foreign and the domestic, even the admiring and the denigrating—about the precise critical elements of a distinctively American model, and about their continuing reality. While such arguments have ranged remarkably broadly, over several centuries of American history, there do appear to be three main strands within them, or at least three main uses of the notion of 'American exceptionalism'.

The first of these concerns simple distinctiveness. What are the elements of American life which deserve to be dubbed exceptional, in the dictionary sense of being clearly and recognizably different from life elsewhere? This use of the term has the obvious advantage of providing a focus for thought about the society in question. It has the additional advantage of encouraging careful consideration and

---

[1] This frequent occurrence is richly analysed in Robert K. Merton, 'On the History and Systematics of Sociological Theory', in Merton, *Social Theory and Social Structure*, enl. edn. (New York: The Free Press, 1968), 1–38.

precise description—a particular kind of comparative defence—of the items selected within that focus. Yet the notion also has the vices of its virtues. Indeed, the key analytic fact about this approach to American exceptionalism is that it does not necessarily make the *American* element consequential. There will, of course, be pieces of American society, or surely combinations of those pieces, which are peculiarly American. How could it be otherwise? Yet the same can be said for many—indeed, any—societies. Said differently, the problem is that all societies, observed closely enough, are distinctive, while all societies, observed with sufficient distance, are simultaneously similar.

For some purposes, this inherent dilemma in the definitional approach to exceptionalism is really not a dilemma at all. In an era when the United States can still lay claim to being the leading economic power on earth, for example, and when it is increasingly the first of only two great military powers as well, the precise contents of any American exceptionalism, even by just this dictionary definition, are more consequential than those which define, say, the Zimbabwean equivalent. Zimbabwean exceptionalism is equally real; American exceptionalism is just more consequential in certain key respects. Yet notions of a putative American exceptionalism—or at least the elements of those notions which have sustained an argument—have always implied more than individual distinction. For much of the life of the concept, in fact, it has, quite explicitly, claimed much more. The character of these implications and claims, in turn, is central to the second main approach to the use of the notion.

Again, at its most fundamental, this second approach revolves around the assertion that there is a general model of societal progression for the developed nations of the world—and the United States does not fit this model. Over time, two distinct branches of this argument have appeared. Initially, there was the more positive, even self-congratulatory branch, arguing that American exceptionalism was an important addition to the human possibility. The ability of the nation to create itself—and the right of the individual within it to do the same—was to be the crucial, diagnostic, American contribution. Much later, there appeared a more questioning, even pejorative branch of the same argument, suggesting that the American experience was inherently unilluminating about the fate of other nations. In this, American exceptionalism was at best a sideshow on the way to societal convergence, at worst an obstacle to that (desired) end.

The first branch of this argument, present almost from the founding of those colonies which were to become the United States, involved the aspirations of a new land to escape the institutionalized vices of the old. This was the version of the new America as a potential 'City on a Hill', a vision articulated by John Winthrop, Governor of the Massachusetts Bay Colony, as early as 1630. When the underlying argument, about a general model of development and the deviance of the American case, was eventually codified under the term 'American exceptionalism', however, it acquired a much more problematic loading. Almost three centuries after Winthrop, American Marxists, in embracing an alleged central dynamic of history while acknowledging that the United States differed from the European societies from which Marx had abstracted that dynamic, simply accepted this difference, argued that it would require a different route to the same ultimate destination, and defended that route by noting that it was necessarily 'exceptional'.

Both these variants of the second main strand in approaches to American exceptionalism, like the definitional approach of the first main strand, have inherent intellectual virtues—and even more serious analytic faults. Each variant does at least move the argument about alleged American exceptionalism away from the merely particularistic and towards patterns—and their violation. Each also contains a stronger if still implicit focus, upon those elements of the American experience which really are different from international patterns, rather than being distinctive solely by virtue of an idiosyncratic combination. Yet both suffer, perhaps fatally in the perspective of our time, from the apparent disappearance of their hypothesized general model (from which the United States was said, so essentially, to deviate) and even, complementarily, from the dilution of the alleged sole and distinctive base of difference.

Thus from one side, the argument for a single, general model from which the United States could deviate has been effectively demolished. The lesser contribution to this demolition came from the failure of the Marxist argument to predict the evolution of the *entire* developed world, of Western Europe and not just of the United States. But the second and more consequential contribution comes from the growth— and apparently growing diversity—of the real world of nations in our time. Even restricting the count to the developed nations alone, the argument has been undermined by the spread of such nations beyond Western Europe and North America, to Japan and South-East Asia as well. From the other side, the maturing of the American republic has made a new and virgin land a decreasingly useful metaphor. Again, the preponderance of nations are newer, less fixed in their evolutionary prospects, and even in many cases less explored. Simultaneously, the bases upon which America *might* be exceptional have actually grown, from newness and a 'fresh start' to the many other, more specific aspects of society in this 'first new nation'[2]—almost all of which have occasionally served as grounds for an argument about 'exceptionalism'.

Both dilutions, of the plausible reality of an external general model and of the focused character of any alleged internal deviation, have made the second main strand in thinking about American exceptionalism increasingly difficult to employ. What has kept the concept alive as a category, then, and what has maintained its vigour as a source of potential argument, is really the third main strand. This is the one which has organized most of the work relevant to the topic in our time; it is also the one which categorizes the essays in this volume. This third strand can perhaps best be described as an effort to highlight distinctively American *clusters* of characteristics, even distinctively American ways of organizing the major *realms* of social life. Such an approach aspires to be more than a focus on individual peculiarities; it accepts the need to be less than a summary of world-wide patterns and their violation.

Said differently, this approach to American exceptionalism looks for peculiarly American approaches to major social sectors—to government, to the economy, to culture, to religion, to education, and to public policy, as we have isolated them in this volume—and to their interaction in the larger society around them. Such an approach has the advantage of bringing a grander focus than 'details producing uniqueness'. It has the advantage at the same time of not requiring some grand and general model by which the *rest* of the world will progress. In essence, it searches for 'the American model', different from other nations in some larger regards, without implying that those other nations follow some single alternative. Such an approach, like its predecessors, also has its own inherent difficulties. By setting out self-consciously to exist between the levels of individual peculiarity and of international abstraction, it can always be accused of drifting one way or the other— so that it must always remain self-conscious about its level of analysis.

Despite that, this third main approach holds out the promise of using American exceptionalism in theoretically fruitful ways, both to analyse a particular society in larger, composite terms and to isolate the elements

---

[2] The phrase belongs, of course, to the author of the overview essay to this volume, Seymour Martin Lipset, in Lipset, *The First New Nation: The United States in Historical and Comparative Perspective* (New York: Basic Books, 1963).

of distinctiveness in that analysis, while not pre-ordaining the outcome of this effort at investigation and interpretation. Which is to say: This third approach to American exceptionalism also permits the essential counter-argument—that the realm in question really is not exceptional. If you find the right societies, you will see that the United States is not different; if you find the proper period, then when the United States enters that period, it will look just the same—or alternatively, when nation X does so, it will look like the United States.

In any case, it is not just this approach but this spirit which animates the essays in this volume. They, of course, have an evolution of their own, though one which is hardly as extended and surely not 'exceptional'. While most essays were later extensively revised, they began as contributions to a conference on the fate of American exceptionalism. It was my colleague, Laurence Whitehead, who suggested that American exceptionalism possessed all of the essential elements for a successful Anglo-American conference at Nuffield College in Oxford, to celebrate, in part, the emergence of a focus on American studies there. The topic, he argued, was intrinsically fascinating; it was large and provocative; it was inherently receptive to different approaches, from a range of disciplines.

Early indications were that he was correct, at least in the sense that it proved remarkably easy to get relevant scholars to assemble *and argue about* the dimensions—and utility—of the notion of American exceptionalism, especially in the late twentieth century. We had already decided to make a serious effort to cover the sectors of American society which form the subdivisions of this book, but otherwise not to define approaches or even themes any more specifically. The title for the conference, 'American Exceptionalism—a Return and Reassessment', did contain an implicit subtheme, the question of whether, in returning to an established debate, there was still a specifically American exceptionalism worthy of consideration and, if there was, whether its elements had shifted in consequential ways. Beyond that, we accepted the fact that these particular participants/ essayists were unlikely to be led away from their own views on the essence of the central phenomenon by any efforts at prior definition.

The conference, then, devoted three days of discussion, and sometimes debate, to the allegedly central elements of the American experience, and to whether these formed a larger, specifically American model. To foster that exchange, we arranged for a keynote paper to introduce the subject through a broad overview (from Seymour Martin

Lipset), and for central papers on the major realms of government (from Daniel Bell), economics (Peter Temin), religion (Andrew Greeley), culture (Aaron Wildavsky), education (Martin Trow), and public policy (Richard Rose). These are the papers which, with one exception, comprise this volume. We also arranged for a designated respondent who would contribute a short, considered riposte to the main paper— from Richard Hodder-Williams on government, Howard Temperley on economics, Richard Carwardine on religion, Steven Fender on culture, Anthony Heath on education, and Jim Sharpe on public policy. A volume containing only the principal conference papers cannot possibly suggest how stimulating these targeted responses were for subsequent discussion, and while I have made some further use of them in my final, integrating essay, their authors remain sadly undercelebrated here.

In any case, the book which follows from this conference was much more substantially shaped by its debates, I suspect, than are most which can be described in similar terms. At least, participants will know how extensively several of these essays have changed in the interim—a change due in every case to ideas, even themes, raised at the conference itself. Two of these larger themes deserve special mention. The first concerns a society with what might best be described as 'populist' values at the personal level, complemented by an institutional structure which emphasizes direct public access and participation and which denigrates and limits the role of intermediaries. The other concerns a society featuring manifestations of 'individualism' in nearly every realm, brought back together in what might best be called 'market arrangements' or 'market solutions', if those terms are understood in a broad and metaphorical sense. I have tried my hand at making these themes explicit in the closing essay of this book, and I have urged individual authors, in revision, to turn their own hands to them. But their versions are, once again, purely their own, and they should not be characterized through mine.

Inevitably, a crucial cast of additional supporting figures made both conference and book possible. Michael Brock, then Warden of Nuffield College and a person deeply concerned with the decline of that external perspective on the USA which the UK has so often historically offered, encouraged the entire project from the start. Nicol Rae, then at Nuffield College and now at Florida International University (and surely as close to a true 'Anglo-American' as any one person could be), managed the full array of logistics of the conference with a grace and intelligence which the term 'logistics' cannot hope to capture. Anthony Jarvis, Jeffrey

Pentland, and Maureen Mancuso—all possessors of the sharp eye which comes from being inside and outside the same tradition simultaneously—provided crucial supporting services during the conference itself. Afterwards, Henry Hardy welcomed the project to Oxford University Press, and our wide-ranging conversations since then have helped the project enormously. Janet Moth then managed the project to completion. All, obviously, have contributed toward this new look at the fate of American exceptionalism.

Oxford   B. E. S.
11 May 1990

Contents

Figures

Tables

Contributors

Daniel Bell, Harvard University
Andrew M. Greeley, University of Arizona and NORC
Seymour Martin Lipset, Stanford University
Richard Rose, University of Strathclyde
Byron E. Shafer, Oxford University
Peter Temin, Massachusetts Institute of Technology
Martin Trow, University of California
Aaron Wildavsky, University of California

1

American Exceptionalism Reaffirmed

Seymour Martin Lipset

The topic which concerns us, American exceptionalism (the phrase is Tocqueville's), could only have arisen in a comparative context.[1] It basically means that America is unique, is different in crucial ways from most other countries. It has been argued by many that the United States has stood out as distinct from other Western countries, in Europe and the Americas, including, as I have tried to document in detail, Canada.[2] In dealing with national characteristics it is important to recognize that comparative evaluations are never absolutes, that they always are made in terms of more or less. The statement that the United States is an egalitarian society obviously does not imply that all Americans are equal in any way that can be defined. This generalization usually means, regardless of which aspect is under consideration (social relations, status, mobility, income distribution, etc.), that the United States is more egalitarian than Europe.

Comparative judgements affect all generalizations about societies. This is such an obvious, commonsensical truism that it seems almost foolish to enunciate it. I only do so because statements about America or other countries are frequently challenged on the ground that they are not absolutely true. Generalizations may even invert when the unit of comparison changes. For example, Canada looks different when compared to the United States from when contrasted to Britain.[3] Figuratively, on a scale of zero to one hundred, with the United States close to zero

[1] Alexis de Tocqueville, *Democracy in America* (New York: Alfred A. Knopf, 1948), ii. 36–7.
[2] S. M. Lipset, *The First New Nation: The United States in Historical and Comparative Perspective* (New York: W. W. Norton, 1979); *Revolution and Counterrevolution* (New Brunswick, NJ: Transaction Books, revised edn. 1988), 37–75; 'Canada and the U.S.: The Cultural Dimension', in Charles F. Doran and John H. Sigler, eds., *Canada and the United States: Enduring Friendship, Persistent Stress* (Englewood Cliffs, NJ and Scarborough, Ontario: Prentice-Hall, 1985), 109–60; and *Continental Divide: The Institutions and Values of the United States and Canada* (New York: Routledge, 1990).
[3] See Lipset, *The First New Nation*, pp. 249–52, 257–9.

on a given trait and Britain at one hundred, Canada would fall around thirty. Thus, when Canada is evaluated by reference to the United States, it appears as more élitist, law-abiding, and statist, but when considering the variations between Canada and Britain, Canada looks more anti-statist, violent, and egalitarian.

The term 'American exceptionalism' became widely applied in the context of efforts to account for the weakness of working-class radicalism in the United States. The issue gave rise to debates within the Communist movement in meetings of Comintern bodies in the 1920s, in particular between the leaders of the American and Soviet sections, the then-secretaries of the two parties, Jay Lovestone and Josef Stalin.[4] Lovestone, pointing to the weakness of American radicalism, both communist and socialist, insisted that the United States was qualitatively different from other capitalist countries. Consequently, the tactics, analyses, and policies which the communist movement developed for industrialized nations in general would not hold for America. Given a unique polity and culture, it was necessary to use different tactics and strategies. Stalin could not accept this line of argument, not only on theoretical grounds—Marxist principles must apply everywhere—but because the logic for a world party controlled from a single centre, Moscow, would not hold if America was acknowledged as qualitatively different. Stalin and the Communist International not only rejected Lovestone's line, they saw to it that he was removed as American party leader and then expelled. American exceptionalism was proclaimed a Marxist heresy.[5]

The major issue subsumed in the concept became: why is the United States the only industrialized country which does not have a significant socialist movement or labour party? That question has bedevilled socialist theorists since the late nineteenth century. Engels tried to answer it in the last decade of his life.[6] The German socialist and sociologist Werner Sombart dealt with it in a major book published in his native language in 1906, *Why is There No Socialism in the United States?*[7]

[4] See S. M. Lipset, 'Why No Socialism in the United States?', in S. Bialer and S. Sluzar, eds., *Sources of Contemporary Radicalism* (Boulder, Colo.: Westview Press, 1977), 64–6, 105–8. See also Theodore Draper, *The Roots of American Communism* (New York: Viking Press, 1957), 247–8, 256, 266; Draper, *American Communism and Soviet Russia: The Formative Period* (New York: Viking Press, 1960), 269–72.

[5] Lipset, 'Why No Socialism?', pp. 65–6.

[6] See 'Unpublished Letters of Karl Marx and Friedrich Engels to Americans', *Science and Society*, 2 (1938), 368, 375; Marx and Engels, *Letters to Americans* (New York: International Publishers Co., 1953), 239; Marx and Engels, *Selected Correspondence, 1846–1895* (New York: International Publishers, 1942), 449.

[7] Werner Sombart, *Why is There No Socialism in the United States?* (White Plains, N.Y.: International Arts & Sciences Press, 1976).

H. G. Wells, then a Fabian, also addressed the issue in the same year, in *The Future in America*.[8] Both Lenin and Trotsky were deeply concerned, for the logic of Marxism, the proposition expressed by Marx in *Das Kapital* that 'the more developed country shows the less developed the image of their future', implied to Marxists prior to the Russian Revolution that the United States, which had the most developed capitalist economy, would be the first socialist country.[9]

The question is still with us today. Since some object to an effort to explain a negative, a vacancy, the query may of course be reversed to ask, why has America been the most classically liberal polity in the world from its founding to the present? Although the United States remains the wealthiest large industrialized nation, it devotes less of its income to welfare and the state is less involved in the economy than others in its class. It not only does not have a viable, class-conscious, radical political movement, but its trade unions, which always have been weaker than those of almost all other industrial countries, have been steadily declining since the mid-1950s. Less than one-sixth, about 15–16 per cent, of the American employed labour force belong to unions, down from one-third in 1955, a smaller proportion than labour organizations elsewhere in the developed world.

The comparison with Canada is particularly striking. The northern country has a structurally comparable, though of course much smaller economy than the United States. Its trade union movement currently encompasses close to two-fifths of all employed people, and its socialist movement, the New Democratic party (NDP), received 20 per cent of the vote in the 1988 national election, and elected a legislative majority in Ontario, the country's wealthiest province, in September 1990.[10] It has been the government in four provinces and the official opposition in others. The Parti Quebecois, a social democratic party, has played these roles in Quebec for well over a decade. Opinion polls gathered in both countries in the early 1980s show Canadians significantly more willing than Americans to identify with a social class, and working-class identifiers are proportionately much stronger in the north. These variations within North America, in two countries which are perceived by outsiders as very similar (anglophone Canada in particular), not only

[8] H. G. Wells, *The Future in America* (New York: Harper and Brothers, 1906).

[9] Karl Marx, *Capital*, i (Moscow: Foreign Languages Publishing House, 1958), 8–9.

[10] S. M. Lipset, 'Anti-Incumbency in Canada, Too', *The American Enterprise*, 1 (November–December 1990), 22–3; Thomas S. Axworthy, 'Left Turn in Canada?' *Public Opinion*, 10 (Sept.–Oct. 1987), 52–4; S. M. Lipset, 'Labor and Socialism in Canada and the United States', Larry Sefton Memorial Lecture (Woodsworth College, University of Toronto, 1990).

suggest that they differ significantly, but revive the issues of why socialism, trade unionism, and class consciousness are weak in the United States.

An emphasis on American uniqueness raises the obvious question of 'different from what?' There is a large literature on the subject dating back at least to the eighteenth century—it goes back earlier in terms of utopias supposedly located in America—trying to specify the special character of the United States in political and social terms. One of the most interesting, often overlooked, is Edmund Burke's speech to the House of Commons proposing reconciliation with the colonies, in which he sought to explain to his fellow Members what the revolutionary Americans were like.[11] He noted that they were different culturally, that they were not simply transplanted Englishmen. He particularly emphasized religion, a point on which I will elaborate. Crevecœur, in his famous book, *Letters from an American Farmer*, written in the late eighteenth century, explicitly raised the question 'what is an American?' He emphasized that the Americans behaved differently in their social relations, were much more egalitarian than other nationalities, that their 'dictionary' was 'short in words of dignity, and names of honor', that is, in terms through which the lower strata expressed their subservience to the higher.[12] Tocqueville, who agreed about religion and egalitarianism, also stressed individualism, as distinct from the emphasis on 'group ties' which marked Europe.[13]

These commentaries have been followed by a myriad—thousands upon thousands—of books and articles by foreign travellers. The overwhelming majority are by educated Europeans. These writings are fruitful because they are comparative; those who wrote them emphasized cross-national variations in behaviour and institutions.[14] Tocqueville's

[11] Edmund Burke, *Selected Works* (Oxford: Clarendon Press, 1904), 180–1.

[12] J. Hector St. John Crevecœur, *Letters from an American Farmer* (New York: Dolphin Books, n.d.), 46–7.

[13] Tocqueville, *Democracy*, ii. 104, 113, 129–35.

[14] Max Berger, *The British Traveller in America, 1836–1860* (New York: Columbia University Press, 1943); Oscar Handlin, ed., *This Was America* (Cambridge, Mass.: Harvard University Press, 1949); Henry Steele Commager, *America in Perspective* (New York: Random House, 1947); J. G. Brooks, *As Others See Us* (New York: Macmillan, 1908); Jane L. Mesick, *The English Traveller in America, 1785–1835* (New York: Columbia University Press, 1922); Robert W. Smuts, *European Impressions of the American Worker* (New York: King's Crown Press, 1953); Frances Trollope, *Domestic Manners of the Americans* (London: Whitaker, Treacher, 1832); Anthony Trollope, *North America* (New York: Alfred A. Knopf, 1951); James Bryce, *The American Commonwealth* (New York: Macmillan, 1912); and Lipset, *The First New Nation*, pp. 101–37.

Democracy, of course, is the best known. He once noted that he never wrote anything about the United States without thinking of France. As he put it, in speaking of his need to contrast the same institutions and behaviour in both countries, 'without comparisons to make, the mind doesn't know how to proceed'.[15] Harriet Martineau, an English contemporary, also wrote a first-rate book.[16] Frederick Engels and Max Weber were among the contributors to the literature. There is a fairly systematic and similar logic in many of the interpretations.

Beyond the analysis of variations between the United States and Europe, various other comparisons have been fruitful. In previous writings I have suggested that one of the best ways to specify American traits is by contrast with Canada.[17] There is a considerable comparative North American literature, almost entirely written by Canadians. They have a great advantage over Americans, since while very few of the latter study their northern neighbour, it is impossible to be a literate Canadian without knowing almost as much as most Americans, if not more, about the United States. Almost every Canadian work on a given subject (the city, religion, the family, trade unions, etc.) contains a great deal about the United States. Many Canadians seek to explain their own country by dealing with differences or similarities south of the border. Specifying and analysing variations among the predominantly English-speaking countries, Australia, Canada, Great Britain, New Zealand, and the United States, is also useful, precisely because the differences among them generally are smaller than between each and non-anglophone societies.[18] Andrew Greeley notes this in his chapter on religion; I have tried to analyse them in *The First New Nation*.[19] The logic of studying societies which have major elements in common was also followed by Louis Hartz in treating the overseas settler societies, United States, Canada, Latin America, Australia, and also South Africa, as units for comparison.[20] Fruitful comparisons have been made between Latin America and anglophone North America, which shed light on each.

[15] Cited in George Wilson Pierson, *Tocqueville in America* (Gloucester: Peter Smith, 1969), 271.
[16] Harriet Martineau, *Society in America* (New Brunswick, NJ: Transaction Books, 1981).
[17] Lipset, *Continental Divide*; S. M. Lipset, 'Historical Traditions and National Characteristics: A Comparative Analysis of Canada and the United States', *Canadian Journal of Sociology*, 11 (Summer 1986), 113–55.
[18] S. M. Lipset, 'Anglo-American Society', in David Sills, ed., *International Encyclopaedia of the Social Sciences* (New York: Macmillan, 1968), i. 289–302.
[19] Lipset, *The First New Nation*, pp. 248–73.
[20] Louis Hartz, *The Founding of New Societies* (New York: Harcourt, Brace and World, 1964).

Some Latin Americans have argued that there are major common elements in the Americas which show up in contrasts with Europe. Fernando Cardozo, a distinguished sociologist and Brazilian political leader, once reported in a conversation that he and his friends—who were activists in the underground left—consciously decided not to found a socialist party as the dictatorship, the military regime, was breaking down. They formed a populist party because, as they read the evidence, class-conscious socialism does not appeal in the Americas. Chile apart, New World left parties from Argentina to the United States (Canada is debatable) are populist. They resemble the American Democrats more than European socialists. Cardozo has suggested that consciousness of social class is less salient throughout most of the Americas than in post-feudal Europe. I do not want to take on the issue of whether the Americas as a whole are exceptional; dealing with the United States (and Canada) is more than enough.

Why No Socialism

The failure of socialist parties in the United States has been explained by numerous factors, so many that the outcome seems overdetermined. These include: the material environment and economic wealth (as Sombart argued, 'all Socialist utopias came to nothing on roast beef and apple pie');[21] political variables, as with the way the American constitution and electoral systems operate to inhibit, if not prevent, third parties; social structural factors particularly the egalitarian elements in the class structure; and values, the special anti-statist and populist beliefs and orientations of Americans which help determine political culture and preferences, that is, the American ideology or national identity.

The revolutionary ideology which became the American creed is liberalism in its eighteenth- and nineteenth-century meanings which stressed anti-statism.[22] The United States is unique in that it started from a revolutionary event and defined its *raison d'être* ideologically. Other

---

[21] Sombart, *Why No Socialism*, p. 106. For a recent overview, see Gary Marks, 'American Exceptionalism in Comparative Perspective', in his book, *Unions in Politics* (Princeton: Princeton University Press, 1989), 195–234.

[22] Louis Hartz, *The Liberal Tradition in America* (New York: Harcourt, Brace and World, 1955), 6 and 234. The word liberal, it should be noted, did not come into existence until the early 19th century and probably did not take on this meaning until the middle. See Giovanni Sartori, *The Theory of Democracy Revisited, Part Two: The Classical Issue*, (Chatham, NJ: Chatham House Publishers, 1987), 370–1.

countries' sense of themselves is derived from a common history, not an ideology. And if they have a historic conservative set of political values, it is Toryism, statist communitarianism, *noblesse oblige*. Winston Churchill once gave vivid evidence of the difference between a nation rooted in history and one defined by ideology in objecting to a proposal in 1940 to outlaw the Communist Party, when it was anti-war. In a speech in the House of Commons, Churchill said that as far as he knew the Communist Party was composed of Englishmen and he did not fear an Englishman. In Europe, nationality is related to community; one cannot become un-English, or un-Swedish. Being an American, however, is an ideological commitment. It is not a matter of birth. Those who reject American values are un-American.

The American Revolution sharply weakened the *noblesse oblige* values of organic community, which had been linked to Tory sentiments, and enormously strengthened the individualistic and anti-statist ones. This is evident in the fact that the United States, as H. G. Wells pointed out over eighty years ago, not only has lacked a viable socialist party, it also never developed a British or European-type conservative or Tory party. It has been dominated by pure bourgeois, middle-class individualistic values. As Wells put it: 'Essentially America is a middle-class [which has] become a community and so its essential problems are the problems of a modern individualistic society, stark and clear.' He enunciated a theory of America as a liberal society, in the classic anti-statist meaning of the term, that was to win wide acceptance a half-century later when described in more detail by Louis Hartz:

It is not difficult to show for example, that the two great political parties in America represent only one English party, the middle-class Liberal party. . . . There are no Tories . . . and no Labour Party . . . [T]he new world [was left] to the Whigs and Nonconformists and to those less constructive, less logical, more popular and liberating thinkers who became Radicals in England, and Jeffersonians and then Democrats in America. All Americans are, from the English point of view, Liberals of one sort or another. . . .

The liberalism of the eighteenth century was essentially the rebellion . . . against the monarchical and aristocratic state—against hereditary privilege, against restrictions on bargains. Its spirit was essentially anarchistic—the antithesis of Socialism. It was the anti-State.[23]

Fighting against a centralized monarchical state, the founding fathers

---

[23] Wells, *The Future in America*, pp. 72–6. For an excellent analysis of liberal party politics in Britain, Canada, and the United States, see Robert Kelley, *The Transatlantic Persuasion: The Liberal-Democratic Mind in the Age of Gladstone* (New York: Alfred A. Knopf, 1969).

distrusted a strong unified government. As the major, modern, classically liberal political theorist, Leo Strauss, noted: 'The United States of America may be said to be the only country in the world which was founded in explicit opposition to Machiavellian principles', to the power of the Prince.[24] The chronic antagonism to the state derivative from the American Revolution has been institutionalized in the unique division of powers, the internally conflicted form of government, that distinguishes the United States from parliamentary regimes, where Parliament, or more realistically the Cabinet, has relatively unchecked power, much like that held by an absolute monarch.

The Political Variables

The first constitution, the Articles of Confederation, did not even provide for a federal executive. Authority was in the hands of the Congress, which had limits on its powers. The second and continuing one is distinguished from all other constitutions in providing for an elaborate system of checks and balances on the executive and the two Houses of Congress, each with a different term of office so as to make concurrence among them difficult. No other elected national government, other than the Swiss, is as limited in its powers, as Byron Shafer elaborates in a piece on exceptionalism in American politics. The American public has indicated in opinion polls that it continues to favour a divided government and a weak state. Whenever samples of the population are asked by pollsters whether they prefer the President and both Houses of Congress to be controlled by one party or divided between two, they choose the latter response by goodly majorities.[25] They also invariably indicate a preference for small governmental units to large ones.

In a brilliant article on 'The State as a Conceptual Variable', J. P. Nettl laid out the enormous differences between the European conception of the state and the American. As he emphasized, the latter is characterized by 'relative statelessness'. In the United States 'only law is sovereign'. The weakness of the state and the emphasis on a constitutionally mandated division of powers gives lawyers a uniquely powerful role in America and make its people exceptionally litigious. Unlike the situation

---

[24] Leo Strauss, *Thoughts on Machiavelli* (Glencoe: The Free Press, 1958), 13.

[25] Byron E. Shafer, ' *"Exceptionalism" in American Politics?*', *PS* 22 (Sept. 1989), 588–94. S. M. Lipset and William Schneider, *The Confidence Gap: Business, Labor and Government in the Public Mind* (Baltimore: Johns Hopkins University Press, expanded and updated edn., 1987), 379–80.

in Europe and Britain, '[i]n the United States, the law and its practitioners have perhaps been the most important single factor making for political and social change and have time and again proved to be the normal instrument for bringing it about'.[26] These have also led to greater juridical guarantees of civil liberties and individual rights than elsewhere.

The institutional (constitutional) structure also inhibits the possibilities for a socialist or any other third party by creating the base for an electoral system which comes close to requiring a heterogeneous two-party system in which a third party cannot really function, by its focus on electing one person as president, who appoints a cabinet responsible to him, not to Parliament. This emphasis, as E. E. Schattschneider convincingly demonstrated, makes for a two-candidate race, for two broad electoral coalitions.[27] Those who attempted to build a socialist party never understood the limits on building a third party, the need for previously unrepresented forces to make their way to power through participation in one of the major party coalitions.[28] Third-party advocates have taken heart from the success of the Republicans, founded in 1854. But the Republicans basically arose out of the break-up of the Whig party on the slavery issues, and included most former northern Whigs.

Ironically, American left-radicalism was also stymied by the progress of populism, the fact that America became more electorally democratic earlier than other countries. Its less privileged strata received the ballot without the kind of class struggle that was required in Britain, Prussia, Sweden, and most countries in Europe. The American workers had the 'free gift of suffrage'.[29] Hence, as Lenin pointed out, socialist movements could not gain strength among the workers in the battle for the vote.[30] He believed that the heavy dose of democracy in the United States was a major obstacle in the path of radicals. They were unsuccessful precisely because as of 1907, when he wrote, the United States had 'no rival . . . [in] the extent of political freedom and the cultural level of the

[26] J. P. Nettl, 'The State as a Conceptual Variable', *World Politics*, 20/4 (1968), 561, 574, 585.

[27] E. E. Schattschneider, *Party Government* (New York: Rinehart and Co., 1942), 65–98.

[28] Daniel Bell, *Marxian Socialism in the United States* (Princeton: Princeton University Press, 1967), 116; S. M. Lipset, 'Socialism in America', in Paul Kurtz, ed., *Sidney Hook: Philosopher of Democracy and Humanism* (Buffalo: Prometheus Books, 1983), 55–9.

[29] Selig Perlman, *The Theory of the Labor Movement* (New York: Augustus M. Kelley, 1949), 167.

[30] V. I. Lenin, *Capitalism and Agriculture in the United States* (New York: International Publishers, 1934); V. I. Lenin, *On Britain* (Moscow: Foreign Languages Publishing House, n.d.).

masses of the population', that there were no 'big nation-wide democratic tasks facing the proletariat'.[31] American socialist leader Morris Hillquit, and the founding and long-term President of the American Federation of Labor, Samuel Gompers, had similar views.[32]

The ultimate source of authority in the American system can be found in the preamble of the Constitution which starts with 'We, the People of the United States'. The greater strength of populism in the United States than in the rest of the democratic world is reflected in the extent to which the public has insisted on the right to elect officials or to change them with the fortunes of elections. Almost all the major figures in law enforcement on the state and local government level, including judges and the heads of the prosecutor's offices and police forces are chosen by the voters, or appointed by elected officials. Most of the almost 60,000 elected county office-holders are 'justices of the peace, county or probate judges, constables, clerks and coroners'. In other countries, legal and police authorities tend to have life tenure, and are not directly involved in politics. Judges are appointed for life. They are not fired when a new party comes to power, and since they are usually prohibited from political activity, they are not under pressure to handle cases in a way that might facilitate their re-election or attainment of higher electoral office.

In the United States, not only are more legal offices open to election, but elections are much more frequent than in any other modern society. As of 1987, according to a US Census Bureau study, there are 504,404 popularly elected officials in the United States, or about one for every 478 citizens. Most of them, 485,691, hold local offices, with 18,171 state offices, about half of the total being administrative officials and judges.[33] This should mean that, including primaries and counting all offices, well over one million such contests occur in every four-year cycle, since many are elected to one- or two-year terms. American states and local governments submit many proposed laws, bond issues, and constitutional amendments to popular votes; other democratic polities rarely or never do. In many states, the citizenry may initiate legislation through initiative petition, a right frequently used; the right hardly exists elsewhere. In 1988, 'a total of 230 propositions were voted on' in the United

[31] Lenin, *Capitalism and Agriculture*, p. 1, and *On Britain*, p. 51.

[32] Morris Hillquit, *History of Socialism in the United States* (New York: Funk and Wagnalls, 1910), 358, 139–40; William M. Dick, *Labor and Socialism in America: The Gompers Era* (Port Washington, NY: Kennikat Press, 1972), 183–4, 116.

[33] Richard Morin, 'A Half a Million Choices for American Voters', *The Washington Post National Weekly Edition* (6–12 Feb. 1989), 38.

States. Austin Ranney, the foremost expert on the subject, has noted the effect of all this on him as a California voter:

On November 8, I, like every Berkeley voter, was called upon to vote on twenty-nine state propositions (we had already voted on twelve propositions in June), five Alameda County propositions, and eight city propositions. But that was not all: I was also asked to make choices for president, U.S. senator, U.S. representative, state senator, state representative, and a number of county and city offices. In the manner of political scientists of my generation, I made a simple count and found that I had a grand total of sixty-one decisions to make![34]

The same differentiating factors seemingly are reflected in varying administrative practices at the governmental level. The dividing line between political appointees and permanent civil servants is drawn higher in most other democratic countries than in the United States. Newly elected presidents, even when they are of the same party as the person they succeeded, as with George Bush, are responsible for thousands of appointments. In a discussion of American politics, Edward Banfield and James Wilson point out that

our government [in the United States] is permeated with politics. This is because our constitutional structure and our traditions afford individuals manifold opportunities not only to bring their special interests to the attention of public officials but also—and this is the important thing—to compel officials to bargain and to make compromises . . . there is virtually no sphere of 'administration' apart from politics.[35]

Such a comment underlines the effects of the populist sentiments and structures that pervade the American polity. The strong egalitarian emphasis in the United States which presses for expression in the 'vox populi' makes Americans more derisive and critical of their politicians and government bureaucrats.

It may be argued that part of the responsibility for the lower turn-out in American elections (only 50 per cent voted in the 1988 presidential contest; far fewer take part in primaries and lower level elections) should be assigned to populism.[36] The prolonged, multi-year campaigns, the frequency with which Americans are called to the polls, and the

[34] Austin Ranney, 'Referendums', *Public Opinion*, 11 (Jan.–Feb. 1989), 15.
[35] Edward C. Banfield and James Q. Wilson, *City Politics* (Cambridge: Harvard University Press and MIT Press, 1963), 1.
[36] Actually, the percentage should be one to two points higher if aliens are excluded from the base, see Walter Dean Burnham, 'The 1980 Earthquake: Realignment, Reaction, or What?', in Thomas Ferguson and Joel Rogers, eds., *The Hidden Election* (New York: Pantheon Books, 1981), 101.

mud-slinging, the character assassination tactics, inherent in contests which focus on individuals rather than the weak parties, all appear to discourage participation. The decline in the power of the organized parties, of what used to be referred to as the 'machines', to nominate candidates and to mobilize people to vote, has meant that fewer people take part.[37] Populism clearly does not explain all of the phenomenon. Many properly point to the greater difficulty Americans face in voting because of eligibility requirements, particularly the need to register to be on the voters' list.[38] But sharp reductions in such requirements since the 1960s, including in some states the elimination of the registration requirements or permitting citizens to register on Election Day and then vote, have been accompanied in such areas by rates of decline in voting paralleling the fall-off in other states, although they have higher ones than those with more stringent requirements. Ironically, as the electorate gains more formal power, the participation gap between the United States and other democracies grows.

Sociological Factors

The societal variables which have reduced the potential for socialism and class consciousness refer mainly to the unique class, religious, and economic systems of the country. The first, the emphasis on egalitarian social relations, the absence of a demand that those lower in the social order give overt deference to their betters and the stress on meritocracy, on equal opportunity for all to rise economically and socially, stemmed from the fact that America was formed as a new settler society. Tocqueville noted these elements in the 1830s when he defined American egalitarianism through two phrases, equality of respect and equality of opportunity. He was, of course, aware of enormous variations in income, power, and status, and of strong emphasis on the attainment of wealth.[39] But he emphasized that regardless of steep inequalities, Americans did not require the lower strata to acknowledge their inferiority, to bow to their betters.

[37] Walter Dean Burnham, 'The Appearance and Disappearance of the American Voter', in Richard Rose, ed., *Electoral Participation: A Comparative Analysis* (Beverly Hills: Sage Publications, 1980), 35–73.

[38] Raymond E. Wolfinger and Steven Rosenstone, *Who Votes?* (New Haven: Yale University Press, 1980); Francis Fox Piven and Richard A. Cloward, *Why Americans Don't Vote* (New York: Pantheon, 1988).

[39] Tocqueville, *Democracy in America*, i. 51.

The emphasis on meritocracy was present early in the ideology of the school system. Martin Trow discusses some of the outcomes in Chapter 6, particularly the tremendous expansion of the system, to the point where the United States has led the world in the proportion attending different levels (elementary, high school, and college) from early in the history of the Republic. He has noted that the 'great, unique feature of American higher education is surely its diversity. It is this diversity—both resulting from and making possible the system's phenomenal growth—that has enabled our colleges and universities to appeal to so many, serve so many different functions'.[40] To this should be added their competitiveness for faculty, students, and resources in fashions that do not exist elsewhere.[41]

Concern for an open and competitive society was also reflected in the emergence of the concept of the common school in the early nineteenth century. Its advocates proposed that everyone regardless of origins, status, or wealth should attend the same school, that there should not be a class-differentiated system. They rejected the models that existed in Britain, France, and Germany. They opposed the European systems as explicitly élitist, limiting access to academic high schools to a small part of the population. It must be noted, however, that the efficacy of the American public school, which seeks to educate all young people in the same system, is low compared to those which seek only to educate a portion of the whole in academically oriented institutions. Cross-national achievement tests in mathematics and native language skills show American school children lagging behind their peers in Canada, Europe, and East Asia. The reasons for this form of 'exceptionalism' are complex, linked among other things to greater social heterogeneity of the American population and the extraordinarily high rates of childhood poverty among minorities. The notable contrast between relative achievement at the level of higher education and failure at lower levels is related by Samuel Huntington to the absence of competition in what is 'overwhelmingly a public monopoly and . . . inferior as a result' in the latter, and 'intense competition' among institutions in the former.[42]

The United States, almost from its start, has had an expanding economic system, one which Peter Temin analyses in Chapter 3.

[40] Martin Trow, 'American Higher Education: Past, Present and Future', *Educational Researcher*, 17 (Apr. 1988), 15.

[41] Henry Rosovsky, *The University: An Owner's Manual* (New York: W. W. Norton, 1990), 31–2.

[42] Samuel Huntington, 'The U.S.—Decline or Renewal', *Foreign Affairs*, 67 (Winter 1988/9), 89.

Although many other countries in Europe and East Asia have developed economically, America is still the world leader by far in per capita real income and the creation of new jobs. As of 1986, in terms of purchasing power parities, the GNP per head for the United States was US$17,360, while Canada was a close second among OECD countries, less than $1,500 behind. West Germany and Japan were well behind with per capita incomes of US$12,793 and US$12,210 respectively.[43] From 1973 to 1987, 30 million jobs were created in the United States, while Western European countries actually experienced a small decline. Japan and Australia also gained jobs over the period, but not nearly as fast.[44] Although the size of the American advantage declined during most of the 1970s, in part because of the incursion into the labour force of many millions of new and inexperienced young and women workers, in

the 1980s U.S. economic performance improved markedly compared to that of other leading countries. . . . During the past five years [1983–87] the U.S. and Japanese economies grew at almost the same rate, with the United States leading in three of these years. In all five years U.S. growth exceeded that of the European Community. The biggest economy has been getting bigger, absolutely and relatively.[45]

The first seven years of the 1980s saw 'the creation of hundreds of thousands of new businesses and 14 million new jobs, far and away the best performance among the advanced countries'.[46] Although some have contended that the great majority of these new positions are low-paying, this argument is not sustained by Bureau of Labor Statistics analysis. Bureau economists report that 'More than half . . . were in occupations—such as managerial/professional, and craft and repair—where the average pay is $22,000 or more.'[47]

The nineteenth-century American economy, as compared to the European

---

[43] 'The Italian Economy', *The Economist* (27 Feb. 1988), survey, p. 9. The data are from OECD.

[44] See Louis Uchitelle, 'Election Placing Focus on the Issue of Jobs vs. Wages', *New York Times* (4 Sept. 1988), 1, 14; Joanna Moy, 'Recent Trends in Unemployment and the Labor Force, 10 Countries', *Monthly Labor Review*, 108 (Aug. 1985), 11.

[45] Huntington, 'The U.S.—Decline or Renewal?', pp. 82–3; Karen Elliot House, 'The 90's and Beyond: For All Its Difficulties, U.S. Stands to Retain its Global Leadership', *Wall Street Journal*, (23 Jan. 1989).

[46] Peter T. Kilborn, 'A Fight to Win the Middle Class', *New York Times*, Business Section (4 Sept. 1988), 5.

[47] Paul Blustein, 'The Great Jobs Debate', *The Washington Post National Weekly Edition* (5–11 Sept. 1988), 20; M. W. Horrigan and S. E. Haugen, 'The Declining Middle-Class Thesis: A Sensitivity Analysis', *Monthly Labor Review*, 111 (May 1988), 3–13.

ones, was characterized by more market freedom, more individual ownership of the land, a higher wage-income structure, all sustained by the national, classically liberal, ideology. From the Revolution on, the United States was the *laissez-faire* country par excellence. Unlike the situation in many European countries, in which economic materialism was viewed by the social and religious establishments—that is, the traditional aristocracy and the church—as conducive to vulgar behaviour and immorality, in the United States hard work and economic ambition were perceived as the proper activity of a moral man.

Writing in the 1850s, a visiting Swiss theologian, Philip Schaff, commented that the 'acquisition of riches is to them [the Americans] only a help toward higher spiritual and moral ends'.[48] Friedrich Engels and Max Weber, among many, emphasized that the United States was the only pure bourgeois country, the only one which was not post-feudal.[49] As Weber noted, 'no medieval antecedents or complicating institutional heritage [served] to mitigate the impact of the Protestant ethic on American economic development'.[50] Similar arguments were made in the 1920s by the gifted Italian communist theoretician, Antonio Gramsci.[51] America was able to avoid the remnants of mercantilism, statist regulations, church establishment, aristocracy, and the emphasis on social class that the post-feudal countries inherited. Each emphasized America's unique origins and resultant value system as a source of its economic and political development. Reacting to a visit to North America in the 1880s, Engels, commenting on the relative economic backwardness of Canada compared to the United States, wrote what the former needed was an infusion of the 'spirit of the Americans' and of 'Yankee blood'.[52] Its secular, Adam Smith, liberal orientation tied in with various aspects derivative from its special religious tradition, especially the dominance of the Protestant sects that, as Weber emphasized, facilitated the rise of capitalism.[53]

---

[48] Philip Schaff, *America: A Sketch of the Political, Social, and Religious Character of the United States of North America* (New York: C. Scribner, 1855), 259.

[49] Engels to Sorge, 8 Feb. 1890, in Marx and Engels, *Selected Correspondence*, p. 467.

[50] Max Weber, *The Protestant Ethic and the Spirit of Capitalism* (New York: Scribner, 1935), 55–6.

[51] Antonio Gramsci, *Selections from the Prison Notebooks* (New York: International Publishers, 1971), 21–2, 272, 318.

[52] Engels to Sorge, 10 Sept. 1888, in Marx and Engels, *Letters to Americans*, p. 204.

[53] Weber, *The Protestant Ethic*, pp. 155–83; and Weber, 'The Protestant Sects and the Spirit of Capitalism', in *Essays in Sociology* (New York: Oxford University Press, 1946), 309, 313.

Americanism as Ideology

The United States is organized around an ideology which includes a set
of dogmas about the nature of a good society. Americanism, as different
people have pointed out, is an 'ism' or ideology in the same way that
communism or fascism or liberalism are isms. As Richard Hofstadter
noted: 'it has been our fate as a nation not to have ideologies but to be
one'.[54] That ideology can be subsumed in four words: anti-statism,
individualism, populism, and egalitarianism. The implications of the
latter two for the failure of the socialist appeal were spelt out by Hermann
Keyserling and Leon Samson, writing in the late 1920s and early 1930s.[55]
They argued that the movement had little appeal because the social
content of socialism, property relations apart (which is of course a big
'apart'), is identical with what Americans think they already have,
namely, a democratic, socially classless society which is anti-élitist. As
Keyserling put it:

The Americans are the only socialists I know of in the true sense of the term
in the Western World. . . . The spirit of the revolutions of the eighteenth century,
the essence of which was revolt against all hierarchy of values still rules
[there]. . . . The United States must obviously be immune to Socialism in the
European sense because of the fact, unheard of in Europe, that the very problem
which the reformers undertake to solve appears solved from the outset.[56]

Leon Samson, a radical socialist, reached similar conclusions from
an examination of Americanism as ideology:

When we examine the meaning of Americanism, we discover that Americanism
is to the American not a tradition or a territory, not what France is to a Frenchman
or England to an Englishman, but a doctrine—what socialism is to a socialist.
Like socialism, Americanism is looked upon . . . as a highly attenuated,
conceptualized, platonic, impersonal attraction toward a system of ideas, a
solemn assent to a handful of final notions—democracy, liberty, opportunity,
to all of which the American adheres rationalistically much as a socialist adheres
to his socialism—because it does him good, because it gives him work, because,
so he thinks, it guarantees him happiness. Americanism has thus served as a
substitute for socialism. Every concept in socialism has its substitutive counter-

[54] Quoted in Michael Kazin, 'The Right's Unsung Prophet', *The Nation*, 248 (20 Feb.
1989), 242.
[55] Hermann Keyserling, *America Set Free* (New York: Harper and Brothers, 1929),
237–40, 244–52; Leon Samson, *Toward a United Front* (New York: Farrar and Rinehart,
1935), 16–17. For my earlier discussions of Samson, see Lipset, 'Why No Socialism in the
United States?', pp. 75–7; and *The First New Nation*, pp. 393–4.
[56] Keyserling, *America Set Free*, pp. 237–9.

concept in Americanism, and that is why the socialist argument falls so fruitlessly on the American ear. . . . The American does not want to listen to socialism, since he thinks he already has it.[57]

Samson noted that conservatives, Republicans, and businessmen, whom he preferred to quote to illustrate his own assumptions, use language, concepts, and goals for American society which in Europe are only voiced by socialists.[58] Thus, he pointed out that Herbert Hoover took Europe as a negative model, saying that in America, 'we resent class distinction because there can be no rise for the individual through the frozen strata of classes'. Hoover emphasized the abolition of poverty as a goal of the American system.

In the early 1970s, the major contemporary leader of American Socialism, Michael Harrington, expressed strong agreement with Samson, noting that 'it was America's receptivity to utopia, not its hostility, that was a major factor inhibiting the development of a socialist movement. . . . [T]he country's image of itself contained so many socialist elements that one did not have to go to a separate movement opposed to the status quo in order to give vent to socialist emotions.'[59] More recently, in August 1988, Harrington reiterated the argument in a television interview in which he said that the United States is more socialist socially than Sweden and other countries governed by social democrats, that social relations among the classes are more egalitarian in America than in other societies, including Canada.

The anti-statist, anti-authoritarian component of the American ideology is another major source of the continued weakness of socialism in the United States. The American radical has been much more sympathetic to anarchism, to libertarianism, to syndicalism, than to state collectivism. Given the emphasis on anti-statist individualism, 'it was the attribute of collectivism or statism . . . that [constituted] the central negative image' of socialism for Americans.[60] If the United States is ever

[57] Samson, *Toward a United Front*, pp. 16–17.

[58] For an intriguing effort to deal with the 'Why No Socialism' question by reference to the almost unique absence of soccer as a popular sport in the United States, see Andrei S. Markovits, 'The Other "American Exceptionalism"—Why is There No Soccer in the United States?', *Praxis International*, 8 (July 1988), 125–50. Markovits argues that both soccer and the socialist movement were 'crowded out' before the First World War, in one case by other sports, American football and baseball, in the second case, by other myths, such as Samson argues, of 'unbound freedom and limitless opportunities, which became one of the most attractive ideologies of the modern world', as well as by its special electoral system (p. 129).

[59] Michael Harrington, *Socialism* (New York: Saturday Review Press, 1972), 118.

[60] Robert N. Bellah, *The Broken Covenant: American Civil Religion in Time of Trial* (New York: The Seabury Press, 1975), 124.

to get a major radical movement, it would be closer to anarchism than to socialism, a notion implicit in H. G. Wells's analysis. This may be seen in the ideology of the American labour movements. The moderate one, the American Federation of Labor (AFL), was syndicalist. The radical one, the Industrial Workers of the World (IWW), was anarcho-syndicalist. Both the AFL and IWW regarded the state as an enemy and felt that state-owned industry would be much more difficult for the workers and unions to resist than private companies. Samuel Gompers, the leader of the AFL for four decades, emphasized that what the state can give, the state can take away—that the workers must rely on themselves. Gompers and the old AFL leadership were not conservative; they were syndicalist and extremely militant. In '1920 Gompers described himself as . . . three quarters anarchist'.[61]

As Dan Bell mentions in Chapter 2, the AFL was much more aggressive than the European labour movements before and immediately after the First World War, as reflected in its greater propensity to strike and use violence.[62] The record of the Congress of Industrial Organizations (CIO) founded in the 1930s is a different story. The Great Depression, as Richard Hofstadter pointed out, introduced 'a social democratic tinge' for the first time in American history, both in politics with the New Deal and in organized labour with the CIO.[63] This tinge, however, was to be drastically weakened in the prolonged post-war prosperity.

The ideological streak in the American experience has been strengthened by its special religious character, one which was discussed in Burke's speech, referred to earlier.[64] He called the Americans the Protestants of Protestantism, the Dissenters of Dissent.[65] The United States is a country formed by the sects and groups known in England as the Dissenters and Nonconformists, the Protestant sects: Methodists,

---

[61] Dick, *Labor and Socialism in America*, p. 84; Melvyn Dubofsky, *We Shall Be All: A History of the Industrial Workers of the World* (Chicago: Quadrangle Books, 1955), 483–4. The New Left of the 1960s was also near anarchist in its ideology and organizational structure.

[62] See also Philip Taft and Philip Ross, 'American Labor and Violence: Its Causes, Character and Outcome', in H. D. Graham and T. R. Gurr, eds., *Violence in America: Historical and Comparative Perspectives* (Beverly Hills: Sage Publications, 1979), 187–243.

[63] Richard Hofstadter, *The Age of Reform* (New York: Vintage Books, 1967), 308; see also S. M. Lipset, 'Roosevelt and the Protest of the 1930s', *Minnesota Law Review*, 68 (Dec. 1983), 273–98.

[64] For an elaboration, see Bellah, *The Broken Covenant*, pp. 36–60; Robert N. Bellah, Richard Madsen, William M. Sullivan, Ann Swidler, and Steven M. Tipton, *Habits of the Heart* (Berkeley: University of California Press, 1985), 28–41, 219–25.

[65] Burke, *Selected Works*, pp. 180–1.

Baptists, and the many others. The majority of the population has always belonged to, or has adhered to, the sects, not to the various denominations which were or are state churches, i.e. Anglican, Catholic, Lutheran, and Orthodox. Religion has been a voluntary institution in the United States, forced to compete to survive. Ministers had to win support.[66] Weber identified sectarian beliefs as the most conducive to the kind of rational, competitive, individualistic behaviour which encourages entrepreneurial success.[67] The epitome of the Protestant ethic was to be found not in the Catholic and Protestant churches, but in the Protestant sects.

In his classic work on the subject, *The Protestant Ethic and the Spirit of Capitalism*, Weber noted that the Puritans brought the values conducive to capitalism with them and, therefore, that 'the spirit of capitalism . . . was present before the capitalistic order'.[68] His principal examples of a secularized capitalist spirit are drawn from the writings of an American, Benjamin Franklin.[69] Weber quotes extensively from Franklin's works as prototypical of the values that are most functional for the emergence of an industrialized system. (Parenthetically, it may be noted that Franklin's ideas appealed to another religious group who helped build market economies, the East European Jews. His writings were translated into Yiddish around 1800 and were read by young Jews in Poland and Russia who found his values kindred to their own. They were committed to rationality and work. Another sociologist, Robert Park, writing in the 1920s, was to suggest that the Jews are the prototypical American ethnic group, that their values are closer to the basic American ones than those of any others, including the English.[70]) The American religious ethic is not only functional for a bourgeois economy, but also, as Tocqueville noted, for a liberal polity. Since most of these sects are congregational, not hierarchical, they have fostered egalitarian, individualistic, and populist values which are anti-élitist. Hence, both the political ethos and the religious ethos have reinforced each other on both sides of the Atlantic.

[66] Tocqueville, *Democracy*, i. 308–14.
[67] Weber, 'The Protestant Sects'.
[68] Weber, *The Protestant Ethic*, pp. 55–6.
[69] Ibid. 48–50.
[70] Robert Park, *Race and Culture* (Glencoe, Ill.: The Free Press, 1950), 354–5; Henry L. Feingold, *A Midrash on American Jewish History* (Albany: State University of New York Press, 1982), 189; and S. M. Lipset, 'A Unique People in an Exceptional Country', in Lipset, ed., *American Pluralism and the Jewish Community* (New Brunswick, NJ: Transaction, 1990), 4–8.

With respect to the extensive participation of Jews in American society, I would reiterate words I wrote in 1963.

To understand the American Jew, it is necessary to be sensitized to factors in American life which used to be discussed in Marxist circles as the problem of 'American exceptionalism'... [T]he United States has sustained a national ideology which defined efforts to emphasize ethnic-religious differences as un-American. The frequent 'nativist' and anti-Catholic movements... [were] put down by the authority structure.[71]

The encouragement to American Jewry to play a full role in society and polity, unique in the annals of the Diaspora, is endemic in George Washington's message to the Jews of Newport in 1790, that in the new United States 'all possess alike liberty of conscience and immunities of citizenship'. Even more significantly, he noted that the patronizing concept of 'toleration... of one class of people... [by] another' has no place in America, that Jews enjoy the same rights as all Americans.[72]

The emphasis on voluntary associations in America which so impressed Tocqueville, Weber, Gramsci, and other foreign observers as one of the distinctive American traits is linked to the uniquely American system of 'voluntary religion'. The United States is the first country in which religious groups became voluntary associations. American ministers and laity consciously recognized that they had to foster a variety of voluntary associations both to maintain support for the church and to fulfil community needs. Tocqueville concluded that voluntarism is a large part of the answer to the puzzling strength of organized religion, a phenomenon which impressed most nineteenth-century observers and continues to show up in cross-national opinion polls taken by Gallup and others, which indicate Americans are the most God-believing people. They also show that Americans are the most church-going in Protestantism and the most fundamentalist in Christendom. The current status of these behaviours and beliefs is documented in Chapter 4 by Andrew Greeley.[73] All the abundant quantitative data indicate the continued validity of Tocqueville's statement: 'There is no country in

---

[71] Lipset, *Revolution and Counterrevolution*, pp. 150–1.

[72] 'Washington's Reply to the Hebrew Congregation in Newport, Rhode Island', *Publications of the American Jewish Historical Society*, 3 (1895), 91–2.

[73] For recent comparative efforts see David Popenoe, *Disturbing the Nest: Family Change and Decline in Modern Societies* (New York: Aldine de Gruyter, 1988), 284, and Ronald Inglehart and David Apple, 'The Rise of Post-Materialist Values and Changing Religious Orientations, Gender Roles and Sexual Norms', *International Journal of Public Opinion Research*, 1 (Spring 1989), 45–75.

the world where the Christian religion retains a greater influence over the souls of men than in America'.[74] In so doing, the United States contradicts a statistically based generalization 'that economic development goes hand in hand with a decline in religious sentiment'.[75] As Kenneth Wald, who has documented this relationship, notes:

The United States, however, is a conspicuous exception to the generalization. This country, with by far the highest score on the index of economic development, was also the most 'religious' of countries as shown by the answers its citizens gave to the interviewers. The magnitude of American 'exceptionalism' can best be gauged by comparing the proportion of Americans who actually assigned great importance to religious belief—51 percent—with the proportion that should have done so on the basis of the pattern in other countries—a mere 5 percent.[76]

The differences between European and American political orientations may be related to variations in religious traditions and church organizations. As noted above, European churches have been state-financed and called on their parishioners to support the political system. They retain structures and values formed and institutionalized in medieval agrarian societies. Structurally, they are hierarchical and have fostered the responsibility of the community for the welfare of its members. Thus, as with the aristocracy and gentry, the European churches have disliked the logic of bourgeois society.

The emphasis on Americanism as a political ideology has led to a utopian orientation among American liberals and conservatives. Both seek to extend the 'good society'. But the religious traditions of Protestant 'dissent' have called on Americans to be moralistic, to follow their conscience with an unequivocal emphasis not to be found in countries whose predominant denominations have evolved from state churches. The dissenters are 'the original source both of the close intermingling of religion and politics that [has] characterized subsequent American history and of the moral passion that has powered the engines of political change in America'.[77] As Robert Bellah has emphasized: 'The millenialism of the American Protestant tradition again and again

[74] Tocqueville, *Democracy*, i. 314. For an excellent current overview, see Edward A. Tiryakian, 'American Religious Exceptionalism: Protestant, Catholic, and Jew Revisited', *Social Compass* (forthcoming).
[75] Kenneth D. Wald, *Religion and Politics in the United States* (New York: St. Martin's Press, 1987), 6. [76] Ibid. 6–7. See also pp. 8–12.
[77] Samuel Huntington, *American Politics: The Promise of Disharmony* (Cambridge: The Belknap Press of Harvard University Press, 1981), 154. For documentation, see pp. 8. 31–2, 84–104.

spawned movements for social change and social reform.'[78] The American Protestant religious ethos has assumed, in practice if not in theology, the perfectibility of humanity and an obligation to avoid sin, while the churches whose followers have predominated in Europe, Canada, and Australia have accepted the inherent weakness of people, their inability to escape sinning and error, and the need for the church to be forgiving and protecting.[79]

Americans are utopian moralists who press hard to institutionalize virtue, to destroy evil people, and to eliminate wicked institutions and practices. They tend to view social and political dramas as morality plays, as battles between God and the devil, so that compromise is virtually unthinkable. This is, of course, part of what some people see as problematic about American foreign policy.[80] As Samuel Huntington has noted, Americans give to their nation and its creed 'many of the attributes and functions of a church'.[81] These are reflected, as Bellah has stressed, in the American 'civic religion', which has provided 'a religious dimension for the whole fabric of American life, including the political sphere'. The United States is seen as the new Israel. 'Europe is Egypt; America the promised land. God has led his people to establish a new sort of social order that shall be a light unto all nations.'[82]

The moralistic tendency generalizes beyond its sectarian origins. A distinguished French Dominican student of American religion, R. L. Bruckberger (who visited the United States in the 1950s and, deciding to stay, wound up as a professor at Notre Dame), criticized his fellow Catholics in *The Image of America* for having absorbed the American Protestant view of religion and morality. He expressed concern that American Catholics had become much more like American Baptists and Presbyterians than European or Latin American Catholics. According to him, the Americans did not sound like Catholics when they spoke out on moralistic issues.[83]

The very emphasis in the Protestant sectarian tradition on the religious chosenness of the United States has meant that if the country is perceived

[78] Bellah, *The Broken Covenant*, p. 48. See also Sacvan Bercovitch, *The American Jeremiad* (Madison: University of Wisconsin Press, 1978), 20, 94.

[79] Lipset, *The First New Nation*, pp. 166–9.

[80] George Kennan, *Realities of American Foreign Policy* (New York: Norton, 1966), 3–50; Robert Bellah, *Beyond Belief* (New York: Harper and Row, 1970), 182–3.

[81] Huntington, *American Politics*, pp. 158–9.

[82] Bellah, *Beyond Belief*, p. 175; Wald, *Religion and Politics*, pp, 48–55.

[83] R. L. Bruckberger, 'The American Catholics as a Minority', in Thomas T. McAvoy, ed., *Roman Catholicism and the American Way of Life* (Notre Dame: University of Notre Dame Press, 1960), 45–7; Bruckberger, *Image of America* (New York: Viking Press, 1959).

as slipping away 'from the controlling obligations of the covenant', it is on the road to hell.[84] The need to assuage a sense of personal responsibility for such failings has made Americans particularly inclined to support movements for the elimination of evil—by illegal and even violent means, if necessary. A key element in the conflicts that culminated in the Civil War was the tendency of both sides to view the other as essentially sinful, as an agent of the devil. Linked to Protestant sectarianism, conscientious objection to military service was until recently largely an American phenomenon. The resisters to the Vietnam War re-enacted a two-century 'Protestant' sense of personal responsibility that led the intensely committed to follow their consciences. In other Christian countries, denominations which have been state churches called for and legitimated obedience to state authority. The American sectarians, however, have taken it as a matter of course that the individual should obey his or her conscience, not the state. Conscientious objection has existed in Britain, but there it stems from the 20 per cent of the population who are dissenters, and consequently has been a less significant phenomenon.

An attempt to compare the extent of anti-war activity throughout American history by Sol Tax of the University of Chicago concluded that, as of 1968, the Vietnam War rated as our *fourth* 'least popular' conflict with a foreign enemy.[85] Widespread opposition has existed to all American wars, with the possible exception of the Second World War which began with a direct attack on the United States soil. Large numbers refused to go along with the war of 1812, the Mexican War, the Civil War, the First World War, and the Korean War.[86] Conversely,

---

[84] Bellah, *The Broken Covenant*, p. 60.

[85] Sol Tax, 'War and the Draft', in Morton Fried *et al.*, eds., *War* (Garden City: Doubleday/ The Natural History Press, 1968), 199–203.

[86] Samuel Eliot Morison, 'Dissent in the War of 1812', in Samuel Eliot Morison, Frederick Merk, and Frank Freidel, *Dissent in Three American Wars* (Cambridge: Harvard University Press, 1970), 3–31; Alice Felt Tyler, *Freedom's Ferment* (New York: Harper Torchbooks, 1962), 407; Frederick Merk, 'Dissent in the Mexican War', in Morison *et al.*, *Dissent in Three Americans Wars*, pp. 33–63; Edward S. Wallace, 'Notes and Comment—Deserters in the Mexican War', *The Hispanic American Historical Review*, 15 (1935), 374; David Donald, 'Died of Democracy', in David Donald, ed., *Why the North Won the Civil War* (Baton Rouge: Louisiana State University Press, 1960), 85–9; James McCague, *The Second Rebellion: The Story of The New York City Draft Riots of 1863* (New York: Dial, 1968); Basil L. Lee, *Discontent in New York City, 1861–65* (Washington: Catholic University of America Press, 1943); Frank Freidel, 'Dissent in the Spanish-America War and the Philippine Insurrection', in Morison *et al.*, *Dissent in Three American Wars*, pp. 65–95, esp. p. 77; H. C. Peterson and Gilbert C. Fite, *Opponents of War, 1917–1918* (Seattle: University of Washington Press, 1957), 39, 123–35, 234.

the supporters of American wars see them as moralistic crusades: to eliminate monarchical rule (the war of 1812), to defeat the Catholic forces of superstition (the Mexican War), to eliminate slavery (the Civil War), to end colonialism in the Americas (the Spanish-American War), to make the world safe for democracy (the First World War), and to resist totalitarian expansionism (the Second World War and Korea).

The long-stalemated struggle with communism was a blow, particularly to American conservatives, to this sense of a moralistic contest which must end with the defeat of Satan. America's initial reaction to communism was often one which implied no compromise. After each major communist triumph—Russia, China, North Korea, Cuba, Vietnam—the United States went through a period of refusing to 're-cognize' the unforgivable, hopefully temporary, victory of evil. This behaviour contrasts with that of Anglican conservatives such as Churchill, or Catholic rightists like De Gaulle and Franco, whose opposition to Communism did not require 'non-recognition'. Franco Spain dealt with Castro soon after he took power. Canada, under Conservative Party leadership, has traded with Cuba and Sandinista Nicaragua and opposes American policy in Central America. Americans have been unique in their emphasis on non-recognition of evil foreign regimes. The principle is related to the insistence that wars must end with the unconditional surrender of the Satanic enemy. Unlike church countries, the United States rarely sees itself merely defending national interests. Foreign conflicts invariably involve a battle of good versus evil. George Kennan, among others, has written perceptively of the consequences of this 'utopian' approach to foreign affairs.[87]

The United States does not ally itself with Satan. If circumstances oblige it to co-operate with evil regimes, they are converted into agents of virtue. Church countries can take the opposite tack. When the Germans invaded the Soviet Union in 1941, Churchill went on the radio to welcome the Soviets as allies, and said that he was prepared to make a treaty with Satan if necessary to defeat the Nazis. The United States, however, converted Stalin into benign, pipe-smoking 'Uncle Joe'. Russia was treated as a free, almost capitalist, country. Eddie Rickenbacker, a right-wing conservative, described the Soviet Union as operating on capitalist principles and presented Stalin in positive terms. Americans must turn the bad guys on their side into good guys.

This emphasis on moralism helps to explain American reactions to

[87] Kennan, *Realities of American Foreign Policy.*

the Vietnam War. That conflict was not fought as an ideological crusade. For a curious reason, it was not defined by the government as a war against evil and Satan. Lyndon Johnson feared that whipping up moralistic sentiment against the communists in Vietnam would result in a new wave of McCarthyism. Ironically, up to 1967, he feared an attack from domestic forces on his right, and deprecated the importance of the anti-war movement on his left. Johnson consciously attempted to restrain anti-communist moralism. The Korean War had produced McCarthyism, whose duration was coterminous with the war, 1950 to 1954. Johnson did not want a renewal of the phenomenon. Hence, the struggle was not sold as an anti-communist crusade. The anti-war movement, therefore, had a near monopoly on morality, and ultimately was able to bring the president down and end the conflict.

Moralistic and movement politics continue today. American conservatives have given expression to these passions in their efforts to outlaw abortion and their support of Reagan's pre-1987 foreign policy, the fight against the 'evil empire'. Liberals equally passionately opposed aid to the Nicaraguan contras, seek to maintain legal abortion (defined as the women's right to control their bodies), and press for full racial and sexual equality through affirmative action quotas. Both see their domestic opponents as advocates of immoral policies.

Philanthropy

Some of the same factors which have affected or been influenced by religion appear linked to the fact that the 'expansion of philanthropy . . . thas gone further . . . in the United States, than in any other part of the word'.[88] The greater commitment to philanthropic activities in the United States has been related historically to the rejection of a powerful central state and of a church establishment. As an English visitor to the United States in the 1830s put it: 'The separation of Church and State, and other causes, have given rise to a new species of social organization, before unknown in history. . . .'[89] Many communal functions which had been handled in Europe by the state or by state-financed churches were dealt with in nineteenth-century America by voluntary associations. The

[88] Aileen D. Ross, 'Philanthropy', in David L. Sills, ed., *International Encyclopedia of the Social Sciences* (New York: Macmillan and The Free Press, 1968), xii. 76.

[89] 'An American Gentleman' (Calvin Colton), *A Voice From America to England* (London: Henry Colburn, 1839), 87–8.

lack of commitment by the state to support communal institutions on the scale fostered by monarchical and aristocratic *noblesse oblige* in Europe has meant that certain institutions have been weaker here. This is most evident in the area of high culture, where opera companies, symphonies, and museums have received much less government backing and, as a result, are in worse financial shape. Conversely, however, a variety of other private institutions, such as colleges and universities and hospitals, have been widely diffused in this country and are supported by the most extensive pattern of voluntary contributions in the world.[90]

The considerable sums, as well as time, that are contributed to philanthropic works, reaching heights undreamt of elsewhere, are also a consequence of the interrelationship between voluntary religion and secular achievements. The emphasis on voluntarism in both areas, religious and secular, has clearly been mutually reinforcing. Men were expected to be righteous, hard-working, and ambitious. Righteousness was to be rewarded both in the present and the hereafter, and the successful had an obligation to engage in good works and to share the bounty that they had attained. A detailed study by Merle Curti of the history of American giving for overseas purposes stresses the role that 'the doctrine of stewardship' played, the belief 'that whatever of wordly means one has belongs to God, that the holder is only God's steward and obligated to give to the poor, the distressed, and the needy. From many diaries, letters and other evidence it is clear that this factor was a dominant one in a great deal of giving.'[91]

Scholarly students of the history of philanthropy in the United States emphasize that the underlying support for private philanthropy has been sustained by American 'individualistic philosophy and suspicion of government control'.[92] Some indication of the strength of these values may be seen in the rejection by the American Red Cross, in January 1931, of a proposed federal appropriation of twenty-five million dollars for the relief of drought victims. The chairman of the Red Cross central committee told Congress, 'All we pray for is that you let us alone and let us do the job.'[93] In spite of the growth of the welfare and planning

[90] Arnaud C. Marts, *The Generosity of Americans: Its Source, Its Achievements* (Englewood Cliffs, NJ: Prentice-Hill, 1966), pp. 4–82.

[91] Merle Curti, *American Philanthropy Abroad: A History* (New Brunswick: Rutgers University Press, 1963), 625.

[92] Ross, 'Philanthropy', p. 76. See essays in Teresa Odendahl, ed., *America's Wealthy and the Future of Foundations* (Washington, DC: The Foundation Center, 1987).

[93] Robert H. Bremner, *American Philanthropy* (Chicago: University of Chicago Press, 1988), 138.

state since the 1930s, these values are not dead, even on the left of American life. In 1971, the National Taxpayers Union, a group whose board included three major New Left figures, Noam Chomsky, Marc Raskin (head of the radical think tank, the Institute for Policy Studies), and Karl Hess (former editor of the left-wing magazine, *Ramparts*), together with a number of conservative free-enterprise thinkers, advocated sharp cuts in the welfare responsibilities of government. To deal with the problem of the 'needy recipients such as welfare people', the group proposed 'a system of tax credits for any individual or group that provides private support for welfare recipients'. It would allow contributions to be deducted as an outright cut from taxes, rather than, as now, from gross income.[94] The fact that such a proposal could have been made in the 1970s by an organization whose leaders included some of the leading left-wing radicals in America attests to the continued vitality of the American individualist emphasis.

The Protestant ethic and the liberal emphasis on individualism and achievement combined in America, as noted earlier, to provide the values that are most conducive for economic development, and for a democratic polity resting on independent secondary powers separate from the central state, which Tocqueville specified as necessary to avoid authoritarianism. The two sets of factors also helped foster the emergence of an élite which took its communal responsibilities seriously. As early as 1807, members of the Boston élite stated in the founding document of the Boston Athenaeum that, in their city,

> the class of persons enjoying easy circumstances, and possessing surplus wealth, is comparatively numerous. As we are not called upon for large contributions to national purposes, we shall do well to take advantage of the exception, by taxing ourselves for those institutions, which will be attended with lasting and extensive benefit, amidst all changes of our public fortunes and political affairs.[95]

Martin Green, who has called attention to this remarkable statement, notes that 'Boston merchants, and to some extent the bankers and industrialists who succeeded them, had the idea that commerce should go hand in hand with philanthropy, and even culture, and should give way to them as soon as the individual had secured himself an adequate sum.'[96] In the nineteenth century, they demonstrated the vitality of this

---

[94] David Deitch, 'Libertarians Unite in Drive to Reduce Tax Burdens', *Boston Globe* (10 Apr. 1971), 7. See also 'What's This?', *Dissent*, 18 (Aug. 1971), 395.

[95] Cited in Martin Green, *The Problem of Boston* (New York: W. W. Norton, 1966), 4.

[96] Ibid. 56.

sense of responsibility by their support for libraries, the symphony, the Perkins Institute for the Blind, the Lowell Institute, Harvard University, and the beginnings of that complex of hospitals which remains at the summit of medical care in America today. The altruistic sentiments voiced by the founders of the Athenaeum were, of course, not the only reasons motivating major contributions by the wealthy. In a fund-raising letter for Harvard in 1886, Henry Lee Higginson, a leading Boston Brahmin, stated, 'educate, and save ourselves and our families and our money from mobs'.[97] James Buchanan Duke, the founder of the Duke Endowment, explained his concern for the expansion of health facilities in a newspaper interview in the 1920s saying, 'People ought to be healthy. If they ain't healthy they can't work, and if they don't work they ain't healthy. And if they can't work there ain't no profit in them.'[98]

But though the philanthropy of the American Protestant wealthy had clear elements of self-interest, it is also true that they exhibited levels of generosity that were unmatched by the rich in other nations. John D. Rockefeller, who gave away more in his lifetime than did any other individual, was frequently attacked, and with good reason, for making his contributions for public relations and political purposes, for seeking to clean the image of 'tainted money'. Yet it must also be noted that, from his days as a teenager on, he would give away a tenth of his earnings to charity. He was a devout Baptist who, in the words of one student of philanthropy, 'apparently felt there was some divine co-operation in the construction of Standard Oil Company'.

'God gave me my money,' he told an interviewer in 1915. After financing establishment of the University of Chicago, Rockefeller told a campus meeting: 'The good Lord gave me the money, and how could I withhold it from Chicago?' In his later years, Rockefeller mused, his wealth was an 'accident of history', possible only because of the peculiar circumstances of oil and the nineteenth century, and that he was only its trustee.[99]

The continued linkage of voluntary religion to voluntary giving on a mass level may be seen in the fact that '72 per cent of all individual giving went to religious institutions' in 1985.[100] Education, health, and

---

[97] Ben Whitaker, *The Foundations: An Anatomy of Philanthropy and Society* (London: Eyre Methuen, 1974), 53.

[98] Joseph C. Goulden, *The Money Givers* (New York: Random House, 1971), 47.

[99] Ibid. p. 28; Whitaker, *The Foundations*, pp. 64–6: Bremner, *American Philanthropy*, p. 106.

[100] Bremner, *American Philanthropy*, p. 210. See also Edward C. Jenkins, *Philanthropy in America* (New York: Association Press, 1950), 91; William S. Vickrey, 'One Economist's View of Philanthropy', in Frank Dickinson, ed., *Philanthropy and Public Policy* (New York:

hospitals are next, but far behind on the list. One study found that 'the ratio of gifts to religious organizations to discretionary receipts was remarkably constant over all the income levels'.[101]

The Great Depression of the 1930s, of course, brought about a fundamental change in the role of philanthropy. The state increasingly took over responsibility for welfare functions, for hospitals, for higher education, and many other activities. Private contributions have continued to increase in absolute size, particularly since the Second World War, but they have become a smaller proportion of the whole, particularly in non-religious spheres. The sources of private philanthropy have also changed. Corporations have replaced wealthy individuals as the large contributors. Corporate gifts have come to be recognized as excellent forms of public relations. One student of philanthropy, Aileen Ross, contends that

the rise in the contributions of corporations has enabled them to take over the control of raising and alloting money to many philanthropic agencies. Management can determine the amount that will be given, and since the same men are often found on the boards of a number of the larger corporations, they have come to form an 'inner circle' which can control both the gifts that are given and the selection of the top executives in the philanthropic agencies and in the more important and prestigious fund-raising campaigns, such as those for hospitals and universities.[102]

It is still true, of course, that a considerable sum continues to come from less affluent contributors. In 1970, it was estimated that 70 million people contributed to charitable causes.[103] Most of the contributions of small donors go to religion-related causes. 'Education, mainly colleges and universities, is getting the largest share of corporation giving, followed closely by health and welfare agencies.'[104] The historic cultural sources of support for philanthropy and voluntary associational activity in America still have vitality.

Each year for more than a quarter century after 1960 recorders of American philanthropy reported that total giving ... had reached new highs. The total for

National Bureau of Economic Research, 1962), 33; George G. Kirstein, *Better Giving* (Boston: Houghton Mifflin, 1975), 59–71. For detailed statistics, see the annual reports, *Giving USA*, published each year by the American Association of Fund-Raising Counsel, Inc., begun in 1954.

[101] Vickrey, 'One Economist's View', p. 45.
[102] Ross, 'Philanthropy', p. 78.
[103] Kirstein, *Better Giving*, p. xiii.
[104] Merrimon Cuninggim, *Private Money and Public Service* (New York: McGraw-Hill, 1972), 169–70.

1985—approximately $80 billion—was more than two and a half times as large as a decade earlier, and more than seven times the amount . . . raised in 1960.[105]

Hospitals, however, find religious-linked contributions are less important than in earlier eras, as relatively few of them are seen to serve denominational purposes. But even though the American state now provides for many activities once almost totally dependent on private support, its population, as the most anti-statist people in the developed world, continues to be the most generous on a personal basis.

Given this emphasis on the generosity of Americans, it is worth reiterating in David Popenoe's words that 'the United States lags well behind most other advanced societies in the creation of welfare state programs . . . it is the only major industrialized nation, for example, that has no general allowance program for families with children and lacks a national insurance plan covering . . . medical expenses'.[106] Detailed documentation of the lesser provisions in the United States, as compared to other developed nations, for dependent populations, particularly children and the elderly, may be found in a comprehensive work on *The Vulnerable*.[107] In discussing 'various explanations . . . for this American "exceptionalism" ', including economic and political structural factors, Stephanie Gould and John Palmer conclude that only two, 'heterogeneity of population and distinctiveness of public philosophy— seem to have explanatory power'. The first, they contend, makes for greater variations among sub-groups in earning capacities and hence more income inequality. The second refers to the discussions reported earlier of 'the peculiarities of the American outlook on public affairs, our extreme emphasis on individualism, our mistrust of central authority, our strong preference for public policies that promote equality of opportunity over those that promote equality of outcome'.[108]

Negative Traits

Thus far, aspects of American exceptionalism most would view as primarily positive have been discussed. But, ironically, it may be argued that the fact that the 'United States is notorious for its high crime rates'

[105] Bremner, *American Philanthropy*, p. 178.

[106] Popenoe, *Disturbing the Nest*, p. 285.

[107] J. Palmer, T. Smeeding, and B. B. Torrey, eds., *The Vulnerable* (Washington, DC: The Urban Institute, 1988).

[108] Stephanie G. Gould and John L. Palmer, 'Outcomes, Interpretations, and Policy Implications', in *The Vulnerable*, pp. 424–8.

and that it has the highest divorce rates in the world may also be linked to some of the special traits of the country as a uniquely liberal, bourgeois, individualistic, and socially egalitarian society.[109] A detailed survey of comparative crime rates in developed countries for the period 1945–85 indicates that 'rates for all categories of crime are approximately three times higher than in other developed nations, and the differences have been growing'.[110] The question is, why?

There is obviously no single answer. Louise Shelley, who has studied the problem comparatively, mentions a number of possible factors: tensions from 'postwar urbanization and population mobility, particularly as reflected among minorities and lower class persons, the drug problem, family structure and social values'.[111] While all these factors seem relevant, the latter set, values, have been noted by various sociologists as particularly important.[112] Robert Merton has emphasized the pressures generated by the interplay between America's basic values and the facts of social stratification in an industrial society.[113] The stress on equality and achievement in American society has meant that Americans are much more likely to be concerned with the achievement of approved *ends*—particularly pecuniary success—than with the use of appropriate *means*—the behaviour considered appropriate to a given position or status. In a country which stresses success above all, people are led to feel that the most important thing is to win the game, regardless of the methods employed in doing so. American culture applies the norms of a completely competitive society to everyone. Winners take all. As Merton has put it:

What makes American culture relatively distinctive . . . is that it is 'a society which places a high premium on economic affluence and social ascent for all its members'. . . . [T]his patterned expectation is regarded as appropriate for everyone, irrespective of his initial lot or station in life. . . .

This leads naturally to the subsidiary theme that success or failure are results wholly of personal qualities, that he who fails has only himself to blame, for the corollary to the concept of the self-made man is the self-unmade man. To the extent that this cultural definition is assimilated by those who have not made

[109] Louise I. Shelley, 'American Crime: An International Anomaly?', *Comparative Social Research*, 8 (1985), 81; Leon Radzinowicz and Joan King, *The Growth of Crime: The International Experience* (New York: Basic Books, 1977), 6–7.

[110] Shelley, 'American Crime', pp. 81, 88–9.

[111] Ibid. 91.

[112] I have drawn on my earlier discussion in *The First New Nation*, pp. 173–7.

[113] Robert K. Merton, *Social Theory and Social Structure* (Glencoe: The Free Press, 1957), 167–9. Merton reports considerable evidence documenting the thesis that pecuniary success is the dominant American value.

their mark, failure represents a double defeat: the manifest defeat of remaining far behind in the race for success and the implicit defeat of not having the capacities and moral stamina needed for success. . . . It is in this cultural setting that, in a significant portion of cases, the threat of defeat motivates men to the use of those tactics, beyond the law or the mores, which promise 'success'.

The moral mandate to achieve success thus exerts pressure to succeed, by fair means if possible and by foul means if necessary.[114]

In contrast, there is more emphasis in nations descendant from more traditionalistic, ascriptive, or aristocratic societies that one should behave in a proper manner. In the morality of aristocracy, to play the game well is more important than victory. All privileged strata seek to develop norms which justify their right to high status and which limit, if they do not eliminate, the possibility that they may be supplanted by 'new men', by the upwardly mobile who succeed by 'innovating'— that is, by ignoring the conventions. To emphasize correct behaviour, manners, and so forth, is to reward the characteristics which those born to privilege are most likely to have. Because of its settler society and revolutionary origins, America entered the era of a capitalistic, industrial, and politically democratic society without the traditions of an aristocratic or deferential order. As a result, the norms of aristocracy, though present to a limited extent among the social élite, have not been able to make much headway. Since the emphasis is on individual success in the United States, those individuals or groups who feel themselves handicapped and who seek to resolve their consequent doubts about their personal worth are under strong pressure to 'innovate', that is, to use whatever means they can find to gain recognition or money.

This pressure to innovate may be reflected in efforts which established groups would not make—for example, the development of new and risky industries by those of recent immigrant background and low status who are barred, by limited economic resources and social discrimination, from advancing up economic ladders. The pressure to succeed may also lead individuals and groups to serve social needs which are *outside* the law, in occupations usually described as 'rackets'. Organized vice—prostitution, bottlegging, drug selling, and gambling—has been open to ambitious individuals from deprived social backgrounds when other fields were closed. The rackets have attracted members of minority ethnic groups who are strongly motivated by the American emphasis on achievement, but who are limited in their access to legitimate means of

[114] Merton, *Social Theory and Social Structure.*

succeeding. The comparatively high crime rate in America, both in the form of lower-class rackets, robbery, and theft, and white-collar and business defalcation, may, therefore, be perceived as a consequence of the stress laid on success. Daniel Bell has logically suggested that large-scale crime may be seen as a natural by-product of American culture:

The desires satisfied in extra-legal fashion were more than a hunger for the 'forbidden fruits' of conventional morality. They also are involved in the complex and ever shifting structure of group, class, and ethnic stratification, which is the warp and woof of America's 'open' society, such 'normal' goals as independence through a business of one's own, and such 'moral' aspirations as the desire for social advancement and social prestige. For crime, in the language of the sociologists, has a 'functional' role in the society, and the urban rackets—the illicit activity organized for continuing profit, rather than individual illegal acts . . . [are] one of the queer ladders of social mobility in American life.[115]

Another source of the high American crime rate may be found in the emphasis here on the 'due process' guarantees for individual rights, which have produced legal inhibitions on the power of the police and prosecutors, including the absence of serious gun-control measures. This may be contrasted to the 'crime control' model, more evident in the Commonwealth, Japan, and Europe, which focuses on the maintenance of law and order, and is less protective of the rights of the accused and of individuals generally.[116] But, as Stephen Cole notes: 'the emphasis on individual rights that makes it difficult to prosecute and punish criminals also gives Americans a degree of civil liberty not found in most other countries'.[117] The American emphasis on due process is accompanied by greater litigiousness, as well as more formal and extensive efforts to enforce the law.[118] The United States has many more lawyers per capita (251 per 100,000 inhabitants as of 1981) than other developed countries, including all the predominantly English-speaking common-law ones.[119]

---

[115] Daniel Bell, *The End of Ideology* (Glencoe: The Free Press, 1960), 116–17.

[116] Herbert Packer, 'Two Models of the Criminal Process', *University of Pennsylvania Law Review*, 113 (Nov. 1964), 1–68.

[117] Stephen Cole, 'Crime as the Cost of American Creativity', *Newsday* (24 Aug. 1983).

[118] 'The United States is the most litigious society known to the world': Alan F. Westin, 'The United States Bill of Rights and the Canadian Charter: A Socio-Political Analysis', in William R. McKercher, ed., *The U.S. Bill of Rights and the Canadian Charter of Rights and Freedoms* (Toronto: Ontario Economic Council, 1983), 33.

[119] Lipset, *The First New Nation*, p. 264.

The United States is also 'exceptional' with regard to high rates of divorce and single-parent families. Its 'marital breakup rate is by far the highest among the advanced societies. . . . The chances of a first marriage ending in divorce in America today are about one in two. While . . . [the] percentage of single-parent families also ranks highest'.[120] The statistics are not to be explained by the presence of a disproportionately black 'underclass', though blacks have higher divorce and teenage birth rates than whites. The rate of teenage pregnancy among whites alone is 'still . . . twice that of the closest European competitor', while 'divorce in America today has become almost as common among the higher classes as among the lower'.[121] In seeking to explain American uniqueness in this area, Popenoe draws on the work of Robert Bellah and his colleagues, who note the importance of 'self-fulfillment' and 'expressive individualism' as major parts of the value system.[122] The lead of the United States in divorce rates which goes back to the nineteenth century presumably reflects in part the strength of individualism.

Interpreting the higher American teenage pregnancy rate, which occurs in tandem with a propensity, especially among whites, to marry to legitimize the birth, is more difficult. The authors of an extremely thorough comparative analysis of *Teenage Pregnancy in Industrialized Countries* seek to account for these seemingly contradictory results as stemming from Americans being more intensely religious, individualistic, anti-élitist, and less law- and rule-conforming than the populations of other countries.[123] The expressive individualism of young Americans leads them to have intercourse at an early age. Their greater religiosity, however, undermines their developing as rational, as instrumental an orientation to use of birth control, as exists among the less religiously committed Europeans and Canadians. The latter are also more disposed to listen to the advice of authority.[124] And when pregnancy occurs, the large majority of teenage white Americans marry; Europeans, particularly in the North, are less likely to.

Regardless of foreign and governmental deficits, evidence of corruption in high places, and higher violent crime rates, Americans

---

[120] Popenoe, *Disturbing the Nest*, p. 287.

[121] Ibid. 288.

[122] Ibid. 289;. Bellah *et al.*, *Habits of the Heart*, pp. 32–5, 48–50, 89, 101–2.

[123] Elise F. Jones *et al.*, *Teenage Pregnancy in Industrialized Countries* (New Haven, Conn.: Yale University Press, 1986), 36, 8–11.

[124] Ibid. 89, 223.

continue to be proud of their nation, to exhibit a greater sense of patriotism and of belief that their system is superior to all others. Opinion polls taken during the 1980s in most European countries, Japan, and North America, find that Americans are invariably more positive— usually much more positive—on items measuring such beliefs than are the citizens of the other industrialized democracies. They continue to believe in America and its superiority as a social system. In the early 1980s, 87 per cent of Americans said they were 'very proud' of their country, another 10 per cent replied 'quite proud'. The corresponding percentages for other countries were: Britain, 58 and 30; West Germany, 20 and 42; and France, 42 and 39.[125] The trend in the United States appears to be moving up. In 1986, Gallup found 89 per cent answered 'very proud', up from 80 per cent in 1981. In line with these findings, Americans also show up as among the most optimistic people, in Gallup Polls taken annually in thirty countries between 1976 and 1987, in response to the question: 'So far as you are concerned, do you think [next year] will be better or worse than [last year]?'[126]

Canada and the United States

The differences in religious, political, and economic terms between the United States and other developed countries may be seen not only with Europe generally, but also as between Canada and the United States. The American Revolution produced two nations. The United States is the country of the revolution, Canada of the counter-revolution.[127] The United States is the part of British North America which successfully seceded, while Canada is the area which remained British. These diverse outcomes have resulted in Canada resembling Europe with respect to the role of national traditions.

In Canada, as in Europe, a common history, rather than an ideological creed, defines the nation. Conservatism in Canada is descended from Toryism. After the Revolution, about 50,000 Tory Americans moved to

[125] Richard Rose, 'National Pride in Cross-National Perspective', *International Social Science Journal*, 37/1 (1985), 86, 93–5; Russell V. Dalton, *Citizen Politics in Western Democracies* (Chatham, NJ: Chatham House Publishers, 1988), 237; Marjorie Hyer, 'Poll Finds Americans Most Proud', *International Herald Tribune* (20 May 1982).

[126] Alex C. Michalos, 'Optimism in Thirty Countries Over a Decade', *Social Indicators Research*, 20 (1988), 178–9.

[127] Lipset, *Revolution and Counterrevolution*, pp. 37–75; 'Historical Traditions', pp. 114–15, 117–18; and *Continental Divide*, pp. 1–18.

Canada. Conversely, some Yankee residents of what was originally northern New England, mainly Nova Scotia, migrated to the new nation. The Revolution produced an interesting transmutation of religion. Congregationalism had been strong in Nova Scotia and New Brunswick, as in the rest of New England before the Revolution. After the Treaty of Paris in 1783, many Congregational ministers moved south.[128] Conversely, many Anglican priests went north. Hence a shift of populations in political and religious terms occurred within English-speaking North America.

Catholic Quebec, which had become a British state in 1763, remained with its conquerors in 1776 for practical reasons. Quebec was totally controlled by the clergy, since almost all the secular élites returned to France after the British conquest. The priesthood of the province understood that they would have much more trouble with the anti-papist Puritan Yankees than they would with the British Anglicans. Other good reasons for staying British soon developed. The French Revolution was anticlerical and materialistic. The francophone clergy, including emigrés from France, deliberately sought to cut off all contact with the mother country. This made Quebec a second counter-revolutionary society. Canada thus became a country of two counter-revolutions. English Canada opposed the American Revolution as did French Canada. But then French Canada rejected the French Revolution.[129]

In Canada, the dominant Tory tradition has meant a strong state, communitarianism, group solidarity, élitism. Most provinces continue to support church-controlled schools. Public ownership, much of its instituted under Conservative Party governments, is considerably more extensive than in the United States. Canadian governments spend more proportionately on welfare.[130] Conversely, her citizens, both corporate and individual, donate much less to charitable causes than Americans.[131] Her criminal justice system has resembled those of Europe, stressing crime control and the rights of the state. As noted earlier, the American emphasis is on due process and the rights of the accused.

Though Canada is often governed by the Conservative Party, its trade

---

[128] Lipset, *The First New Nation*, pp. 88, 160.

[129] Northrop Frye, *Divisions on a Ground: Essays on Canadian Culture* (Toronto: Anansi, 1982), 66.

[130] Robert Kudrle and Theodore Marmor, 'The Development of Welfare States in North America', in Peter Flora and Arnold Heidenheimer, eds., *The Development of Welfare States in Europe and America* (New Brunswick: Transaction Books, 1981), 91–3; Lipset, 'Canada and the United States', pp. 128–34.

[131] See Lipset, *Continental Divide*, pp. 142–9.

unions and socialist party are very much stronger than in the United States. The proportion of organized workers is double that south of the border.[132] As indicated previously, the Canadian social democrats, the New Democratic party (NDP), are an important force in national politics, whilst socialists are close to non-existent in electoral terms in the United States. In Canada, moreover, all three parties—the Conservative, the Liberal, and the NDP—support the welfare state.

In the United States, on the other hand, conservatism is associated with the national tradition of suspicion of government. Ronald Reagan and Milton Friedman, the two names most identified with this ideology, define conservatism in America. The word still means *laissez-faire*. It also involves rejection of aristocracy and social class hierarchy. As recently as the April and June 1987 issues of the British magazine *Encounter*, two leading trans-Atlantic conservative intellectuals, Max Beloff (Lord Beloff) and Irving Kristol, debated the uses of titles. Kristol argued that Britain 'is soured by a set of very thin, but tenacious, aristocratic pretentions . . . [which] foreclose opportunities and repress a spirit of equality that has yet to find its full expression'. Hence the frustrations of many 'which makes British life . . . so cheerless, so abounding in ressentiment'. Like Tocqueville, he holds up 'social equality', as making 'other inequalities tolerable in modern democracy'. Beloff, a Tory, contended that what threatens Conservatism in Britain 'is not its remaining links with the aristocratic tradition, but its alleged indifference to some of the abuses of capitalism. It is not the Dukes who lose us votes, but the "malefactors of great wealth" '. He wondered 'why Mr. Kristol believes himself to be a "conservative" ' since he is 'as incapable as most Americans of being a conservative in any profound sense'. Lord Beloff concluded that 'Conservatism must have a "Tory" element or it is only the old "Manchester School" ', i.e. Liberal.[133]

Canada's most distinguished Conservative intellectual, George Grant, emphasizes in his *Lament for a Nation*, that

Americans who call themselves 'Conservatives' have the right to that title only in a particular sense. In fact, they are old-fashioned liberals. . . . Their concentration on freedom from governmental interference has more to do with nineteenth century liberalism than with traditional conservatism, which asserts the right of the community to restrain freedom in the name of the common good.

[132] Lipset, 'North American Labor Movements', pp, 425–6.
[133] Max Beloff, 'Of Lords, Senators, & Plain Misters', *Encounter*, 68 (Apr. 1987), 69–71; 'An Exchange Between Max Beloff and Irving Kristol', *Encounter*, 69 (June 1987), 69–71.

Grant bemoans the fact that American Conservatism, with its stress on the virtues of competition and links to business ideology, focuses on the rights of individuals and ignores communal rights and obligations. He notes that there has been no place in the American political philosophy 'for the organic conservatism that pre-dated the age of progress. Indeed, the United States is the only society on earth that has no traditions from before the age of progress.' Writing in the mid-1960s, he reiterated the words of H. G. Wells, voiced over half a century earlier. The Americans' ' "right-wing" and "left-wing" are just different species of liberalism'.[134]

Still, it must be recognized that American politics have changed. The 1930s produced a qualitative difference.[135] The Great Depression resulted in a strong emphasis on planning, on the welfare state, on the role of the government as a major regulatory actor. An earlier upswing in statist sentiment immediately prior to the First World War, which took the form of significant support for the largely Republican Progressive movement led by Robert LaFollette and Theodore Roosevelt and increasing strength (up to 6 per cent of the vote nationally) for the Socialist Party, failed to change the political system. Grant McConnell explains the failure of the former as stemming from 'the pervasive and latent ambiguity in the movement' about confronting American anti-statist values. 'Power as it exists was antagonistic to democracy, but how was it to be curbed without the erection of a superior power.'[136]

The New Deal, which owed much to the Progressives, was not socialist. Franklin Roosevelt clearly wanted to maintain capitalism. But the New Deal did increase the statist strain in American politics, in tandem with increased public support for trade unions.[137] The new labour movement which arose concomitantly, the Committee (later Congress) for Industrial Organization (CIO), unlike the AFL, was social democratic in its orientation. In fact, socialists and communists played important roles in the movement. The CIO was much more politically active than the older Federation and helped to press the Democrats to the left. The Depression led to a kind of Europeanization in American politics as well as in labour organizations. Class factors became more important in differentiating party support.[138] The Conservatives, increasingly con-

[134] George Grant, *Lament for a Nation* (Princeton: D. Van Nostrand Co., 1965), 64–5.
[135] Hofstadter, *The Age of Reform*, p. 308.
[136] Grant McConnell, *Private Power and American Democracy* (New York: Random House, 1966), 38.
[137] Lipset, 'Roosevelt and the Protest of the 1930s', pp. 273–98.
[138] Samuel Lubell, *The Future of American Politics* (New York: Harper & Row, 3rd edn., 1965), 55–68.

centrated among the Republicans, remained anti-statist and *laissez-faire*, but many of them grew willing to accommodate an activist role for the state. This pattern, however, gradually inverted after the Second World War as a result of long-term prosperity.

The United States, like other parts of the developed world, has experienced what some call the economic miracle. The period from 1945 on has been characterized by considerable growth, an absence of major economic downswings, higher rates of social mobility both on a mass level and into the élites, and a tremendous expansion of higher educational systems—from a few million to eleven or twelve million going to colleges and universities—which fostered mobility. As noted earlier, America has done particularly well economically, leading Europe and Japan by a considerable margin in terms of new job creation. A consequence of these developments has been a refurbishing of the classical liberal ideology, i.e., American Conservatism. The class tensions produced by the depression have lessened, reflected in the decline of the labour movement, and lower correlations between class position and vote choices. Even before Ronald Reagan entered the White House, the United States had a lower rate of taxation, a less developed welfare state, and very few government-owned industries, as compared to Canada and most other industrialized nations. Conversely in Canada, which has no classically liberal tradition to return to, trade union membership and socialist support have grown.

Conclusion

To what extent is it still possible to speak of American exceptionalism? It is obvious that America and the rest of the Western world have changed greatly over the past two centuries. They have all become industrialized, urbanized, better educated. The post-feudal elements that existed in many European countries have declined enormously, with the partial exception of England. In social structural terms, they are becoming Americanized. One of the more striking examples is the emergence of Margaret Thatcher and the so-called 'drys' as the dominant faction within the British Conservative Party. Thatcher represents the trend towards social modernization, the Americanization of Britain and Europe. She seeks to eliminate post-feudal values and institutions, including mercantilist socialist policies. She much prefers self-made entrepreneurs, like her successor, John Major, to the aristocracy. She has transformed the Conservative Party into a classically liberal one in the process of trying to create a fully bourgeois nation, that is, one which is more like the United States.

The changes that have occurred, however, still leave many differences. The United States and Canada, for example, continue to vary along lines that flow from their distinctive national traditions, although Canada today resembles her southern neighbour in economic structural terms. In a sense, it may be argued that the trans-national changes are like movement up railway tracks on parallel lines so that the gap between the nations remains, even though the movement in behaviour and values over time is enormous. Still, the United States is more religious, more patriotic, more populist and anti-élitist (the number of elective positions increased between 1977 and 1987 by over 10,000, while direct involvement of the electorate in the candidate nomination process continues to grow), more committed to higher education for the majority, hence to meritocracy, more socially egalitarian, more prone to divorce, less law-abiding, wealthier in real income (purchasing power) terms, markedly more job-creating, and less disposed to save, than other developed countries. It remains the least statist Western nation in terms of public effort, benefits, and employment as Richard Rose notes.[139] Not surprisingly, cross-national polls continue to reveal that Americans are less favourable to an active role for government in the economy and large welfare programmes than the citizens of Canada and European countries. Conversely, Americans continue to show a marked preference for private efforts in welfare as in industry; they lead the world in philanthropic giving. As Nathan Glazer reports, 'non-public resources in American welfare are greater than is found in any other major nation'.[140]

There are, however, two major exceptions or changes which have contradicted the original 'creed' with its emphasis on individual rights.[141] These include the introduction of a planning, welfare-state emphasis in the 1930s, accompanied by greater class consciousness and trade union

[139] Richard Rose, 'How Exceptional is American Government?', *Studies in Public Policy*, 150 (Glasgow: Centre for the Study of Public Policy, University of Strathclyde, 1985).

[140] Nathan Glazer, 'Welfare and "Welfare" in America', in Richard Rose and Rei Shiratori, eds., *The Welfare State East and West* (New York: Oxford University Press, 1986), 62; Harold Wilensky, *The Welfare State and Equality* (Berkeley: University of California Press, 1975), 28–39; Arnold Heidenheimer *et al., Comparative Public Policy: The Politics of Social Choice in Europe and America* (New York: St. Martin's Press, 1983).

[141] For a sophisticated analysis of the changes which have been attempted, and which have survived or failed, see Hugh Heclo, 'The Emerging Regime', in Richard A. Harris and Sidney M. Milkis, eds., *Remaking American Politics* (Boulder, CO: Westview Press, 1989), 290–320.

growth, subsumed in Hofstadter's phrase 'social democratic tinge', and the focus on ethnic, racial, and gender rights in the 1960s and beyond, to which Aaron Wildavsky calls attention in Chapter 5. The first change has had continuing impact in the form of a much-expanded government which remains committed, even under Reagan and Bush, to many welfare and regulatory objectives. But, as noted earlier, the growth has been slowed, in some cases reversed. Popular sentiment seeks to limit welfare and opposes some state involvements in the economy that once had considerable support. Trade union membership has fallen greatly as a share of the labour force, and the significance of class as a variable related to partisan support is much reduced. At the end of the 1980s, the economic role of government was weaker in the United States than in any other industrialized economy.

The focus on non-class forms of group rights which came to a head in the 1960s is, however, still a dynamic force. Affirmative-action quotas, first introduced in 1969 in the Nixon administration by administrative fiat, implicitly assume the Euro-Canadian emphasis on group rights and the socialist concern for equality of results. The policy did not derive from pressure from the American left or working-class groups. Rather it reflected an effort by the white élite to meet the militant demands of blacks for economic equality. A conservative Republican, now a Reagan judicial appointee, Laurence Silberman, then Assistant Secretary of Labor, concluded that individual redress to the courts for anti-discrimination judgements would not do much to open discriminatory parts of the labour market to blacks. He drafted an administrative order providing for a quota for blacks in the Philadelphia construction industry. The Nixon and subsequent administrations have applied the principle of 'communal rights', in Grant's language, to other minorities and women and to many areas of the society, including universities.

This policy clearly involves an effort to guarantee equal results to groups. It has persisted through liberal and conservative administrations, even though opinion polls have repeatedly reported that overwelming majorities of whites and pluralities of blacks believe that the principle of equal opportunity should apply to individuals, that special preference or quota guarantees should not be accorded to members of groups, like blacks, who are underrepresented in privileged job or educational categories. Seemingly, the American élites, including many Republican and most Democratic leaders, felt the national creed had to be amended to make up for the past treatment of blacks. This concern was then extended to other groups, perceived as lacking equal rights because of ascriptive or biological traits: Hispanics, Native Americans, Asians (though their success has undermined their place), women, the handicapped, and, to some degree, homosexuals. The fact that such significant changes could occur, much like those stemming from the Great Depression, demonstrates that the creed is not inviolate, that it is not written in stone, that further change is possible.

The success of blacks in modifying the emphasis on individual rights in American values stems, of course, from the fact that slavery and racism have been the foremost deviation from the American creed throughout the history of the republic. Thomas Jefferson voiced his concern over its impact on the future, noting in 1781 that 'I tremble for my country when I reflect that God is just'.[142] In his classic analysis of American racism, *An American Dilemma*, Gunnar Myrdal noted in 1944 that, in spite of their racist practices, white Americans, including Southerners, believed in the creed, in egalitarianism. They believed that they believed in equality for all. From this assumption, it could be anticipated that if blacks organized to demand their rights, the whites would give in.[143] This is what has happened. And in yielding politically, the white male political élite has acquiesced to the demand for group rights, for a form of equality of results. But this change does not affect economic class rights, or the strength of the meritocratic belief that those who work hard will succeed.

These changes, however, have not basically modified the emphases on individual success, on equality of opportunity rather than of results. Affirmative-action group rights have been defended from the 1960s on as 'compensatory action', since compensation for past discrimination is consistent with the egalitarian creed and essentially makes the conditions of competition 'fairer' without violating the notion of a competitive system.[144] And as indicated earlier, America continues to be exceptional among developed nations in the low level of support it provides for the poor through welfare, housing, and medical care policies. As a result, though the wealthiest country, it has the highest proportion living in poverty among developed nations, according to the detailed statistical

---

[142] Thomas Jefferson, *Notes on the State of Virginia* (New York: Harper & Row, Torchbooks edn., 1964), 156. On the complexity of Jefferson's views see Edmund S. Morgan, 'Slavery and Freedom: The American Paradox', *Journal of American History*, 59 (June 1972), 5–29.

[143] Gunnar Myrdal, *An American Dilemma* (New York: Harper & Row, 2nd edn., 1962), 460–2.

[144] For a detailed discussion, see Lipset, *The First New Nation*, pp. xxxiv–xxxv.

analyses of the Luxembourg Income Study data, the most comprehensive available. The United States also ranks last among ten countries (six in Europe, plus Australia, Canada, and Israel) as most unequal in comparisons of income distribution. But it should be noted that complex composite measures of inequality, which include items like social security programmes, physicians per capita, infant mortality, caloric and protein consumption per capita, educational attainments, social mobility, as well as income distribution, place the United States close to the top, most equal (only Switzerland is possibly higher) among 120 polities.[145]

It is important to recognize that various seemingly contradictory aspects of American society are intimately related. The lack of respect for authority, anti-élitism, and populism contribute to higher crime rates, school indiscipline, and low electoral turn-outs. The emphasis on achievement, on meritocracy, is also tied to higher levels of deviant behaviour and less support for the underprivileged. Intense religiosity is linked to less reliance on contraception in pre-marital sexual relationships by young people. The same moralistic factors which make for patriotism help to produce opposition to war. Concern for the legal rights of accused persons and civil liberties of all is tied to opposition to gun control and difficulty in applying crime control measures. The stress on individualism weakens social control mechanisms which rely on strong ties to groups, and facilitates diverse forms of deviant behaviour.[146]

I would like to conclude with some thoughts derived from a Canadian scholar who was named after two executed Italo-American anarchists, Sacvan Bercovitch, an American political scientist, Samuel Huntington, and a communist theorist, Antonio Gramsci. The first two note that an emphasis on a national consensus, a national myth, is not an alternative to a stress on conflict.[147] A consensual myth may foster bitter controversy. Huntington notes periods of credal passion in America, intense conflicts seeking to bring 'institutions and practices in accord with these values and beliefs are associated with political change. In a political

[145] Michael Don Ward, *The Political Economy of Distribution: Equality versus Inequality* (New York: Elsevier, 1978), 43, 65.

[146] Brigitte Buhmann *et al.*, 'Equivalence Scales, Well-Being, Inequality, and Poverty: Sensitivity Estimates Across Ten Countries Using the Luxembourg Income Study (LIS) Database', *Review of Income and Wealth*, 34 (June 1988), 126–33; Timothy M. Smeeding and Barbara Boyld Torrey, 'Poor Children in Rich Countries', *Science*, 242 (11 Nov. 1988), 873–7.

[147] For a discussion of the complementary interrelated character of consensus and conflict in societies, see S. M. Lipset, *Consensus and Conflict* (New Brunswick: Transaction Books, 1985), esp. pp. 1–109.

system produced by a major revolution . . . efforts may be made from time to time to renew or reaffirm revolutionary values.' Such conflicts and patterns of change can only take place 'in a society with an overwhelming *consensus*' on 'values'. They could not occur 'in societies with traditional ideological pluralism, such as most of those of western Europe' and Canada.[148]

Americans fight each other in their efforts to defend or expand the American creed. Pre-Civil War leaders of the anti-slavery struggle such as Frederick Douglas and William Lloyd Garrison, or founder of American feminism Elizabeth Cady Stanton, like mid-twentieth-century American communists, demanded changes in order, in Douglas's words, to live up to 'the genius of American institutions, fulfill its sacred mission'.[149] Bercovitch, who cites these radical exponents of the creed, first entered the United States during the conflict-ridden 1960s. Expressing his reaction to the credal passions of the era, he writes:

My first encounter with American consensus was in the late sixties, when I crossed the border into the United States and found myself inside the myth of America. Not of North America, for the myth stopped short of the Canadian and Mexican borders, but of a country that despite its arbitrary frontiers, despite its bewildering mix of race and creed, could believe in something called the True America, and could invest that patent fiction with all the moral and emotional appeal of a religious symbol. . . . Here was the Jewish anarchist Paul Goodman berating the Midwest for abandoning the promise; here, the descendant of American slaves, Martin Luther King, denouncing injustice as a violation of the American way; here, an endless debate about national destiny . . . conservatives scavenging for un-Americans, New Left historians recalling the country to its sacred mission.

Nothing in my Canadian background had prepared me for that spectacle. . . . It gave me something of an anthropologist's sense of wonder at the symbol of the tribe. . . . To a Canadian skeptic, a gentile in God's country . . . [here was] a pluralistic, pragmatic people . . . bound together by an ideological consensus.

Let me repeat that mundane phrase: *ideological consensus*. For it wasn't the idea of exceptionalism that I discovered in '68. . . . It was a hundred sects and factions, each apparently different from the others, yet all celebrating the same mission.[150]

[148] Huntington, *American Politics*, pp. 130–1, 85–109 (my emphasis).
[149] Quoted in Sacvan Bercovitch, 'The Rites of Assent: Rhetoric, Ritual, and the Ideology of American Consensus', in Sam B. Girgus, ed., *The American Self: Myth, Ideology and Popular Culture* (Albuquerque: University of New Mexico Press, 1981), 21; see also Bercovitch, *American Jeremiad*, pp. 140–51, 176.
[150] Bercovitch, 'Rites of Assent', pp. 5–6 (emphasis in original).

Gramsci, who also believed that Americanism is the national ideology, wrote in the 1920s that before Italy could become socialist it had to Americanize socially as well as economically, a development he viewed positively. Like earlier Marxists, he saw the United States as the epitome of a bourgeois democratic society, one that lacked the traditional pre-capitalist elements which were still to be found in Italy and other European cultures.[151] Of course, as noted, the industrialized European countries have begun to resemble the United States economically, as more affluent, and less status-conscious socially. In the process, their socialist movements (and the Italian Communist Party, now renamed the Party of the Democratic Left) have redefined their objectives in terms which resemble those of the American Democratic Party. Their conservatives, like Margaret Thatcher, increasingly accept the classical liberal ideology, one which is also impacting on their lefts. In line with Marx's anticipation, cited earlier, that 'the more developed country shows the less developed the image of their future', the United States is less exceptional as nations develop and Americanize.[152] But, given the structural convergences, the extent to which it is still unique is astonishing.

[151] Gramsci, *Selections*, pp. 21–2, 272, 318.
[152] Lipset, *Consensus and Conflict*, pp. 187–217.

2

The 'Hegelian Secret': Civil Society and American Exceptionalism

Daniel Bell

The rise and fall of nations and empires is a puzzle that has recurrently attracted, if not seduced, philosophers and historians, tempting them to grand visions of a ghostly demiurge that drives reflective consciousness, as with Hegel, or some Wagnerian drama of challenge and response, of purification and heroism, as with the self-wrapped robes of Arnold Toynbee.

There is a mystery. What accounts for the sudden gathering of energies that spurs a people to a surge of might which sweeps across continents, and then lies spent—whether it be the Near East Empires of the Assyrians or Egyptians, never to rise again; or the Mongols and the Asiatic hordes which in the thirteenth century embraced all of China and by the middle of the fourteenth century had stretched across Russia to Budapest, and then collapsed. In the long succession of Western history we often begin with the rise and fall of Rome and, after a long hiatus, the shift of strength to the Atlantic littoral, with the unexpected rise and the expected falling away of the Spanish and Portuguese empires, and, in our own time, the expansive spread and then the contraction of the British empire.

An arabesque interpretation was given by the Berber philosopher of the fourteenth century, Ibn Khaldun, who in his beguiling book *The Muqaddimah* (Arnold Toynbee called it 'undoubtedly the greatest work of its kind that has ever been created by any mind in any time or place') externalized the cycle of Plato's 'fevered city', destroyed by the desire for luxury, and elaborated it into a philosophy of history: the rude barbarians, ruthless and amoral, storm the older centres of civilization; their children consolidate the gains and build the great cities and palaces; and their children, soft and sybaritic, given over to the perfumed arts and sexual peccadillos (the permissive society?), become unable to resist the new barbarians at the gates.[1]

[1] Ibn Khaldun, *The Muqaddimah: An Introduction to History*, tr. from the Arabic by Franz Rosenthal (Bollingen Series 43; New York: Pantheon Books, 1958).

Any such simplifications are inherently suspect. In their single-threaded story-line, they are more fitting for a Cecil B. DeMille extravaganza (but then, Hollywood has also declined) than for the prosaic sociological analysis that is our wont today. (Though Ibn Khaldun's idea of *asabiyah*, or primordial group feeling, as the basis of the emotional unity of a regime, is clearly a relevant insight.)

And since the mystery remains, historians and sociologists seek answers by searching for more mundane and even grand, though no longer dramatic, images. Brooks Adams, the brother of Henry Adams and himself an historian of large ambition, exulted in 1900 that Great Britain was passing from the stage of history to be succeeded by the United States. The reason, however, was no longer military might, as in the past, but the character of industrial production—in this instance, the production of steel—which indicated that the United States was forging ahead and becoming the mightiest industrial power on earth. For Brooks Adams, all this was fated not by some inscrutable cunning of reason, but because the access to and control of strategic resources (metals and minerals), combined with energy and national will, was the basis of power. In *The New Empire* (1902), he skilfully traced the pattern of the exhaustion of resources as the fault lines of economic history— the tremors, one might say, of geology and geo-politics. (And, in an intriguing side glance, Adams remarked on the shadow of Japan waiting in the wings, waiting for its sun to rise.)[2]

What is striking is that each nation, when it begins to gather its energies—military, political, or economic—to make a decisive entry on to the 'stage of history', defines itself with respect to its uniqueness and exceptionalism. In Japan today that debate is emerging over the question of the uniqueness of Japanese social development: how to explain why Japan seems to confound Max Weber's generalization that capitalism could begin only in the west, and not in the orient, and why it has made that 'leap' in a shorter time than Western social development.[3]

---

[2] Brooks Adams, *The New Empire* (New York: The Macmillan Co., 1902). As Adams wrote about Japan (p. 195): 'The Japanese have developed a higher order of energy than the Russians, and such a supposition is hardly to be entertained. Yet the only path by which Japan can expand is through Korea: if she occupy Korea she will flank the Russian trade-routes and the Russian empire will totter'.

[3] I have in mind the major effort of Murakami, Kumon, and Sato, in their huge work, *Bunmei to shite no ie-shakai*, to pose a distinctive Japanese form of social organization, the *Ie*, as one of the category of 'historical civilizations' comparable to Greece, Rome, India, and China and, of course, the contemporary Western civilization. For a summary of this debate, see Murakami Yasusuke, '*Ie* Society as a Pattern of Civilisation', *Journal of Japanese Studies*, 10/2 (Summer 1984), the large symposium on this thesis in the *Journal of Japanese Studies*, 11/1 (Winter 1984), and the reply by Professor Murakami, in the same journal, 11/2 (Summer 1985).

But when the sense of mortality begins to take hold, there arises the question of exemption. Is one always fated to pass away from greatness? Many such speculations—and hopes—centre on the theme of some form of 'exceptionalism'. In the United States there has been the belief, so strong since the beginning of the Republic, in an American exceptionalism. From the start there had been the self-consciousness of a destiny that marked this country as being different from others; that the greatness was laid out like a magnetic field which would shape the contours of the nation from one ocean to the other, and finally, when it confronted the rest of the world from that magnetic core, this would become 'the American Century'. The expansion across the vast continent in the nineteenth century seemed to confirm that manifest destiny. And the evidence of American strength after the Second World War, when the United States emerged as the paramount power (or to use the current jargon, as the hegemonic nation), seemed to confirm that coming century. Yet now, forty or more years later, arise doubts whether America can maintain its greatness, and equally the fear that the curtain is falling on the American play.

I

In all these speculations and debates, three different historical questions are intertwined, and I wish to sort these out, both to distinguish the separate questions and to concentrate on the one that has the greatest interest (in the sense of being the most fruitful) for a sociologist.

The first and most spectacular question is the one with which I began—the puzzle of the rise and fall of empires, and its possible application now to the United States. About a decade and a half ago, the economic historian Charles P. Kindleberger foresaw in a few years 'an American climacteric' (the male equivalent of the menopause), based on the proposition that the United States was losing the exuberant energy that had made it the economic and technological leader in field after field. And in the last year or two, there have been a number of books which have emphasized the theme of decline: Walter Russell Mead's *Mortal Splendor*, David P. Calleo's *Beyond American Hegemony*, and, with the warning that top-heavy military expenditures and low productive investment would repeat for the United States the conditions which toppled France, Spain, and the United Kingdom, Paul Kennedy's *The Rise and Fall of the Great Powers: Economic Change and Military Conflict from 1500 to 2000.*[4]

---

[4] Charles P. Kindleberger, 'An American Climacteric?' *Challenge*, 17/1 (Jan.–Feb. 1974),

There are many reasons to appreciate the suggestiveness of these works. And many reasons to be sceptical. As Samuel P. Huntington has wryly remarked: 'In 1988 the United States reached the zenith of its fifth wave of declinism since the 1950s'. And, going on more combatively, Huntington declared: 'With some exceptions, declinist writings do not elaborate testable propositions involving independent and dependent variables.'[5] True, but then, which statements about macro-historical phenomena or political sociology do, other than some micro-mini circumscribed propositions? (The inherent difficulty of the social sciences, as S. M. Lipset once observed, is that there are too many variables and too few cases.)

These issues are unmanageable for other reasons. Methodologically, there are often no clear time-frames: when to start the count, when to mark the point of inflection, i.e. the mid-point of change, and when to mark the downturn to a conclusion. The problem is similar to the various efforts to create a 'social physics', from Henry Adams to Derek de Solla Price, which sought to plot a logistic curve, an S-curve, based on initial exponential rates of change—the doubling rates, of vehicular speed, of the number of different scientific journals, of population increases—and to identify the falling-off phase as an inverse rate of the early swarming period. The parameters (in the technical, not metaphorical sense) simply cannot be stated accurately. Sociologically, there is the difficulty that the nation may be less and less the relevant unit of analysis as different structures emerge in world society—an international set of markets for

35–45. Walter Russell Mead, *Mortal Splendor: The American Empire in Transition* (Boston: Houghton Mifflin, 1987); David P. Calleo, *Beyond American Hegemony: The Future of the Western Alliance* (New York: Basic Books, 1987); Paul Kennedy, *The Rise and Fall of the Great Powers: Economic Change and Military Conflict from 1500 to 2000* (New York: Random House, 1987).

[5] Samuel P. Huntington, 'The U.S.—Decline or Renewal?', *Foreign Affairs* (Winter 1988/ 9) 76, 77. Apropos the Kennedy thesis, it may be instructive to look at other explanations of 'decline', particularly for the United Kingdom. Mancur Olson, in his *The Rise and Decline of Nations: Economic Growth, Stagflation, and Social Rigidities* (New Haven, Conn., Yale Univ. Press, 1982), makes structural rigidities the focus of his explanation, rigidities created by the networks of collusive relations which we would call 'corporatist'. Martin Wiener, in his book *English Culture and the Decline of the Industrial Spirit: 1850–1980* (Cambridge: Cambridge Univ. Press, 1981), attributes the decline to the ethos of the gentleman and the power of a status system that held economic success in low esteem. And this thesis has been elaborated most recently by Corelli Barnett in *The Pride and the Fall: The Dream and Illusion of Britain as a Great Nation* (New York: Free Press, 1987). There the slackness of British life is deplored, and the size of the welfare state made the butt of Britain's economic burden after the Second World War. But these are 'sociological' explanations and a far cry from Paul Kennedy's emphasis on the burdens of military expenditure and the disproportion between these and productive investment. And what is one to say, too, of Mrs Thatcher who has shaken up the British economy so vigorously, and seemingly belied all these putative explanations of decline?

capital, integrated in real time; a continental scale of trade, as with the European Community or the North American continent; and regional economies in the new systems of production. And in culture, we see a syncretism in which 'Dallas' and 'Dynasty', and 'Nintendo' and 'Masterpiece Theatre', permeate popular culture, children's culture, and middle-brow culture everywhere.[6] So, if for economic and sociological reasons, the nation is losing its boundaries, what do we mean by the 'rise and fall' of nations or empires?

The second, very different kind of question is that of the uniqueness of each nation or culture. That wise Harvard psychologist Henry A. Murray once remarked that each of us is in some ways like *everybody* else, in some ways like *somebody* else, and in some ways like *nobody* else. What is true of individuals has also been true, at least metaphorically, of countries and nations. All societies face the problems of exercising authority and power, of organizing and allocating resources. Many societies are alike in being, say, democratic or market societies. And each society has an idiosyncratic history shaped by topography and location, traditions and culture, and that less definable element of *esprit* or *moeurs* which gives a distinctive imprint to its culture and people. That idiosyncratic contour—call it national character or, since character is an ambiguous term, national style—is often the overriding feature we have had to identify in order to understand the history, politics, or character of the country. A work such as Louis Hartz's *The Liberal Tradition*, with its emphasis on the lack of a feudal past, points to a historical uniqueness which is the ground of American manners and political institutions, just as B. H. Sumner's *Survey of Russian History* makes vivid the role of the steppes and climate in shaping Russian swings of mood, or the studies from Glanville to Maitland on the development of English law or of Harrington on property give us an understanding of the centrality of liberty in the unfolding of English political institutions. If, as Herder observed, a culture and a people are marked off from each other by language and history, so too were political institutions, at least until the convergences and syncretism of the second half of the twentieth century.

But uniqueness is not 'exceptionalism'. All nations are to some extent unique. But the idea of exceptionalism, as it has been used to describe

---

[6] On the first of these issues, time-frames, see the section 'The Measurement of Knowledge' in my book, *The Coming of Post-Industrial Society* (New York: Basic Books, 1973), 177–87. On the second issue, of the different emerging structures, see my essay 'The World and the United States in the year 2013', *Daedalus* (Summer 1987).

American history and institutions, assumes not only that the United States has been unlike other nations, but that it is exceptional in the sense of being exemplary ('a city upon a hill'), or a beacon among nations; or immune from the social ills and decadence that have beset all other republics in the past; or that it is exempt from the historical course of 'social laws' of development which all nations eventually follow. Thus it is the idea of exceptionalism as a distinct historical theme, not 'uniqueness' or 'rise and fall', that I wish to pursue.

In the United States, the theme of 'exceptionalism' has been argued in diverse ways. Sometimes the United States is conceived of as being the *exemplary* nation, fated by Providence or by following the wise course laid down by the founding fathers; or as an *exempt* nation, exempt from the laws of decadence or the laws of history; or as the *first new, self-conscious nation*, able to control its own fate and future, which is the mark, presumably, of the modern. Much of the discussion of American exceptionalism, I believe, has been confused because the different and sometimes overlapping facets indicated by my italicized terms have been taken as the central meaning of the idea. Since there are several different conceptions, I would like to sort these out and then, in this paper, add a fourth. None of these, I should add, are mutually exclusive. Historical interpretation is never exhausted by a single idea.

II

For intellectuals, and particularly for radicals who think of themselves as the standard-bearers of the intellectual class, the theme of American exceptionalism is interwoven with the question first raised by Werner Sombart in 1906, 'Why is there no Socialism in the United States ?' The formulation is ambiguous, if only for the literalness of the translation from the German. In 1896, Sombart, then a professor at the University of Breslau, had published a small book, based on eight lectures, under the title *Socialism and the Social Movement in the 19th Century*. Social movement in this context, a translation from the German word *Sozial*, meant simply socialist movement. If socialism was the necessary, evolutionary outcome of capitalist development, the socialist movement was also inevitably brought into being by capitalism, as part of the class divisions of society.

The book was a review of the ideas of various socialist thinkers, in particular Marx, and dealt as well with the history and spread of working-class movements in England, France, and Germany. As John Bates Clark, the professor of political economy at Columbia University (and one of the founders of the theory of marginal productivity), wrote in his introduction to the American edition:

The structure of the world of industry is changing. Great establishments are exterminating small ones, and are forming federations with each other. Machinery is producing nearly every kind of goods, and there is no longer a place for such a middle class as was represented by the master workman, with his slowly learned handicraft and his modest shop. These facts construed in a certain way are the material of socialism. If we see in them the dawn of an era of state industry that shall sweep competition and competitors out of the field, we are evolutionary socialists.

We may need a doctrinal basis for our view of evolution that is going on; and we may find it in the works of Marx and others. . . . Marxism, in practice, means realism and a reliance on evolution, however little the wilder utterances of Marx himself may suggest that fact. Internationalism is also a trait of this modern movement. . . . It is a natural affiliation of men of all nations having common ends to gain.[7]

Sombart's book was an immediate success. In five years, it went through four editions and was translated into eleven languages. In 1905, when a fifth edition appeared in Germany (to be translated into seventeen languages, including the Japanese), the book was two and a half times longer, and included detailed historical material on the development of the 'social movement' in Germany, France, and England, as well as cursory surveys of eleven other countries. Its general themes were summed up in the chapter and subject headings: 'The tendency to uniformity', 'the social movement cannot be stayed', 'its present form necessary'. The theme, repeated in the conclusion, is that 'the Social movement is inevitable', and 'the movement has taken the only form possible'.[8]

Yet there was the puzzle of the United States. In 1905, Sombart (now a professor at the commercial school in Berlin) wrote a number of long essays in the *Archiv für Sozialwissenschaft und Sozialpolitik* (one of whose editors was Max Weber), entirely devoted to the United States.

---

[7] Werner Sombart, *Socialism and the Social Movement in the 19th Century*, tr. by Anson P. Atterbury with an introduction by John B. Clark (New York: G. P. Putnam's Sons, 1898), pp. viii, ix.

[8] *Sombart's Socialism and the Social Movement*, tr. (from the 6th edn.) by M. Epstein (New York : E. P. Dutton, 1909), pp. xiv–xv, pp. 280–1.

This appeared in book form in German the following year, and was translated, with a curious history, into English as *Why Is There No Socialism in the United States?*[9]

It was a puzzle because Sombart assumed that there *had* to be a growing socialist movement in the United States, since 'modern Socialism follows as a necessary reaction to capitalism'. And, of course, 'the United States is the country where the model of the Marxist theory of development is being the most precisely fulfilled, since the concentration of capital has reached the stage (as described in the famous penultimate chapter of *Capital*) at which the final cataclysm of the capitalist world *is near at hand*' (emphasis added). In 1905, no less.[10]

Why then was there no socialist movement in the United States, as in Europe? Why did socialism have little appeal to the American worker? To answer his questions, Sombart drew heavily on the earlier work of James Bryce (he himself had never visited the United States) and on official statistics, and made some shrewd observations about the 'capitalist mentality' of the American worker, the populist character of the electorate, the high standard of living, the expectations of social mobility, and he tried to show, to put it crassly, how the American worker had been 'bought off' by the capitalist class. Amusingly, Sombart's work had begun to be serialized in the *International Socialist Review*, the theoretical journal of the Socialist Party, but when Section Two of Sombart's work appeared, on the success of American capitalism, the translation ceased, and in the next number, in a slashing review of the work, the editor remarked: 'When we came to the nonsense on the conditions of the American worker, we stopped further publication.'

But the *International Socialist Review* had stopped too soon. In the end, Sombart could not accept his own evidence. As with every good academic, theory triumphed over the existent reality—it is the heritage of Hegel—and Sombart concluded in the penultimate paragraph of his book (all in italics, for emphasis): '*However, my present opinion is as follows: all the factors that till now have prevented the development of Socialism in the United States are about to disappear or to be converted into their opposite with the result that in the next generation Social-*

---

[9] Werner Sombart, *Why is There No Socialism in the United States?*, tr. by P. M. Hocking and C. T. Husbands (London: Macmillan, 1976), 6.

[10] Sombart, drawing on John Moody's *The Truth About the Trusts* (New York: Moody Publishing, 1904), cited data on the concentration of capital in the hands of seven 'greater' trusts and various 'lesser' trusts, and concluded: 'Just think! Eighty-five thousand million marks concentrated in the hands of a few capitalists.' (Ibid. 6.)

ism in America will very probably experience the greatest possible expansion of its appeal.'[11]

The weakness of that expectation is obvious. Just as Marx stated in his introduction to *Capital* that he had found (using Newton's terminology) 'the laws of motion' of capitalism, which would apply not only to England but (*De te fabula narratur!*) to all capitalist societies, Sombart, following Marx, believed that economic relations shape political and all other relations in capitalist society, and that the inevitable class divisions would lead to the polarization of society. And with his own rhetorical flourish, Sombart proclaimed in his broader work that we are in the midst of 'one of those great historical processes' whose trajectory cannot be denied, much as a 'mountain torrent rushes down from the highest peaks into the valley below in accordance with nature's unchangeable laws'.[12]

Yet if one reads Sombart's American book—putting aside the introduction and the conclusion, but looking at his own evidence—the obvious title would be: *Why Should There Be Socialism in the United States?*[13] There is no exception, perhaps, because there is no rule.

A different kind of historical issue of exceptionalism is posed by Max Weber on the relation of religion to economic development. In *The Protestant Ethic*, Weber argued, as we know, that the Calvinist strand of Protestantism was a necessary condition for the development of modern capitalism because of the rational principles common to both; their 'elective affinity' reinforced each other. Religion spurred methodical work and habits; it provided legitimacy to capitalist profit; it gave dignity, and even status, to achievements in work rather than in military occupations.

[11] Sombart, *Why is There No Socialism?*, 119. This is a statement repeated as well in the 6th edn. of Sombart's broader and more famous works, *Socialism and the Social Movement* (1908), where he concludes: '[in America] the Social Movement is beginning to show the same tendencies as in Europe . . . the result is as obvious as it is unavoidable' (p. 278).

[12] *Socialism and the Social Movement*, (Epstein edn., pp. 279–80).

[13] There is a very different question which Sombart and most commentators on the fate of the socialist movement rarely addressed, namely: why is it that the American Socialist Party, through most of its history, remained sectarian in its orientation, much like H. N. Hyndman's Social Democratic Federation in Britain? Rather than move (to the extent possible) to the creation of a Labour Party, as in England, the American Socialist Party, by and large, rejected that course. Why, in effect, did the Socialist Party fail to recognize the situation and adapt to the realities? I have tried to answer that question in my monograph, 'Marxian Socialism in American Life', appearing originally in the volume *Socialism and American Life*, ed. by Donald Egbert and Stow Persons (Princeton: Princeton University Press, 1952), and published independently with a new introduction and a bibliographical essay, as *Marxian Socialism in the United States* (Princeton: Princeton University Press, 1967). My answer, briefly, was that the Socialist Party was trapped, first by its belief in inevitable success, which brooked no ideological compromise, and later, under Norman Thomas, by its moralism,

But Weber also expressed the view that the further rationalization of society would mean the *entzauberung der welt*; the spread of the secular would mean the de-sacralization of beliefs. It is true that many European societies, in particular the United Kingdom and Sweden, have become largely 'secularized', so that church attendance is low and theological questions (other than the ideological defence of the traditional Anglican Book of Common Prayer by otherwise agnostic neo-conservatives) have little appeal in intellectual or cultural life.

Yet what can one say of the United States, the land where, more than any other nation, industrialization has raged unchecked, where pragmatism (I mean, of course, the vulgarization of the word, not the ethics of Dewey or James) is the ready and easy way in business and politics. Yet fundamentalist and evangelical movements have surged forth time and again, never more so than in the past eight years when demands for school prayer and the pledge of allegiance, under God, have become salient political issues; or where religious themes are of serious interest to intellectuals, often in the guise of communitarianism and other non-utilitarian values.

Is this another instance of American exceptionalism, a deviation from the 'sociological law' of secularization? I think not. As I have argued previously, the term secularization is deceptive in that it conflates two very different processes—changes on an *institutional* level (and the role of religious authority in secular matters), and the more variable and fluctuating nature of *beliefs*—and the two are not isomorphic or even strongly coupled. Religious beliefs are not an epiphenomenal reflection of underlying social structures. Nor are they creeds that are erased by the unfolding of a 'rational' consciousness. It is quite striking that every Enlightenment thinker, from Voltaire to Marx, thought that religion would disappear by the twentieth century. They conceived of religion as fetishism, animism, superstition, and the like, an aspect of the 'child-hood' of the human race, which would be replaced by reason. There was the belief, too, that science, with its unveiling of exact laws, and practical activities such as economics or engineering, would *show* the mundane relations between persons or things as against 'magical beliefs'. Yet they completely misunderstood the nature of religious beliefs, since these have served, as for Kierkegaard, to give an 'answer' to the paradoxes

in living 'in but not of' the world, which rendered it ineffective. The thesis has been hotly debated and is discussed by John Laslett with a reply by myself in John H. M. Laslett and S. M. Lipset, eds., *Failure of a Dream? Essays in the History of American Socialism*, rev. edn. (Berkeley: Univ. of California Press, 1984).

and absurdities of life; or, for contemporary writers such as Geertz and Bellah, to provide significant meanings in symbolic form to life situations; or to provide, as I have argued, some coherent responses to the existential predicaments—such as death, tragedy, obligation—that confront every culture and single individuals in their lives.[14] Religious beliefs fall and rise variously in different cultures, and at different times.

Again, the problem of *entzauberung* was wrongly put. There was no exceptionalism, but a fallacy of misplaced abstraction.

There is, however, a third, persistent, and more manifest exceptionalism. This is the belief, intertwined with the philosophical views of the founding fathers, that ours would be the providential nation, the redeemer nation, the one whose dedication to liberty and individual worth would be the foundation of a new moral society. And since that morality was constitutive of the political order, we would avoid the decadence and degeneration of previous republics. This was Madison's reading of Montesquieu, especially on the fate of Rome. It was that of John Adams on Davila and the outcomes of revolution.

This was not a wholly unqualified belief in exceptionalism. Those like Jefferson, who were deists, saw America as God's design worked out in a virgin, paradisaical land. But others, such as Franklin, more worldly and sceptical, saw none the less the possibility of the United States being *exemplary*, and thus a hope for the future. But has it all foundered? In the international sphere, Wilson's idealism proved feckless in the face of old-world realism. In the political realm, morality has given way to moralism. And in recent years, the regimes of several of our presidents have been tissues of lies, webs of deceit, or rhetorical excesses of self-righteousness.

And yet other elements do remain: the initiative on human rights begun in the Carter administration which may yet become the minimal foundation of Kantian morality in a fragile world order; the continuing commitment to constitutionalism and the rejection of a rigidity which would limit the role of the court as an arbiter, if not legitimator, of change.

Our future may be more uncertain than at any time in the past two hundred years, yet some enduring values of character and even idealism

[14] I have tried to expand this theme in my Hobhouse lecture, 'The Return of the Sacred?: The Argument on the Future of Religion', printed in my collection of essays, *The Winding Passage* (New York: Basic Books, 1980), 324–54. What I have argued is that the answers to these predicaments vary, for that is the *history* of the human race, shaped by different sociological circumstances and environments; but the questions are the same, and always recur.

persist.[15] One senses, in reflecting on American political development, that there was something *exceptional* about the nation's history and character, exceptional not necessarily in the sense of being exempt from some presumed laws of social evolution, but as providing, in the theological and political nuances of the term, *a saving grace* which makes us still exemplary for other nations.

III

In reflecting about a two-hundred-year history, one is drawn inevitably to comparison with France, which has just celebrated (though not unanimously) the bicentennial of its Revolution. The 'conventional' wisdom is that France, at least the Jacobins, attempted a *social* revolution that would instaurate a blissful new order, 'the religion of human-ity'—and, given the nature of man, it was bound to fail. And the United States attempted a *political* revolution which, more limited in its aims, could succeed, presumably by leaving the economic order alone and thus allowing men an outlet for their passions while the political order mediated their interests.

Yes, there is a degree of truth in this. But the easy division between the political and the economic masks the fact that a new kind of social order *was* attempted on this continent. This conception of society, an insight I derive from Hegel, may be one of the more relevant explanations of the 'success' of American society, success in the sense of being able to create an *institutional* foundation that has protected individual liber-ties and rights, and provided a degree of continuity and consensus, and thus a social stability, unmatched in the history of political societies. It is to this 'secret' that I now turn.[16]

Ideas rarely emerge full-blown in one great conceptual vision or tangible fact, such as Minerva out of the head of Zeus. The first tantalizing thought which over time led to this 'secret' came more than twenty years ago, when in 1964 I initiated an enterprise, the Commission

[15] These are questions that I explored more than a dozen years ago in an essay, 'The End of American Exceptionalism', which is referred to in a number of papers contributed to this volume. It is reprinted in *The Winding Passage*, pp. 245–71.

[16] In a number of different writings, notably in my *Cultural Contradictions of Capitalism* (New York: Basic Books, 1976), I have dealt with the social structure (economy and technology) and culture as embodying contradictory purposes which create tensions for the society. I think the analysis is still valid. This essay, in its focus on political institutions as the ground (or 'substructure') of society, is one way of seeing the resolution of some of these contradictions.

on the Year 2000, of the American Academy of Arts and Sciences. To
find financial support, I wrote a memorandum for a foundation official
arguing the need for forecasting institutions. At the time, the idea was
a novel one, and the man was intrigued. Give me an instance of a
prediction, he said. It is very difficult to predict, I replied; and besides
we are more interested in tracing out the consequences of policies now
being enacted than in sketching an amorphous future; after all, the way
city streets were laid out in the nineteenth century constrains the patterns
of traffic in the twentieth; we wish to suggest 'alternative futures' for
decisions now being taken. True enough, he said, but much depends on
the kinds of futures you see; so give me an instance. And, smiling
mischievously, he said: if you cannot give me *one* prediction, you do
not get the money!

To paraphrase Dr. Johnson, there is nothing like the loss of money
to concentrate the mind, so without much forethought, and quite spon-
taneously, I blurted out: 'This is the spring of 1964. In November, there
will be an election for the Presidency, again in 1968, in 1972, 1976,
1980, . . . 2000!' He looked at me somewhat incredulously, as if to
underscore the banality of the statement, and said irritably: that's a
damned trivial prediction. Yes, I replied, it may be, but there are about
130 nations in the world today. About how many can you make such
a prediction?

It was a striking, and sobering, thought, and the puzzle—that of
institutional stability and continuity in a world of change—has stayed
with me since. Other than a handful of nations, pre-eminently the United
Kingdom and the United States, about how many countries can one, con-
fidently, make such a prediction? This was the time when, just a few
years before, the French army in Algeria, under Generals Salan and
Challe, were poised to send the paratroopers to seize Paris. And if the
weak Guy Mollet had not been replaced by Charles de Gaulle, coming
back from his second exile, the outcome in France might have been vastly
different. One thought of other situations that had actually seen such
disruptions. In the 1920s and 1930s, a large number of parliamentary
regimes in Europe—Italy, Portugal, Austria, Germany, Spain—had
collapsed and gone fascist or authoritarian. In the last century, almost
all of Latin America has had intermittent military or authoritarian dic-
tatorships. One-party states abound in most of the 'stable societies' of
the world. Only the United Kingdom, since the end of its civil war in
the seventeenth century, and the United States (with the exception of its
'war between states'), plus a handful of smaller nations (Switzerland and

the geographical fringe societies of Scandinavia), have achieved political stability and consensus. How was this accomplished?

Let me focus on the United Kingdom and the United States. There were some obvious, common factors, particularly a degree of geographical insulation. The United Kingdom has not been invaded since 1066, and 'foreign rule' (the houses of Orange and Hanover) was quickly assimilated into the façade of monarchy. The United States, since 1812, has not been invaded, and its wars (including the Mexican, Spanish–American, and the World Wars) were fought outside the major continental borders.

There was expanding material wealth and various outlets, geographical and social, for potentials of discontent (in Great Britain, administrative or military positions in the empire, for the 'second sons', and Australia for the convicts; in the United States, the free farms of the Homestead Acts, free public education, new expanding industries, and the promise of opportunity for the next generations).

There was a factor, common largely to the United Kingdom and the United States, which has been less noticed: the legal system. As against the continental legal system, with its powerful inquiring magistrates, Anglo-American legal procedure has been an adversarial one, with an emphasis on rights. The continental legal system seeks to uncover 'truth'. The Anglo-American system seeks to establish guilt. Thus the power of the state and its courts is mitigated by the protection of rights and due process created by the common law, equity, and torts, and the Constitution.

But what of the United States itself? Is there a distinctive element in its history and sociological make-up which has contributed to that stability? I think there is, and that answer begins with Hegel.

For Hegel, the United States was always the embodiment of modernity, 'the land of the future . . . the land of desire for all those who are weary of the historical lumber-room of old Europe'. Yet Hegel also said, in the introduction to his lectures on the philosophy of history, that America was still only a dream, and in tracing the vicissitudes of the *Begriff*, he retreated to 'the Old World—the scene of World's history'.[17] Today, if we are mindful of what *is* (even if it is not rational), we have to be concerned with the United States, though as we approach the twenty-first century we may be seeing a great historical shift of economic power to the Pacific rim, and the reappearance of Clio in samurai dress. (If that occurs, more may also be at stake, for it could signal the passing

[17] G. W. F. Hegel, *The Philosophy of History*, tr. by J. Sibree (New York: 1944), 86–7.

of the Euro-centred civilizations, which have been at the heart of world history for the past 2,500 years, to a new cultural centrum.)

Still, tattered and frayed, the twentieth remains the American century, as historians will have to acknowledge, though the dreams of some of those who fashioned that hope have turned into nightmares. The United States is still the foremost military and technological power, and the dollar the uneasy foundation of the world economy. And, *pace* Paris and London, it is the cultural marketplace, if not the cultural centre, of the world. If there is no outright hegemony, the United States is still the paramount power, unmatched by the Soviet Union. More importantly, it remains, with the United Kingdom, one of the few nations of the world to maintain its institutional stability, so that investors, or the rich in other nations, still turn to the United States as a haven. The understanding of the 'secret', then, may be one of the important sociological contributions to political theory.

What is the distinguishing feature of the United States, one that has been its strength throughout its history—and may, perhaps, now be its weakness? It is simply that the United States has been the complete *civil society*, perhaps the only one in political history. Hegel thought that England, as a bourgeois nation, exemplified civil society in its self-interest and its utilitarian character. But Hegel, at the beginning of the nineteenth century (and Marx, who lived in England for almost all of his adult life), never understood the thick character of England: the symbolism of the Crown, the strength of the landed classes, the Centrality of an established church, the desire of the bourgeoisie, or its sons, to become gentry or gentlemen, the weight of the Establishment, and the lure of titles and honours—the fact that England was a society in which a status order dominated the political and economic orders. The Manchester liberals, such as Cobden and Bright, did *not* wish to rule, for not only (as they said) did they not know how to govern, they sought the autonomy of the economic order from the state, the freedom to pursue trade, industry, and wealth. British imperialism of the late nineteenth century, as distinct from the colonialism of the eighteenth, was, as Schumpeter cogently argued, not a necessity of capitalism, but an extension of the status order, allied with finance, an outlet through the Army and administration overseas for the 'second sons' disinherited by primogeniture, and a means, by emphasizing the primacy of empire (and pomp and glory), of cowing the staid bourgeois classes.[18]

[18] Joseph Schumpeter, *Imperialism and Social Classes*, tr. by Heinz Norden (New York: World, 1951), see especially pp. 84–5 and p. 118.

The United States was from the start a rejection of the old social order by a motley class of *novi homines*, vagabonds, adventurers, convicts, dispossessed cavaliers, and dissident Protestants, from Quakers to Puritans, reinforced in the next century by a flood-tide of immigrants from all the countries of Europe, from southern Italy to northern Scandinavia. It was an open society. Each man was free to 'make himself' and (he hoped) to make a fortune. Marx was constantly warning the German radicals not to go to the United States, for he saw, as happened with Hermann Kriege and August Willich and dozens of others, that the democratic atmosphere of the United States, its basic egalitarianism, would supplant the old European-bred socialist beliefs. For them the attraction of the future was not some cosmological *telos* of universalism, but the yearning to be treated as a person and a desire for opportunity and advancement—a feature Marx himself recognized, but only in the footnotes of *Capital*, where he writes with amazement of the number of individuals who could move about freely and change their occupations, 'much as a man could change his shirt, egad'.[19]

In Hegel's sense—and it is a central starting-point for my analysis—there was no *state* in the United States, no unified, rational will, only individual self-interest and a passion for liberty. In every European nation (with the partial exception of Britain), the state ruled *over* society, exercising a unitary or quasi-unitary power (enforced by a military class and a bureaucracy); and the state itself was the focus of power. Revolution, as Marx and Engels knew, meant the seizing of state power. Paradoxically, the United States probably experienced more internal violence (the Civil War apart), call it even class struggle, than most countries of Europe: the agrarian struggles against the moneyed interests and, more focused, the labour conflicts with the capitalists. By any set of rough indicators—more strikes, longer strikes, more dynamiting, more times troops called out, more lives lost in the period from the railway strikes of the 1870s to the auto and steel strikes of the 1950s—the American labour struggles were more prolonged and more violent than any in Europe. But these were not (nor could they be thus interpreted) attempts to seize state power. They were primarily economic conflicts, against particular corporations and, in the instances of the great union actions of the 1930s, in coal, steel, auto, and rubber, against entire industries; but they were not contests for state power. Paradoxically, those tremendous organizing actions of the 1930s were undertaken with the support of the New Deal political administration against economic

[19] Karl Marx, *Capital*, i (Chicago: C. H. Kerr, 1906), 534 n. 1.

Daniel Bell

corporate power. It would not be too much to say that the AFL–CIO could not have been maintained without the support of the Democratic administration, and the power of bargaining extended by the Supreme Court.

If there was no state, what was there?[20] To make a semantic yet substantive distinction, there was a *government*. The government was a *political marketplace*, an arena in which interests contended (not always equally) and where deals could be made. Fortuitously, for it was not planned (nor were these powers specified in the Constitution), the Supreme Court became the final arbiter of disputes, and the mechanism for the adjustment of rules, which allowed the political marketplace to function, subject to the amendment of the Constitution itself—which then again was interpreted by the court. The Constitution and the court became the bedrock of civil society.

There was an underlying philosophical theme expressed in the Declaration of Independence: the theme of *rights*, inalienable rights, rights naturally endowed. But these rights inhered in each person, not in a group, and institutions were designed to embody and protect them.[21] The Constitution of the United States was a *social contract*, a contract initially between the several states, yet transferred over time as a social contract between the government and the people. It may be the only successful social contract we know in political history; perhaps because the state was so weak and often non-existent.

Behind this contract lay a distinctive political culture. In the early

---

[20] In a recent paper, Quentin Skinner has argued that the word 'state' came to be recognized when political philosophers (he singled out Hobbes) sought a term that would identify an emerging realm of power distinct from *res publica* or *civitas* (since those terms designated popular sovereignty), and from the literal power-holders, such as a monarch, who insisted on fealty sworn to them, as persons, rather than to an institution. The state, thus, was an entity that doubly abstracted sovereignty from rulers and ruled, and combined the rights alienated from them into the *persona ficta* of 'the State'. (This theme of alienation of rights is found in Hobbes, where the individual surrenders his natural rights to the commonwealth, the Leviathan, and later in Rousseau, where, in the 'social contract', each person submerges himself and his rights into the general will.) If one defines the state by this vocabulary, then it is certainly clear that there was no state in the United States, for the very character of the founding documents denied the idea of alienated rights and expressed sovereignty in 'We, the People'.

[21] And this is also why there is so much litigation in American society, and such an expansive role of the courts, for if the foundation of the society is one's individual rights, then one sues to defend and protect them. When the question arose as to whether business corporations could come under the jurisdiction of the 14th Amendment, which established the primacy of the Federal Government in extending due process to the protection of persons, the court ruled, by creating a fiction, that the corporation was also a *person* and could thus be protected.

years of the country's formation, there was a self-consciousness about being the first *new* nation: not a new quasi-religious utopia as proclaimed in the French Revolution, but of going back to the origins of government and founding a new, free world; thus the expression on the Great Seal of the United States: 'Novus Ordo Seclorum', a new order of the ages.[22] There was equally a strong republican emphasis and a civic (not state) consciousness of republican virtue, derived from reading the history of the Roman Republic and the desire to avoid the degenerative diseases— civil strife spawned by faction, the use of mercenaries rather than a citizens' army, and the arbitrary concentration of power—that had crippled the republics of the past. One sees this double consciousness, as I have remarked, in the Federalist Papers, with its echoes of Montesquieu, and in the writings of John Adams.

There was, self-consciously, an intellectual (and *intellectualist*) foundation. But as the nation expanded and political parties developed— for political parties had not been foreseen or even desired by the founding fathers—the competition in the political marketplace spurred the egalitarianism and populism which have been, since the 1830s, the distinguishing features of American politics. This is why some writers have argued that the political structure of the United States was transformed from a republic to a mass democracy. As I will argue later, this is true, but on one level only.

What one did see was a shift from intellectualism and thought (the Lockian emphasis, in a sense) to sentiment and emotion (a strange Rousseauian twist), for while intellectualism implies a hierarchy of thought and respect for the learned, sentiment affirms egalitarianism and a common feeling among all men. And this was reflected as well in a turn away from history and from Europe, the turn inwards to the land and the moving frontier. All this was symbolized in the election of General Andrew Jackson, the first 'Western' president, in 1828 (and the throwing open of the White House to the people), and was ratified, so to speak, in the 'cider barrel' election of 1840, when the Whigs, seeking to broaden their appeal, nominated another war hero, General William Henry Harrison (nicknamed Tippecanoe for his battles against the Indians), for president. A Democratic publicist in the East sneered at him as a man who wanted nothing better than to live in a log cabin and drink

---

[22] 'It has been the will of heaven,' John Adams wrote in 1776, 'that we should be thrown into existence at a period when the greatest philosophers and lawgivers of antiquity would have wished to live. A period when we have an opportunity of beginning government new from the foundation. . . How few of the human race have ever had any opportunity of choosing a system of government for themselves and their children!'

cider. The whigs picked up the sneer and it became part of their slogan, to show that they were as deeply connected to the masses of the people as their Democratic rivals.[23]

The other transforming element of American politics was the rule of money, the rise of the plutocracy and the easy use of money to buy politicans, gain influence, or induce outright corruption, a feature that reached its apogee in the administration of another war hero, General Ulysses S. Grant, and disgusted the fastidious scion of the (now patrician) Adams family, the historian Henry Adams—a scene portrayed in Adams's novel entitled, significantly, *Democracy*.[24]

The outcome of these changes is the strange structure of domestic American politics, which few foreigners, and not even many Americans, understand. The American political order is a two-tiered structure: the presidency is a plebiscitarian referendum, in which the person, not the party, is the cynosure of identification and judgement, the focus of mass *passions*, while the Congress, the Senate and the House, are elected by a responsiveness to group *interests*. though today not necessarily the moneyed interests.

It is no accident that so many Presidents have been 'heroes' or celebrities, so many of them generals, from Washington to Eisenhower, usually elected after a war, in a country that has never had a large standing army. Heroes were considered to be 'above' party; while during periods of normalcy the Presidents have been colourless neuters such as McKinley, Harding, or Coolidge. (The one certified intellectual, Woodrow Wilson, a political-science professor who had once been president of Princeton University, was elected in 1912 because of a three-way split, the only instance of its kind in American history, and he was re-elected during the war in Europe on the ground that he would keep America out of the war.) Such presidents of the post-Second World War years as Truman, Nixon, Carter, and Reagan have been unabashed populists,

[23] Harrison's campaign also introduced the fashion of slogans as an electoral technique. Bracketed with his vice-presidential candidate, who succeeded him on his early death in office, the banner across the cider wagon read: 'Tippicanoe and Tyler too'. The most fascinating discussion of this campaign is contained in that witty book by Ignazio Silone, *The School for Dictators*, where the potential American dictator, coming to Europe for instruction, is told of this initial populist turn in his own historical backyard.

[24] Though the end of the century saw the rise of large corporate power and indeed, huge concentrations, there was no national 'ruling class'. Mark Hanna sought to create one through the National Civic Federation, seeking to weld the plutocracy together as a political force, but the effort foundered. In the economic realm, the anti-trust movement, populist at its source, broke up many of the trusts, as later the Glass-Steagall Act, in the early years of the New Deal, sundered the financial union power of investment and banking. One can say that in the US there have always been economic and political élites, but not a unified ruling class.

running against the Establishment and often minimizing party identification.[25]

Yet the elections to the Congress show a very different pattern. One could see this two-tiered structure with startling clarity in 1984. Ronald Reagan, one of the most popular presidents in history, who carried all the states in the nation except one (Walter Mondale's home state of Minnesota), won in the state of New Jersey by one million votes, yet the Democrat, Bill Bradley, won the Senate seat in that state by one million votes. Reagan carried Massachusetts by a half-million votes, yet John Kerry, a left-liberal Democrat, won by a half-million votes. The same pattern was repeated in 1988. George Bush carried the state of Ohio, but Howard Metzenbaum, one of the strongest liberal voices in the Senate, was also re-elected. Since the Second World War, though the Presidents have come largely from the Republican side, the Congress has more often been Democratic, and the House consistently so.

Populist in politics, that mentality also affected the small-town culture (not the modern mass-media culture), which was largely a religious culture. Protestant, moralizing, and fundamentalist, it was also, given its emphasis on the literalism of the Word, anti-intellectual and anti-institutional. There was, of course, no aristocratic tradition or strong artistic heritage: the arts were crafts—plain, simple, and utilitarian. And the Catholic tradition, which in Europe provided a firm intellectualist foundation in theology and dogmatics, beauty in litany and liturgy, and a set of distinctive styles in architecture and sculpture, all of which became fused with an historic high culture, was in the United States embodied in the Irish church, made up largely of immigrants or rude self-made men, so that (with the exception, say, of a John Courtney Murray) until recently it has lacked intellectual weight and made little contribution to American thought and culture.

Thus we find a society deeply individualist and populist, its fluid modernity shaped by the open expanse of geography (a natural world

---

[25] Harry Truman, who became president on the death of Franklin D. Roosevelt, won his own election in 1948 by running against a Republican Establishment candidate, Thomas E. Dewey. Yet Truman did accept the Establishment figures fully in international affairs because the Cold War required their experience in foreign policy. But the Vietnam War destroyed the moral authority of the Establishment, and foreign policy has become the focus of passions and ideologies crossed with national interest. For those reasons, it has lacked a consistent focus or a sense of long-range purpose. For a shrewd history of this early post-war period, and the men who shaped American foreign policy, see *The Wise Men: Architects of the American Century* (New York: Simon & Schuster, 1986) by Walter Isaacson and Evan Thomas, a 'group biography' of Acheson and Harriman, McCloy and Lovett, Kennan and Bohlen.

that could easily be plundered without remorse) and in the economy, by the rule of money, the riches going to the rugged men bent on pursuing their own ends. Both environment and economy were unencumbered by the polity. Indeed, from the 1870s to the 1930s, the court consistently struck down most efforts of social legislation and regulation, other than anti-trust laws. Freedom was defined principally in individualistic economic terms. That was the consensus. That was the framework of the civil society.

In the last half-century, the lineaments of a state—the creation of institutional structures to shape and enforce a unitary will over and above particular interests—have emerged in the United States, and it begins with the New Deal of Franklin D. Roosevelt. The New Deal has usually been interpreted ideologically (from the left) as saving capitalism, or (from the right) as creeping socialism because of the growth of statist institutions. While there are relevant truths in both arguments, neither is very satisfactory. The rise of a state in American society, I would say, was unplanned and not at all consistently ideological, but a response, during crisis, to three elements: the changes in the 'scale' of the society, . the outcome of changing political realignments, and the logic of mobilization for war.

The problem of scale was foundational. By 1930, the United States became a national society; from 1900 to 1930 there arose national corporations and national markets banded together by the transportation systems. But the 'countervailing' political power was distributed, ineffectively, among the states. When the economy broke down in 1929–32, the Roosevelt administration responded first with the National Industrial Recovery Administration, setting up national industry codes and price-fixing schemes in the major industries. It adopted, in fact, the principles of the corporatist state as urged by many capitalists, such as Gerard Swope of General Electric, and the du Ponts. When this was declared unconstitutional, the New Deal began to move away from the corporatist planning and to rely more on regulatory mechanisms to control markets. Out of this came the Securities and Exchange Commission for financial markets and, to ensure labour stability, a National Labor Relations Board for collective bargaining. The New Deal thus became a 'matching of scales', creating national political institutions and national political rules to match national economic power.

The logic of stabilization and control led to the increasing reliance on fiscal policy to direct spending, and the emerging state became a major actor in the allocative and growth processes of the economy. Fiscal sociology, as Joseph Schumpeter once noted, means the rise of the 'Tax State', and tax policy becomes the fulcrum of economic activity. But economic activity also has redistributive effects. And the domestic political realignment, in which labour, farmers, and minorities swung into the Democratic camp, led to national farm subsidies and protection of disadvantaged groups; more broadly to a welfare state: the need for protection against economic and social hazards; the desire for the 'inclusion' of the disadvantaged into the society; the ethics of income redistribution to provide at least a 'safety net' to keep people from dropping below a poverty line—and to the idea of entitlements and a social-service state.

The third great impetus to statism was war and foreign policy. In almost every society, war has been the most decisive instrumentality for the creation of a state. War focuses emotions against a dangerous enemy; it is necessary to impose a unitary point of view to rally the society; and the needs of war force the state to mobilize the resources of the society, men and material, for single objectives. A mobilizing society—for economic development or for war, or to meet great disasters—becomes the forcing house of a state.

In the period after the Second World War, the new role of the nation in underwriting and sustaining a destroyed international economy groping towards reconstruction, and the pointed conflict with the Soviet Union on an ideological and political and military level—embodied in the Cold War and expressed concretely in the Berlin blockade, the war in Korea, the Cuban missile crisis, and the protracted conflict in Vietnam—all combined to enlarge the presence of a state.

Significantly, the external foreign-policy pressures and the internal domestic factors were *not* intertwined. Foreign policy was not a reflex of domestic pressures, despite the military–industrial complex. The spread of subsidies and entitlements during the Johnson administration, to the aged, the poor, and to education, was not dependent on the mobilization for defence purposes. In fact, as the financial pressures expanded, the two became more and more competitive, which to a large extent made it easier for the Reagan administration to reduce regulation, subsidies, and entitlements in the domestic arena while substantially expanding the defence budgets for the military. There was never, philosphically, a unitary national state.

All these activities are registered in the growth in the size of government, the number of public-sector employees, the incidence of taxation, the proportion of the gross national product initiated in the 'state sector' (including defence), and the astounding rises in the last decade in the budget deficits and the ballooning national debt. And all of this is reflected in rising discontents: in many societies, taxes are understood to be the purchase of public services that individuals cannot buy for themselves; in the United States many (most?) persons feel it is 'our' money that is being taken by 'them'. The growth of regulations in all areas of economic and social life has led to resentment against government intrusion (and also to the cultural contradiction of those who resist government intrusion in their economic affairs but urge moral tutelage and social regulation of personal and sexual conduct). One finds the amazing rhetoric of a President, Mr. Reagan, who tells the people, 'Don't trust your government, and get them off your back', while running up a larger government debt in eight years than in any previous hundred.

But beyond these 'idiosyncratic' contradictions, it is evident that the problem of 'the state' has become a central one for political theory and political practice. As I argued more than ten years ago, the question of state-society relationships, of the public interest and the private appetite, is clearly the salient problem for the polity in the coming decades. And in the expansion of the scale of economic and political activities, the national state has become too small for the 'big' problems of life (i.e. the tidal waves of the capital and currency markets) and too big for the 'small' problems of life (i.e. the problems of neighbourhood and community).[26] Foreign policy, which has been one focusing prism for unitary decision, has become a chaotic area as the idea of a consistent national interest has tended to founder, while ideological passions have risen and fallen. The idea of a managed economy has retreated in the face of the difficulties of fine tuning, and there has been a return to market mechanisms. Bureaucracies have become too centralized and burdensome in most societies. Individuals increasingly wish to find the means of managing social and welfare issues, environment, and quality of life, on scales commensurate with their ability to control such decisions. What is striking, in fact, in country after country—I think of Poland and Italy, where such views are being articulated—the idea of a 'civil society' rather than 'the state' as the primary arena of political activities has become a major theme of exploration and debate, in particular as the old ideologies have faded.

[26] 'The Future World Disorders,' in *The Winding Passage*, pp. 226–7.

IV

We see, then, the return of the idea of civil society. But of what kind? For Hegel, the character of civil society was that of an anarchic self-interest, of economic individualism which had destroyed the older institutions of *sittlichkeit*—the customary institutions of family and village—but could not replace them with *moralität*, the abstract rational beliefs of a unified and universal will. Hegel was wrong in his romanticism, this contrast of an unmediated traditionalism with a self-centred appetitive utilitarianism, which could only be mastered by a state. This romanticism has run like a scarlet thread through German thought. In the social sciences it has given us the simplicities of the *gemeinschaft–gesellschaft* dichotomy, with its patina of a *naturwille* and a *kürwille*, as two different kinds of social bonds and two different wills.[27] In philosophy and politics it has given us the demonic view embodied in Heidegger's allegiance to the Nazis, of a heroic *volkstum* and *staatstum* against the hated commercial and bourgeois society. Yet these contrasts, and the denigration of civil society as anomic cruelly misread the complexities of a modern society and the difficulties of establishing the limits of freedom and civility.

The return to civil society is a return to a manageable scale of social life, particularly where the national economy has become embedded in an international frame and the national polity has lost some degree of its independence. It is an emphasis on the voluntary association, on the church and community, on the self-management of resources on a local scale, outside the bureaucracy and state, in the areas of work and welfare. Utopian? Possibly. But more possible now, given the new technologies, with their potential for the decentralization of industry and the downsizing of firms.

Nor is this idea of civil society the return to civic humanism or republican virtue, the tradition espoused now by Quentin Skinner and

[27] In their collection of Toennies's writings—since those terms are his—Werner Cahnman and Rudolf Heberle seek to defend Toennies against the charge, in particular by Ralf Dahrendorf, that he was an 'enemy of modernity', who romanticized the pristine innocence of *gemeinschaft*. Toennies himself was a democrat and a supporter of labour, and in a courageous act joined the Social Democratic party in 1932, leading to his dismissal from his chair by the Nazis a year later. Yet the fact remains that the somewhat fevered and clumsy language of his famous book (written in 1887) is soaked in these images of community as a 'community of blood' while *kürwille* becomes translated as 'arbitrary will', rather than 'purposive intention', which would be a somewhat different value reading of the term. All this is a cautionary tale about the use of language. See W. J. Cahnman and Rudolf Heberle, *Ferdinand Toennies, On Sociology* (Chicago: University of Chicago Press, 1971).

J. G. A. Pocock. Republican virtue—it was *not* the republicanism of Adams or Jefferson—was one in which the community was prior to the individual, so much so that, in its extreme form, private property was abolished. The common good was a unitary good. But a modern civil society—a heterogeneous and multi-racial society within the bounds of citizenship—has to establish different rules: the principle of toleration and diversity, and the consensus by plural communities on rules of procedure and rules for negotiation, within the frame of constitutionalism.

All of these are issues which engage political philosophy today—and, understandably, are outside the province of this paper. I have only been able to assert my ground. The fact of civil society, however, has been, as I have tried to show, a distinctive American theme which, though it began in the more benign version of 'republican virtue', became transformed, institutionally, along the contrasting and complementary axes of rugged individualism and radical populism. Yet, to the extent that the theme of civil society has again become urgent for a new kind of social order which limits the state and enhances individual and group purposes—a definition, once more, of liberalism!—it is also one more twist in the long tale of American exceptionalism.

3

Free Land and Federalism: American Economic Exceptionalism

Peter Temin

The American economy has seemed unique to generations of foreign observers. Its growth was a wonder of the Western world for more than a century. The organization of economic life provided a model for others to emulate. For a while after the Second World War, the United States even appeared capable of transforming the world economy into a larger version of itself. These images all seem to be fading like an old photograph. Before they disappear completely, it is appropriate to take a closer look at the development of the American economy and ask how it was unique, if indeed it was. This chapter is a contribution to that effort.

I shall argue that the American economic experience until very recently was unique. Its uniqueness derived from two characteristics of the economy. First was the pervasive effect of 'free land'. The abundance of rich American farmland in favourable climates and close (in terms of the cost of transportation) to English markets provided a hospitable setting for economic growth. The land, for example, was far better than the also largely vacant lands in Canada (too northerly) or Australia (too distant).

The second influence emanated from the federal system of American government created in the late eighteenth century that limited the political power of large land-holders. As in Germany, there was a struggle between the industrial areas and the regions of concentrated staple agriculture. But unlike Germany, the large landowners were disenfranchised and restricted in control of their workers when the showdown came in the late nineteenth century. The settlement was not peaceful; the Civil War left far more scars than the process of resolution in Germany. But for all the draconian cost, the outcome was far different.[1]

---

[1] Alexander Gerschenkron, *Bread and Democracy in Germany* (Berkeley: University of California Press, 1943).

This paper is composed of four substantive sections. The first section lays out a theory of 'free land' and applies it to the American North. The second applies this framework to the South and discusses the defeat of Southern landowners in the Civil War. The third section focuses on the government and the economy. The fourth describes the effect of these factors on the growth of the American economy and assesses current prospects for a continuation of past patterns.

I

Domar proposed an impossibility theorem.[2] He showed that it was not possible to have simultaneously free land, free labour, and a land-owning aristocracy. The reasoning is straightforward. If there is no land available for the taking at a moderate cost, then it is possible to have free labour and a landed aristocracy, as in England. Ownership of the scarce land gives the aristocracy its power. But if land is freely available, then the aristocracy needs another source of power. If it can, it will subjugate the populace as serfs or slaves. If not, it will disappear. Preservation of the aristocracy is incompatible with the maintenance of free labour.

The North American colonies were quintessentially the location of free land. When the young people in mid-seventeenth-century Sudbury, Massachusetts, found their economic opportunities barred by their elders, they went off and founded their own town of Marlborough on lands granted to them by the General Court of Massachusetts.[3] The opportunity to move westward was present long before Horace Greeley called attention to it in the nineteenth century.

The question, then, is which of the other two characteristics would obtain, for only one was possible. No theoretical process gives a unique answer. It is part of the unusual character of American history that it was not even answered the same way throughout the North American colonies. In the North, the westward migration of free labour precluded the development of a landed aristocracy. In the South, by contrast, the enslavement of African labourers allowed the growth of a land-owning (and slave-owning) aristocracy.

Expansion in the North in the eighteenth century was accomplished

---

[2] Evsey D. Domar, 'The Cause of Slavery or Serfdom: A Hypothesis', *Journal of Economic History*, 30 (Mar. 1970) 18–32.

[3] Sumner C. Powell, *Puritan Village: The Formation of a New England Town* (Middletown, Conn.: Wesleyan University Press, 1963).

by what would be called yeoman farmers in England. They were both prosperous and, as the British learned, independent. Agricultural expansion was joined in the nineteenth century by industrial development, a development that seemed peculiar and peculiarly American to many observers.

Alexander Hamilton found it necessary to argue the legitimacy of industrial development. He claimed modestly that his 'suggestions are not designed to inculcate an opinion that manufacturing industry is more productive than that of Agriculture. They are intended rather to show that the reverse of this proposition is not ascertained.'[4] If it is not, then the Physiocratic argument for free trade fails, and tariffs to promote industry are legitimate and, Hamilton concluded, desirable. English visitors a half-century later were amazed at the progress of American manufacturing in the face of a prosperous agriculture. They asked themselves Hamilton's implict question: how could manufacturing be as productive as agriculture ? They answered: 'On account of the high price of labour the whole energy of the people is directed to improving and inventing labour-saving machinery.'[5]

This has given rise to two related debates. The first asks why there was manufacturing in the American North. The second asks why that industry used labour-saving machinery. The two questions are close, but not identical. If, as the mid-nineteenth-century visitors asserted, American manufacturing existed because it used labour-saving machinery, then answering the second question also answers the first. But if American manufacturing grew in the early nineteenth century for other reasons, then it is necessary to answer the second in the context of those reasons.

The first question suffered some historical neglect after Hamilton. Habakkuk, for example, analysed at length the second of these two questions.[6] He did not state explicitly its relation to the first, suggesting that manufacturing in America existed only because of the labour-saving machinery. But Habakkuk brought in the tariff to explain why there was manufacturing at all. He then tried to infer how this sector would work.

I think that Habakkuk was correct in this aspect of his argument; the tariff was a critical enabling factor in the growth of American manufacturing, as Hamilton knew it had to be. The tariff of course

[4] Alexander Hamilton, *Report on Manufactures* (1791) reprinted in Jacob E. Cooke (ed.), *The Reports of Alexander Hamilton* (New York: Harper and Row, 1964).

[5] *Report of the Committee on Machinery of the United States of America*, UK Parliamentary Papers, 50/1–(1854–5).

[6] H. J. Habakkuk, *American and British Technology in the Nineteenth Century: The Search for Labour-Saving Inventions* (Cambridge: Cambridge University Press, 1962).

was imposed by government. A complete explanation of American industrial growth therefore has to include an account of government action. Let me defer this part of the story to the third section, below.

Returning to the second question, there is a paradox. American industry had to offer high wages to attract workers from agriculture. It seems logical that they used labour-saving machinery to do this. But if they raised the productivity of labour by increasing the quantity of machinery used per worker, then the rate of return on machinery should have gone down. While wages would have been higher in Britain, the interest rate would have been lower. But, alas for clarity in simple models, it was not.[7]

Many authors have proposed ways out of this paradox. Clarke and Summers used a very general model, in which all sorts of cross-effects were possible.[8] It then was possible to raise the productivity of labour in manufacturing by several different means. But when the model was restricted to allow more concrete conclusions to be drawn, the paradox reappeared. Clarke and Summers then suggested that the demand for agricultural goods was inelastic, so that the large supply of land *depressed* the price of agricultural goods and therefore agricultural wages. This was not a resolution of the paradox; it only replaced one anomaly by another. Instead of having to reconcile free land with a high interest rate, one would have to reconcile it with *low* agricultural wages.

An alternative approach was tried by Field.[9] In order to accommodate the high American interest rate, he argued that industry in the United States used capital-saving rather than labour-saving practices. Like Clarke and Summers, Field replaced one anomaly with another. This one has a lot of appeal. Single tracking on American railroads, hard driving in blast furnaces, flimsy wooden machinery, all can be interpreted as saving capital. But while there is some evidence of capital scarcity in the United States, the distinctive feature of American economic growth is the massive investment in transportation and production facilities that raised labour productivity. We observe both high interest rates and high wages.

This leads us back to back to Hamilton and Habakkuk: the tariff mattered. A protective tariff allowed profitable investment in American

---

[7] Peter Temin, 'Labor Scarcity and the Problem of American Industrial Efficiency in the 1850s', *Journal of Economic History*, 26 (Sept. 1966), 361–79.

[8] Richard N. Clarke and Lawrence H. Summers, 'The Labor Scarcity Controversy Reconsidered', *Economic Journal*, 90 (Mar. 1980), 129–39.

[9] Alexander J. Field, 'Land Abundance, Interest/Profit Rates, and Nineteenth Century American and British Technology', *Journal of Economic History*, 43 (June 1983), 405–32.

industry even with the high American wage. It does not seem historically accurate, however, to think of the supply of capital in the United
States as fixed. Americans borrowed from Britain throughout the nineteenth century, albeit at different rates at different times. In the 1840s,
for example, the inability of English investors to understand the critical
distinction between the United States and the several states—that is,
the difference between United States and Michigan bonds—led to a
temporary halt in the capital flow. But this was the exception rather than
the rule. In more normal times, there was a relatively free flow of capital
between England and America, and the interest rates moved together.[10]

Protected by the tariff and by transportation costs, American manufacturers created something that was known as the American System,
emphasizing its unique character. There can be no doubt, I think, that
the American System owed its origins to the factors just described: free
land, free labour, hospitable conditions for industry. But Yankee culture,
rampant Protestantism, and the universal education they gave rise
to, were important as well. The mechanism by which these factors
produced the American System is unclear, and the suspicion remains
that economic variables reveal only part of the story.

The American System was based on the use of interchangeable parts.
As the English visitors at mid-century noted, it was concentrated in light
manufacturing: locks, clocks, and small arms. This practice made it
possible for Americans to produce goods in volumes and at prices
unattainable in England. Chauncy Jerome, a Connecticut Valley clock-
maker, introduced a one-day brass clock for less than fifty cents about
1840. He exported some to England in 1842. English customs reserved
the right to confiscate goods at their invoice valuation to protect themselves against undervaluation. The clocks were clearly under-valued by
English standards, and they were confiscated. This was fine for Jerome;
he had sold his shipment at full price quickly and easily. He sent another,
larger load, which was duly confiscated. But when he sent a third, still
larger load, the customs authorities dropped their English blinkers and
allowed it in.[11]

The American System did not, however, emerge from the private
economy. It began in arms production, at United States government
armouries. The first step was taken by Thomas Blanchard at the Spring-

[10] Peter Temin, 'Labor Scarcity and Capital Markets in America' (paper prepared for
Festschrift Conference in honour of Sir John Habakkuk, 1985).
[11] Joseph W. Roe, *English and American Tool Builders* (New Haven, Conn.: Yale
University Press, 1916).

Peter Temin

field Armory, who introduced a sequence of fourteen special-purpose lathes and machines to make gun stocks out of sawn lumber. These machines were noted prominently by the English visitors in the 1850s. They demonstrated the potential of the sequential use of special-purpose machines.

The next step was taken by John Hall at the Harpers Ferry Armory. Hall realized that the problem in making interchangeable parts was to keep the gauges (patterns) used to make individual parts from getting worn away through use. The thousandth piece needed to be matched against a gauge that was the same as the gauge used for the first piece. But the action of comparing and sizing gradually wore away the gauges, causing the pattern to 'drift'. Hall introduced a second level. There had to be gauges for the gauges. These would be kept safely away where they would not wear. They would be brought out only periodically to recalibrate the gauges used to size the actual production. The gauges used in production then only would vary within limits set by the time period between recalibrations, assuring interchangeability.[12]

The American System spread throughout American manufacturing, but only slowly. The use of a two-tier set of gauges does not seem to be very complex, but it took a long time to be widely adopted. The Singer Sewing Machine Company, a leading producer of new products with new techniques, still needed to stamp the serial number of each machine on all its component parts in the 1860s. To assemble a machine, it was important to know when in the run the machine was made and to be able to match it to a part made at a similar stage. There must have been 'drift' in the gauges used to make the parts in order for this to have been important. The pattern gauges were not yet stable. Singer sewing mechines made in the 1880s, by contrast, did not have serial numbers stamped on all their parts; the standard of workmanship had become uniform enough to obviate the separate dating of each component of the machine.[13]

The use of interchangeable parts reduced manufacturing costs by reducing the cost of fitting the pieces together. Any saving in repair costs after the machine was in use was secondary to the savings upfront. Singer was never completely successful in eliminating the fitting stage, an expensive, labour-intensive process. Only in the manufacture of

[12] Merritt Roe Smith, *Harpers Ferry Armory and the New Technology* (Ithaca, NY: Cornell University Press, 1977).

[13] David A. Hounshell, *From the American System to Mass Production, 1800–1932* (Baltimore: Johns Hopkins University Press, 1984).

transportation equipment—bicycles and then Ford automobiles—was the system of mass production with interchangeable parts perfected. This *fin-de-siècle* development was coincident with the rise of large business firms, of which more below.

Free land in the American North, then, led to free labour, which led in turn to the American System of manufactures. The last step in this progression is still obscure. But it is clear that mass production was at least partly the result of free land, free labour, and federal government policies. The role of the federal structure of the United States government and the policies it generated will be discussed below.

II

The economic history of the American South has been very different from that of the North. This contrast can be attributed to the different resolution of Domar's dilemma. Forced to choose between free labour and a land-owning aristocracy, Southerners chose the latter.

Southerners were able to make a different choice from Northerners because their labour force was drawn from a different location. In both regions, the demand for labour rose rapidly in the seventeenth and eighteenth centuries, too rapidly to be accommodated by the rate of natural increase of the population. Northern immigrants came from Europe, predominantly England in the Colonial period, and were absorbed into the society. Southern immigrants came from Africa and were not.

There were many differences between English and African immigrants. The importance of racism and xenophobia should not be underestimated as influences on attitudes toward African immigrants and thereby on the institutional forms into which they were placed.[14] But I want to focus here on the economic differences between European and African immigrants, that is, on differences that might have differentiated the choice of labour system in the North and South even if Africans had been English-speaking whites.

The critical economic difference between the Northern and Southern immigrants was who made the decision to immigrate. In the North, the European immigrant decided whether or not to come to the American colonies. He or she typically did not have the resources to finance the

[14] David Brion Davis, *The Problem of Slavery in the Age of Revolution: 1770–1823* (Ithaca, NY: Cornell University Press, 1975).

trip across the Atlantic. The immigrant therefore borrowed against his or her future earnings to pay for the journey; he or she became an indentured servant for a fixed term of years. It was not stated this way at the time, but we may see this interval as the time needed to pay off the immigrant's loan. As the demand for labour in America grew and the supply of labour from England shrank with a slower rate of population growth, wages in the colonies also grew. It took less time for an immigrant to pay for his or her transportation. And, as this analysis suggests, the average term of indenture fell from an average of more than five years to somewhat less.[15]

The African immigrant was entirely different. He or she did not make the decision to emigrate. The emigrant instead was a captive, usually as a result of the tribal wars that were endemic in sub-Saharan Africa. The captor exchanged his captives for goods brought by European traders, and the captives became the property of the Europeans. They were taken initially to the West Indies, where they were sold again to sugar planters. Slaves were used to grow sugar both because the hard, simple tasks of sugar cultivation facilitated coercion and because the rapid growth of the demand for labour could not be accommodated by the free market.[16]

The rising demand for labour in America was not confined to the North. American planters were willing to pay more to get labour in both the North and the South. But they paid different people. In the North, as just noted, they paid the immigrant. In the South they found it cheaper to buy and use slaves from the West Indies. Africans were preferable to Europeans for growing rice for the same reasons as for sugar and additionally because many of them had prior experience with rice cultivation. Planters in South Carolina first imported slaves from Barbados. The slave trade spread throughout the South and grew to include direct importation from Africa.[17]

The immorality of this enslavement has haunted American history. It was a major factor in antebellum politics; it was a critical factor in

[15] David Galenson, 'The Rise and Fall of Indentured Servitude in the Americas: An Economic Analysis', *Journal of Economic History*, 44 (Mar. 1984), 1–26.

[16] Stefano Fenoaltea, 'Slavery and Supervision in Comparative Perspective: A Model', *Journal of Economic History*, 44 (Sept. 1984), 635–68. Barbara L. Solow, 'Capitalism and Slavery in the Exceedingly Long Run', *Journal of Interdisciplinary History*, 17 (Spring 1987), 711–37.

[17] Peter H. Wood, *Black Majority: Negroes in Colonial South Carolina from 1670 through the Stono Rebellin* (New York: Alfred A. Knopf, 1974). Richard S. Dunn, 'Servants and Slaves: The Recruitment and Employment of Labor', in *Colonial British America: Essays in the New History of the Early Modern Era* (Baltimore: Johns Hopkins Press, 1984).

the Civil War. The role of blacks in American society continues to be an issue today. I want to focus here on one small part of this issue, the effects of slavery on the Southern economy.

Slaves have far different incentives to work than free labour. Much ink has been spilt on the implications of this observation for the efficiency of the Southern economy. There seems little doubt that slaves were more or less as productive as free labour in unskilled agricultural activities. Hire prices of slaves rose with the wages of free men, and they approximated the same level.[18] The picture is less clear when the region as a whole is described.

The South grew rapidly first on the basis of a diversified agriculture and then on the basis of cotton. The voracious appetite for cotton in Lancashire was matched by the growing cotton production of the South, even after the slave trade was abolished in 1808. Southern expansion has been attributed to the vitality of slave institutions by some authors and to the availability of cotton-growing land by others. It has proved difficult to disentangle these two influences because the extent of American slavery in the nineteenth century and of cotton production were very much the same.[19]

This question—albeit complex and fascinating—is not the relevant one here. The Northern experience was one of efficient agriculture and a shift out of agriculture. The antebellum Southern experience was only the former. Was this the result of the peculiar institution?

Slavery inhibited the industrialization of the South in at least three distinct ways. First, as noted already, the incentives of slaves and free men were opposed. While the identification of slaves with the fortunes of their owners varied, there was far less than that of free workers and their employers. The American System, while encouraged by good management, seems to have originated in the efforts of machinists to make a better and cheaper product. There was little scope for a Blanchard or a Hall in the antebellum South.[20]

---

[18] Lewis C. Gray, *History of Agriculture in the Southern United States* (Washington: Carnegie Institution, 1932), 467.

[19] Robert W. Fogel and Stanley L. Engerman, *Time on the Cross: The Economics of American Negro Slavery* (Boston: Little, Brown, 1974). Paul A. David *et al.*, *Reckoning with Slavery* (New York: Oxford Univeristy Press, 1976). Gavin Wright, *The Political Economy of the Cotton South: Households, Markets and Wealth in the Nineteenth Century* (New York: W. W. Norton, 1978). Paul A. David and Peter Temin, 'Explaining the Relative Efficiency of Slave Agriculture in the Antebellum South: Comment', *American Economic Review*, 69 (Mar. 1979), 213–18.

[20] Kenneth M. Stampp, *The Peculiar Institution: Slavery in the Ante-Bellum South* (New York: Alfred A. Knopf, 1956).

Second, slavery was better able to fit the economy to the demands of agriculture. Ricardo asserted that land became poorer on the frontier, but the American experience was the opposite; land was more fertile as antebellum settlers moved West. Agriculture in both the North and South moved westward as the nineteenth century progressed. But even though many Northerners followed Horace Greeley's advice to move west, there was a substantial pool of labour in Eastern cities for industrial growth. Many of the European immigrants who came to America through these cities also were not pulled off into the west. They stayed to create an industrial laour force. In the South, by contrast, slaves— who again did not have the choice of where to live—were moved west as the price of slaves in the west rose. The fate of old cotton states was depopulation, not industrialization. Paradoxically, the South's very success in adapting itself to cotton production inhibited the movement out of agriculture.[21]

Third, the political climate created by slavery was inimical to industrialization. The federal nature of the United States allowed these views to be embodied in state governments and expressed in state actions. The absence of large landowners in the North allowed industrialists to acquire political power in Northern states. Government activity therefore favoured urban industrial growth. Southern state governments were dominated by large slave-owners, Domar's landed aristocracy. Economic policy in the South favoured the growth of cotton agriculture.

The variation in local economic policies can be seen in several areas. The growth of transportation facilities was encouraged far more by Northern states than by Southern. Most canal and railroad building in the antebellum United States therefore was in the North.[22] Education was widespread in the North, but restricted to whites in the South. Slaves had no more choice in their education than they had in their location or   occupation. From the slave-owners' viewpoint, slaves had no need for learning, and learning might foment rebellion as well.[23]

[21] Alexander Field, 'Sectoral Shifts in Antebellum Massachusetts: A Reconsideration', *Explorations in Economic History*, 15 (Apr. 1978), 146–71. Claudia Goldin and Kenneth Sokoloff, 'The Relative Productivity Hypothesis of Industrialization: The American Case, 1820 to 1850', *Quarterly Journal of Economics*, 99 (Aug. 1984), 461–87.

[22] Carter Goodrich, *Government Promotion of American Canals and Railroads, 1800–1890* (New York: Columbia University Press, 1960). George R. Taylor and Irene D. Neu, *The American Railroad Network, 1861–1890* (Cambridge, Mass.: Harvard University Press, 1956).

[23] Bernard Bailyn, *Education in The Forming of American Society* (New York: W. W. Norton, 1972).

And Southern Congressmen vehemently opposed tariffs, while their Northern counterparts favoured them. Northerners wanted tariffs to encourage the growth of industry; Southerners wanted free trade to encourage the export of raw cotton (and the importation of English cotton textiles).

The contrasting resolutions of Domar's dilemma in the North and South thus led to increasing tension between the regions as the free-labour economy and polity diverged ever more strongly from the landed-aristocracy system. Sooner or later, there had to be a struggle for supremacy, as there was in many Western European countries. Germany, France, Italy, etc., went down one road with the adoption of heavy tariffs in the late 1870s and 1880s. The United Kingdom went down another by adhering to free trade. In each case, the decision was made peacefully.[24]

The struggle came earlier in the United States than in Europe. And it was bloodier. The Civil War was precipitated by tariff disputes, even though the morality of slavery was an underlying issue.[25] From the perspective of this paper, these two disputes were expressions of the same underlying cause. Slavery was the cause of the Civil War, both directly (by arousing moral indignation in the North) and indirectly (by maintaining the Southern power structure favouring agriculture and therefore free trade). Slavery undoubtedly was the cause of the violence as well, making a peaceful resolution of the conflict impossible.

The Civil War placed an enormous burden on the American economy. In addition to diverting resources to the conduct of the war, it also destroyed people and the capital accumulated by them. Even though the resolution of the political conflict affected by the war was desirable, the war itself was a tragedy, It has proved difficult to quantify the cost of the war itself, both because of the variety of the its effects and because of its coincidence with other events—most notably a slowing in the world demand for cotton. The best estimates show the cost to the North to have been between 10 and 20 per cent of consumption in the North throughout most of the 1860s and 1870s. The cost to the South was above 20 per cent of hypothetical consumption (that is, the probable consumption in the absence of the war) from 1862 to 1874 and above 30 per cent

[24] Peter A. Gourevitch, 'International Trade, Domestic Coalitions, and Liberty: Comparative Responses to the Crisis of 1873–96', *Journal of Interdisciplinary History*, 8 (Autumn 1977), 281–313.

[25] Kenneth M. Stampp, *And the War Came: The North and the Secession Crisis 1860–1861* (Baton Rouge, La.: Louisiana State University Press, 1950).

82 *Peter Temin*

throughout the 1860s. This considerable cost surely is part of the burden of Southern history.[26]

The victory of the North in the Civil War showed the dominance of the society based on free labour. In contrast to Europe, the expression of industrial political power in the United States was high tariffs. The reason for this difference is clear. The United States was an agricultural exporter; Western European countries, importers. Free trade therefore meant the destruction of agriculture in Western Europe and its encouragement in the United States.

High tariffs were not the only problems facing Southern agriculture after the Civil War. The demand for cotton grew more slowly after the war as the expansion of the British cotton industry slowed and other sources of supply emerged. Equally important, the supply of labour to Southern agriculture dramatically decreased. Both slave men and women had worked in the fields before the war. After the war, freedmen and women could make their own choices. They opted for the pattern shown by free American labour. They did not work as hard as they had under the coercion of slavery. And the men worked in the fields while the women brought up the family and worked closer to the house. Labour supply of black farm workers was reduced by about 30 per cent. The decline in Southern incomes therefore was partly a fall in welfare (due to the lower demand for cotton) and partly a voluntary shift of consumption (towards leisure).[27]

Black incomes rose after the war, but the gap between black and white incomes did not close. Research has tried to explain this persistent discrepancy. One school maintains that it is the result of continuing discrimination. Black tenant farmers, for example, were said to be coerced into growing more cotton than they should have. Without the ability to dictate the use of labour, the merchants who replaced land and slave owners as Southern captains of agriculture had to fall back on costly methods of control. This argument seems overdrawn. There is no evidence that the cropping pattern of the post-bellum South was inefficient. The claim that farmers were coerced into inefficient patterns therefore loses its rationale.[28]

[26] Claudia G. Goldin and Frank D. Lewis, 'The Economic Cost of the American Civil War: Estimates and Implications', *Journal of Economic History*, 35 (June 1975), 299–326. Peter Temin, 'The Post-Bellum Recovery of the South and the Cost of the Civil War', *Journal of Economic History*, 36 (Dec. 1976), 898–907.

[27] Roger L. Ransom and Richard Sutch, *One Kind of Freedom: The Economic Consequences of Emancipation* (Cambridge: Cambridge University Press, 1977), 44–6.

[28] Roger L. Ransom and Richard Sutch, *One Kind of Freedom: The Economic Con-

More evident patterns of coercion came late in the nineteenth century with the growth of segregation and Jim Crow laws. Perhaps the most important part of this discrimination for black economic opportunity was its effect on education. Slaves had not been educated, and segregated schooling perpetuated the educational gap between blacks and whites.[29]

Others have argued that the persistent gap is the result of the poor conditions of freedom after the Civil War. Radical Republicans wanted to give each freedman '40 acres and a mule', but their programme did not pass. Freedmen were left with no physical assets and no human assets (education, training) after the war. The argument from initial conditions asserts that this handicap was too great to be overcome in any short time.[30]

There is no need to choose between these alternatives. The history of American blacks contains both elements. Freedmen and women drew a bad hand after the war, albeit better than they had held before. At best, they were not helped to overcome their initial deficit by governmental policy. At worst, they were actively opposed. Only in the twentieth century has the balance of governmental policy shifted clearly toward integrating blacks into the national economy on an equal footing. And only in the second half of the twentieth century has this been a conscious policy, as distinct from reactions to national emergencies like wars and depression.

III

Although my main theme so far has been the varied but pervasive effects of free land, the government has reared its head at several points in the discussion. It is time to bring in the American form of government as a separate compelling influence on American economic history.

Two characteristics of the United States government are of interest here. First is its popular nature, which ensured that political power conformed to the economic interests just described. Second is the federal nature of the government, which ensured that much of American politics is local politics. This in turn limited the power of the national government

sequences of Emancipation. Peter Temin, 'Freedom and Coercion: Notes on the Analysis of Debt Peonage in One Kind of Freedom', *Explorations in Economic History*, 16 (Jan. 1979), 56–63.

[29] Robert Higgs, *Freedom and Coercion: Blacks in the American Economy, 1865–1914* (Cambridge: Cambridge University Press, 1977).

[30] Stephen J. DeCanio, *Agriculture in the Postbellum South: The Economics of Production and Supply* (Cambridge, Mass.: MIT Press, 1974).

and left economic forces relatively free to operate. State governments were hardly divorced from economic activity. Rather they tended to be responsive to emerging economic interests.[31]

Despite the volume of writing on American political thought, there has been little attention paid to the origins of federalism in the United States. Sovereignty was located in the people, according to the founding fathers. But the individual colonies also retained some of the sovereignty granted them by the English Crown. This slight wobble in the ideological gyroscope of the revolution does not seem to have attracted a lot of attention; it seems natural to us looking back—as it apparently did to the leaders at the time—that the American government should be organized by states.[32]

Slavery was a state institution, and the agreement to let the states go their own ways endured for a while. But as abolitionist morality grew, there had to be a series of compromises at the national level limiting what states could do about slavery. This interplay between the state and federal governments is a continuing theme in American economic history.

The politics of the tariff, for example, illustrate the interaction. Francis Lowell, the founder of the Boston Manufacturing Company, found himself in need of protection for his nascent cotton mill at the close of the war of 1812. The mill employed power looms copied after English looms Lowell had seen on a visit to England. Given the primitive state of American power-loom technology, the Boston Manufacturing Company machinery was designed to weave a coarse, heavy cloth. Lowell designed the relevant part of the Tariff of 1816 to protect this end of the cotton market.

The tariff bill was a response to the influx of cheap British goods following the end of the war with Britain. It set a duty of 25 per cent on cotton textiles, but—in response to an argument by Lowell—introduced a minimum valuation of 25 cents. The tariff, in other words, was a specific duty of 6.25 cents for all fabrics priced below 25 cents a yard and an *ad valorem* duty for finer fabrics.

---

[31] Oscar Handlin and Mary F. Handlin, *Commonwealth, A Study of the Role of Government in the American Economy: Massachusetts, 1774–1861* (New York: New York University Press, 1947). Louis Hartz, *Economic Policy and Democratic Thought: Pennsylvania, 1776–1860* (Cambridge, Mass.: Harvard University Press, 1948). Morton J. Horwitz, *The Transformation of American Law, 1780–1860* (Cambridge, Mass.: Harvard University Press, 1977).

[32] Gordon S. Wood, *The Creation of the American Republic, 1776–1787* (Chapel Hill, NC: University of North Carolina Press, 1969). Bernard Bailyn, *The Ideological Origins of the American Revolution* (Cambridge, Mass.: Harvard University Press, 1967).

Lowell lobbied for a minimum in order to protect his nascent Waltham mill. His product was designed, in Nathan Appleton's words, 'to imitate the yard wide goods of India, with which the country was then largely supplied'. But even with the power loom, the Massachusetts mill could not compete with the Indian producers. Lowell needed a very high tariff to survive. But he knew he could not get Congress to levy a high enough *ad valorem* rate; Souther cotton-growers sold most of their output on the British market, and they refused to agree to anything that would decrease the demand for English cotton textile products or that might provoke retaliation.

Lowell therefore proposed a tariff structure that would discriminate against Indian cottons, but not the higher-priced English fabric. He sent a memorial to Congress to that effect. In Lowell's words: 'The articles, whose prohibition we pray for, are made of very inferior materials, . . . No part of the produce of the United States enters into their composition. They are the work of foreign hands on foreign materials.' The minimum, in other words, would exclude only Asian cloth made from Asian cotton; it would not affect the demand for higher quality English cloth made from American cotton. This argument won the support of South Carolina, which saw the minimum as a measure to protect the domestic market for their raw cotton, and assured passage of the tariff.[33]

Lowell's successful efforts show the need to get a consensus between the states on tariff policy. This co-operative spirit was hard to maintain. South Carolina responded to the Tariff of 1828 by passing a Nullification Act, asserting that the federal government lacked power to dictate to the states. At a time when compromises over slavery seemed to be holding, agreement on the tariff was eroding.

The tariff was more than a political symbol; it had an important impact on American manufacturing. Not only the minimum but the whole structure of the cotton tariff protected the bottom end of the cotton market more than the top. It served to segment the American market between American and English producers by quality. With the tariff, the American producers could expand at the lower end. Without it, Lancashire would have supplied the entire range of American consumption.[34] The tariff on iron, considerably less controversial than the cotton duty, reached its antebellum peak in the Tariff of 1842, but iron

[33] Peter Temin, 'Product Quality and Vertical Integration in the Early Cotton Textile Industry', *Journal of Economic History*, 48 (Dec. 1988), 891–907.
[34] Mark Bils, 'Tariff Protection and Production in the Early U.S. Cotton Textile Industry', *Journal of Economic History*, 44 (Dec. 1984), 1033–46.

producers were unable to maintain this high level. Econometric work has confirmed that the tariff rate had a strong effect on the growth of American iron production.[35]

More generally, the tariff promoted industrial growth in the North. It enhanced the return to industrial capital enough to offset the pull of agriculture. American manufacturing therefore owed its vigour partly to the characteristics of people and land in the North and partly to the structure of the federal government that could support a favourable commercial policy.

The growth of industry in the North strengthened its hand in the military contest with the South. Industrial growth enhanced the North's ability to provide war material for the conflict. State policies had encouraged the expansion of railroads to move men and *matériel* around. The prosperity of the North had drawn immigrants from Europe to provide a basis for production and the army. And the will of free labour proved very strong as well.

These factors are not enough to explain why the American resolution of the agrarian–industrial conflict was so different from the German or French. Other factors—like the success of Charles Francis Adams in keeping England out of the war—mattered too. But, whatever the cause, the North's victory in the Civil War placed a federal government in power that was strongly sympathetic to the growth of industry. The Republican tariff introduced during the war remained in force after its end. It was a losing partisan issue for the Democrats for the rest of the century. The Fourteenth Amendment (guaranteeing due process) introduced to provide for freed slaves during the war was reinterpreted after the war to provide legal growing room for corporations. The state militias turned from sectional divisions to preparation for the anticipated class war in which they would have to defend property against the working-class mob.[36]

One aspect of public policy was particularly important for the economy and peculiarly American. The transition from the American System to mass production has been described already. This change in the technique of manufacturing was coincident with and connected to the emergence of what Chandler has called the modern business

[35] Robert W. Fogel and Stanley L. Engerman, 'A Model for the Explanation of Industrial Expansion during the Nineteenth Century: With an Application to the American Iron Industry', *Journal of Political Economy*, 77 (May/June 1969), 306–28.

[36] Robert M. Fogelson, *America's Armories: Architecture, Society, and Public Order* (Cambridge, Mass.: Harvard University Press, 1989).

enterprise. These multi-layered industrial corporations and their managerial hierarchies made their appearance in the 1880s as firms integrated mass production and mass distribution.

Chandler identified three types of industries in which these large firms were most likely to appear. In some industries, the invention of new machines created the capacity for continuous production from a few plants large enough to saturate the market. The need to manage the large volume of production and the returning cash flow led to the growth of administrative networks that provided 'the pioneering enterprises their greatest competitive advantage'. In other industries, the centralized production of perishable products like meat, beer, and butter, required manufacturers to get involved with distribution. For while the wholesaler might not be affected by the spoilage of goods from one producer, the manufacturer concerned about the reputation of his product could easily be hurt. Still other industries produce products like sewing machines or agricultural machinery that needed customer service. The retailer could not be trusted to give enough service to promote the use of new products, and manufacturing firms expanded all the way into the retail distribution and support of their products. The Singer Sewing Machine Company, mentioned earlier for its manufacturing techniques, was cited as well by Chandler for its marketing and service operations.[37]

These large firms were an American phenomenon. There were large companies in Europe, to be sure, but they were limited to a much narrower spectrum of industries than in the United States. An increasing number of them also were connected with their American counterparts; the United States exported managerial expertise at the turn of the twentieth century.[38]

This American phenomenon grew out of the technology developed in the hospitable conditions of the northern United States. It also flourished in the favourable legal environment of America. The Sherman Antitrust Act was passed in 1890 to restrain the trusts and holding companies that were the legal forms of the large firms. But its effect was swiftly blunted by judicial decisions restricting its applicability.

The *Knight* decision confirming the legality of the Sugar Trust was the first under the new law. The Supreme Court said the trust was

[37] Alfred D. Chandler, jun., *The Visible Hand: The Managerial Revolution in American Business* (Cambridge, Mass.: Harvard University Press, 1977), 298.
[38] Alfred D. Chandler, jun., and Herman Daems, *Managerial Hierarchies: Comparative Perspectives on the Rise of the Modern Industrial Enterprise* (Cambridge, Mass.: Harvard University Press, 1980). Chandler, *Scale and Scope: The Dynamics of Industrial Capitalism* (Cambridge, Mass.: Harvard University Press, 1990).

engaged in production, not commerce, and therefore was beyond the reach of the law. This decision can only be understood in the context of the federal nature of American government. For the issue in front of the court was jurisdictional; should antitrust be a policy of the states or of the federal government? The court reaffirmed the power of the states by reserving antitrust policy to them. This had the perverse effect, however, of gutting antitrust policy as the states competed with each other for the charters of new firms. This unintended reaction therefore was the result of the federal structure of American government as much as a deliberate policy to promote business.[39]

The tilt of government towards business also had implications for labour. Jacoby argues that the government's toleration of business combination and expansion contributed to managerial hostility toward collective bargaining.[40] This in turn restricted the options open to American labour unions, opposed by management and unsupported by government. Finding themselves unable to reach the broader institutional goals of their European counterparts, the American labour unions adopted the conservative emphasis on jobs and pay that has characterized them ever since.

The orientation of American government also had consequences for the organization of what are called public utilities in America. Railroads, telephones, and power generation and distribution are private in the United States and public in most other countries. The government drew back from these activities—although it took over some utilities, like municipal transport, when private companies failed. Instead of direct governmental control, the government opted for indirect control through regulatory commissions. The record of economic regulation has been patchy, but the American reaction has been to deregulate the private companies, rather than to nationalize them.[41]

One prominent recent example shows the continuing importance of American federalism. AT&T had managed the American telephone network for a century as a private regulated utility. It was broken up into

[39] C. W. McCurdy, 'The Knight Sugar Decision of 1895 and the Modernization of American Corporate Law, 1869–1903', *Business History Review, 53* (Autumn 1979), 305–42.

[40] Sanford M. Jacoby, 'American Exceptionalism Revisited: The Importance of Management' in Jacoby, *Masters to Managers* (New York: Columbia University Press, 1991).

[41] Thomas K. McCraw, ed., *Regulation in Perspective: Historical Essays* (Cambridge, Mass.: Harvard University Press, 1981). Id., *Prophets of Regulation: Charles Francis Adams, Louis D. Brandeis, James M. Landis, Alfred E. Kahn* (Cambridge, Mass.: Harvard Univeristy Press, 1984).

eight pieces in 1984 in the resolution of an antitrust suit that provides a curious counterpoint to *Knight*. A primary accusation against the telephone company was that it was cross-subsidizing its competitive activities to restrain competition illegally. This tangled issue was misunderstood by most of the actors in the law-suit, in large part because they saw only the federal government and ignored the states. For the cross-subsidies actually ran the other way, from competitive to monopoly activities. They ran that way to satisfy the demands of state regulators for low local-service rates. The federal antitrust unit in this case overwhelmed the states' influence through the regulatory process, leading to the dismembering of AT&T and—not surprisingly—rising local telephone rates. If AT&T had not been forced to accede to the wishes of state regulators and judges over many years, it might well have avoided its unhappy fate.[42]

The exceptional growth of American industry therefore has twin roots. Its mother, so to speak, was the abundant and fertile American soil. The accessible land tenure system of the North gave rise to manufacturing and the American System. The father was the federal form of American government that created the permissive legal setting that favoured mass production and the modern business enterprise. As usual, both parents have affected the appearance and behaviour of the offspring.

IV

The phenomena I have described comprise only a partial description of the American economy. There were other activities and other influences coexisting with these trends. It is appropriate to ask if the factors analysed here have left their traces in the aggregate record. Was the aggregate growth of the American economy in any way exceptional ?

Some data collected by Kuznets provide the answer. I have selected a subset of the countries he described, and I have placed them into three 'tiers', as seen in Table 3.1. The United Kingdom and the Netherlands were the richest countries of the eighteenth century and the source of modern commerce and industry. In the century or so prior to 1970, their per capita incomes grew at an average rate of 13 per cent per decade. The second tier includes the first group of large follower countries.

[42] Peter Temin, *The Fall of the Bell System: A Study in Prices and Politics* (Cambridge: Cambridge University Press, 1987).

Despite the well-known and much-discussed differences between France, Germany, and the United States, their average per capita growth rates were all higher than the countries in the first tier and practically identical. The third tier of more recent follower countries exhibited even faster growth in per capita income.

TABLE 3.1. *Percentage growth rates per decade in the century prior to 1970*

Country	National income	Population	Income per head	Years in sample
First Tier				
U K	23	8	13	106
Netherlands	28	13	13	100
Second Tier				
France	21	3	17	99
Germany	31	11	18	110
U S A	39	19	17	105
Third Tier				
Italy	31	7	23	68
Japan	48	12	32	88
Sweden	37	6	29	100

Source: Simon Kuznets, *Economic Growth of Nations: Total Output and Production Structure* (Cambridge, Mass.: Harvard University Press, 1971).

The United States fits comfortably within this scheme; there seems little that is exceptional about its long-term economic growth. Closer inspection, however, reveals one important uniqueness. While the United States is in the middle of these countries in the long-term growth of per capita income, it is an outlier in the long-term growth of population. No other country even comes close to the American rate. The United States was able to absorb the highest rate of population growth while keeping pace with its industrializing peers in per capita income.

This high rate of population growth was the result of a high rate of natural increase and the extraordinary immigration to the United States, in roughly equal proportion. Had there been no immigration after the Revolution and the same rate of natural increase in the colonial population as there was in the presence of immigration, then the population in 1920—roughly the end of the great immigration period—would have been one-half its actual size.[43] The emphasis on the nature of

[43] Lance E. Davis *et al.*, *American Economic Growth* (New York: Harper and Row, 1972), 126.

immigration in this exposition therefore is not misplaced. The exceptional quality of aggregate American economic growth was its simultaneous absorption of massive immigration and rapid growth in income.

Baumol has asserted that countries' per capita incomes converge to a common level, that is, that their rate of growth in the century before 1979 was inversely proportional to their 1870 income ranking.[44] If he is correct, then no country's growth will show a unique pattern. But his claim cannot be sustained. Baumol used a sample of sixteen countries, taken from Maddison, who reported in many cases the same data as Kuznets.[45] There are two problems. First, underestimates of income in early years will bias upwards the estimated rate of growth, producing a negative correlation between initial income and growth that reflects errors in the variables rather than the path of history. Japan, for example, may appear as the most rapidly growing country in Table 3.1 because we have underestimated its income at the Meiji Restoration.[46] Second, Maddison's sample included only those countries that have industrialized. If one takes a sample of countries identified by their characteristics in 1870—rather than in 1979—then the tendency towards convergence disappears.[47]

There are real differences between countries, even in their rate of growth. But the sense that *industrial* countries are becoming more homogeneous remains. America was unique in the nineteenth and early twentieth centuries. Is it still exceptional?

Nowhere near as much as it used to be, seems the answer, at least on the dimensions analysed here. Let me comment briefly on them by turn. Free land disappeared long ago; twentieth-century America is a fully settled country. And while the modern business enterprises that grew from this fertile soil are still dominant economic institutions, there is a suspicion that they are becoming obsolete. Economic growth in our day may be generated more easily by alternate forms of organization. Flexible specialization and matrix management have

[44] William J. Baumol, 'Productivity Growth, Convergence, and Welfare: What the Long-Run Data Show', *American Economic Review*, 76 (Dec. 1986), 1072–85.

[45] Angus Maddison, *Phases of Capitalist Development* (Oxford: Oxford University Press, 1982). Simon Kuznets, *Economic Growth of Nations: Total Output and Production Structure* (Cambridge, Mass.: Harvard University Press, 1971).

[46] Susan B. Hanley, 'A High Standard of Living in Nineteenth-Century Japan: Fact or Fiction?', *Journal of Economic History*, 43 (Mar. 1983), 183–92.

[47] Bradford De Long, 'Have Productivity Levels Converged? Productivity Growth, Convergence, and Welfare: Comment', *American Economic Review*, 78 (Dec. 1988), 1138–54.

replaced management hierarchies as the hallmark of the new organizations.[48]

Slavery of course is long gone, even though the social problems attendant on racial integration still remain. They are not, however, Southern problems. The South has become integrated into the national economy. Both economic problems and achievements have become national in scope; the sharp regional differentiation that was such a feature of nineteenth-century America is no longer economically significant.[49]

Federalism, while still very much alive, seems ever more tenuous in its economic effects. Government regulation and its support for economic activities emanate chiefly from Washington, DC. Despite the volume of rhetoric about the independence of the states, they are less independent of Washington and smaller relative to large corporations than they have ever been. I do not want to say that states do not matter—they do—but only that economic policy formation today shows less effect of federalism than it did at earlier times.

In short, America was exceptional. Its history is unique, both in the aggregate and in its composition. The contradictions of the early nineteenth century, resolved bloodily in the Civil War, gave rise to a distinctive American economy that provided an example to the world both of aggregate growth with immigration and of managerial forms for corporate economic life. In our generation, however, the distinctive quality of American economic life is fast disappearing.

Disappearing, but not yet gone. Free land and slavery are long gone; federalism is much attenuated. But there is still an American approach to many problems. This world-view can no longer be attributed to the factors discussed here, but they may be regarded as the result—perhaps an echo—of a history replete with these factors. This, however, is the end of a chapter on the history of the American economy, not the start of one on its future. A few words on the legacy of free land and federalism will suffice.

The American population no longer grows at the extraordinary rate shown in Table 3.1. The United States none the less has remained somewhat open to the immigration of Asians and Latin Americans. These new Americans are being absorbed into the economy and society

[48] Michael J. Piore and Charles F. Sabel, *The Second Industrial Divide: Possibilities for Prosperity* (New York: Basic Books, 1984). Mel Horwitch, *Post-modern Management: Its Emergence and Meaning for Strategy* (Detroit: Free Press, 1988).

[49] Gavin Wright, *Old South, New South: Revolutions in the Southern Economy Since the Civil War* (New York: Basic Books, 1986).

of the United States in a free-wheeling fashion reminiscent of frontier settlements. Individuals are free to go their own way, and the success of individuals is celebrated. American education is very open and inclusive, providing an avenue for immigrants of all sorts to make their way into the higher levels of the economy in a very few generations.

But while there are ample signs of social progress and individual achievement, the integration of black Americans into the economy has been slow and difficult. The very individualism that has welcomed, say, Asians into the mainstream has seemed to hamper blacks. Reservations about affirmative action reflect both resistance to equality—that is, racism—and adherence to the ideology of the frontier. Great strides toward equality have been made in the years since the Second World War, but the relative position of blacks seems to have stopped improving in the 1980s, just as the distinctive features of the American economy are eroding.

It may not be too far from the mark to suggest that a decisive issue for the future of the American economy is how to resolve the tensions between the immigrant and resident groups whose economic prospects differ so sharply. This conflict is hardly as servere as the historical one leading to the Civil War. It is not too fanciful, however, to see it as a reprise of the tensions of the mid-nineteenth century. The South and the descendants of slaves have been integrated into the economy, but not completely and not without problems.

American business no longer appears as distinctive as it did thirty or forty years ago. The change here is twofold. As mentioned above, the American business firm is losing its distinctive focus on mass production and standardized products. More importantly, firms in other countries have adopted many of the American innovations. Business has become multinational.

The internationalization of economic life is too complex to be described here. The point is simply to generalize the previous paragraph. The interaction goes both ways. The United States economy is losing its exceptional character as it adapts to growing international competition. And other economies are recasting themselves in a more American mould through privatization and *perestroika*.

If the latter influence is stronger, American economic exceptionalism may be disappearing more because the rest of the industrial world is acquiring 'American' traits—without a history of free land and federalism—than because the United States economy is escaping from its exceptional history.

4

American Exceptionalism:
The Religious Phenomenon

Andrew Greeley

I propose in this chapter to present a sketch of religion in the United States based on my professional tools, survey research data, to ask whether this portrait does indeed make American religion 'exceptional', and to suggest some reasons why religion in the United States might differ from religion in Great Britain and on the continent. This is not an essay about the nature of religion. It is rather a much more modest effort to determine whether the tools of survey research are able to confirm the hypothesis that self-reported religious behaviour in America has diminished in the last four decades. To use the language of the logic of social research: can one safely reject the null hypothesis that the survey indicators show no major change in American self-reported religious behaviour?

To anticipate my conclusions:

1. There have been only marginal changes in American religious attitudes and behaviours since the first years when survey material was available to us. Projections based on age and cohort analysis suggest that there will be no major changes in the years immediately ahead.

2. There is some question as to whether the high levels of religious devotion in the United States are 'exceptional' in the English-speaking world of the North Atlantic. More probably, if there is an exception, it is Great Britain not the United States—and only in one component of the British population.

3. Religion in the United States seems to differ from religion in Great Britain in that it has more capability to confer identity in the former than in the latter. In those British groups where one may assume that religion does have some identity-conferring potential, the levels of religious devotion do not differ from those in the United States.

Because my argument may seem strange even to some of my American colleagues—counter-intuitive, opposed to what everyone knows to be true—I must set the argument in the context of my own approach to research, a context which at the very beginning must express systematic scepticism about what everyone knows to be true. Whatever I may be when I wear other hats, I am an empiricist when I am doing social research; that is to say, I begin by seeking evidence to disconfirm the null hypothesis at the start of my investigations. In this case the null hypothesis is that there is no social change. Only when I can reject that hypothesis do I endeavour to explain the social change I have tentatively established.

Another way of describing this approach is to say that if a proposition cannot be falsified it cannot be verified. If research is not structured in such a way that the thesis of the researcher is not subject to falsification, then it cannot be established as even provisionally true. Thus when Professor Bellah and his colleagues tell me that civil responsibility in America has declined and individualism has increased during the last hundred years, I beg to be excused from accepting such an assertion in the absence of any serious attempt to falsify it, to confirm the null hypothesis that there is no such change.[1] The intensity with which Professor Bellah and his colleagues feel the truth of their argument is not a substitute for the search for evidence to disconfirm it. The evidence does not have to be survey evidence of the sort I use in my own work. Obviously surveys were not taken during the last century. But I want some evidence which, if the indicators go the 'wrong' way, would disprove their thesis. Until I observe the search for such evidence, I simply will not accept an argument as anything more than a deeply felt opinion.

Secondly, I am interested in the behaviour of people and not of church leaders, theologians, or church organizations. When someone purports to describe the changes in American religion by detailing the changing stands of theologians, the changing editorials of church publications, or the changing resolutions of clergy in solemn assembly, I take these data as proving only that there have been changes in institutional leadership. That some priests march on picket lines indicates only an upswing in clerical involvement in politics and *not* a change in political attitudes of the men and women who belong to the institution.

Thirdly, while I am aware of the weaknesses of my own data and willingly accept other data sources, I will not apologize for survey data.

[1] Robert N. Bellah *et al.*, *Habits of the Heart: Individualism and Commitment in American Life* (Berkeley: University of California Press, 1985). See also Bellah, *The Broken Covenant: American Civil Religion in Time of Trial* (New York: Seabury Press, 1975).

Everyone uses samples of some sort and everyone asks questions. The issue is how the samples are chosen, how the questions are worded, how the data are collected, and how the data are analysed. What a professor hears at a cocktail party, what a pastor thinks about his parish, and what everyone knows to be true are also findings that represent results of informal surveys. I am not prepared to admit that my data are inferior.

Minimally, I expect scholars using other data sources to take survey findings seriously, especially when such findings challenge their own conclusion. Survey results may not capture the whole of reality; neither do any other kinds of data. But they do measure at least one aspect of reality and hence cannot be lightly dismissed, especially when they run against what everyone knows to be true. I confess to a certain impatience with some historians and humanists who dismiss survey scholarship from the lordly position of their own wisdom, or assert that respondents are not telling the truth, or try to refute survey findings with anecdotes.

In each case, their own methods are not more solid but only less explicit. The historian tries to recreate the past from documents which are a sample of possible descriptions of the past, usually a sample with a powerful élite bias. Moreover, the historian picks and chooses from the testimony of his or her documents, usually without any explicit description or explanation for the decisions made about judging testimony. Finally, the anecdote-teller's stories may be more interesting than survey results and more entertaining than survey tables. None the less, he or she is reporting from a sample of data and, like the historian, is also sampling within the data sets available in his or her memory. The only real difference between these two kinds of wise and witty critics and the survey scholar is that the latter has eliminated personal bias from the process of sample selection and has been forthright about the limitations of his data.

'But there has been change', some critics say of my failure to find much change in American religion in the last half century. Surely some things have changed, but some things have remained remarkably consistent too. The consistencies must not be dismissed merely because everyone knows that they cannot be true—not when a legitimate mode of analysis demonstrates that what everyone knows to be true is not *in fact* true. For a number of years I worked on a board of an international Catholic magazine which wanted (or thought it wanted) an American empiricist among its members. Whenever I would present an article about the work of my colleagues and myself, continental theologians would first of all label it as 'positivism', as though such a label dismissed it out of hand. Then they would ask why I had not taken into account the theories of the Marxists or of the Frankfurt school. To which I would reply that I did not give a damn about either unless they had evidence that called into question my own evidence. I cite this not to establish the correctness of my position but rather to illustrate what my position is.

The conventional wisdom among those Americans who write about religion—clergymen, journalists, academics, even sociologists not specializing in empirical sociology of religion—is that American religion is 'declining'. When I was asked by the Social Science Research Council to write a monograph on American religion for the Harvard University Press social indicators series on America, I was told that my principle task would be to document the ever-increasing power of secularization in American society. I replied that I would be happy to write the book, but no one should count on that being the finding. It took a year-and-a-half struggle with referees who 'knew' that I had to be wrong before the book was finally forced towards publication. Something had to have changed, had it not?

The problem is that those who write on religion and most academics are not religious themselves. Neither are their families or friends. Since many of them came from religious backgrounds, they naturally assume that their own biographies are typical. Scholarly restraint ought to incline them to scepticism about their own typicality. But, on the subject of religion, scholarly restraint is a notoriously weak quality.

A typical élite position on American religion was expressed one night on the NBC evening news when Tom Brokaw reported that the latest edition of the Statistical Abstract contained one more piece of evidence for the declining importance of American religion: there had been no increase in the previous year in church membership. When the absence of an increase is taken to be proof of a decline we have left behind all the rules of logic and entered the area of religious faith! *Credo ut intelligam.* (I believe so that I may understand.) Incidentally, while one can hardly expect TV news writers to be aware of it, any decline or indeed any levelling off of increase in a society with a disproportionately youthful population (as the United States still is, under the impact of the 'baby boom') must be examined to determine whether the change is the result of age composition and not of cultural or structural change.

Alongside the conventional wisdom that American religion is in decline is the opposite conventional wisdom of a 'surge' of religious fundamentalism, of the 'emergence' of the 'religious right' or the 'moral majority'. On the one hand, the forces of secularization are eroding religion; on the other, the radical fundamentalists are increasing in numbers, importance, and influence: this, I submit, is the conventional wisdom not only of the national press but also of the faculty dining rooms.

How can such positions be held with any consistency? Since both of them are in fact pre-conscious imagery and not explicitly articulated propositions, there is no necessity for consistency. One can feel, on the one hand, quite confident that science and education are diminishing the importance of religion and, on the other hand, frightened about the effect of massive waves of fundamentalists on society. If one strives for some sort of consistency, one can always use the strategy of Peter Berger and talk about 're-sacralization', a countervailing force to 'secularization'.

One can use such an approach if one has no concern about empirical evidence. Yet it is very difficult indeed to find any—I repeat, *any*—evidence of either phenomenon in the survey data. When George Gallup, sen., asked the first question about whether you 'happened' to attend church or synagogue last week in the early 1940s, the proportion that had 'happened' to attend church was 40 per cent. It's still 40 per cent almost a half-century later.

In the first Roper question about belief in life after death, also in the 1940s, a little more than 70 per cent of Americans said that they were 'certain' about such continuance of life. In the 1987 NORC General Social Survey the proportion was exactly the same. Nor does such a conviction correlate with age or education at either point in time; both the young and the old, the college-educated and those who did not even attend secondary school, believe in survival in almost exactly the same proportions.

As to the 'rise' of the fundamentalists, twenty years ago some 22 per cent of Americans believed in the literal interpretation of the Bible, described themselves as 'born again', and said that they had tried to convert someone else to Jesus. This proportion has not changed. Indeed, acceptance of the literal interpretation has not declined, as we shall see shortly. The 'fundamentalist' right is now, as it was two decades ago, about a fifth of the American population. It has always been an important part of the American religious scene. The First Great Awakening, after all, occurred in 1744. The change in the last decade is that the élite media in New York, under the impact of the Reagan election, have rediscovered the fundamentalist fifth of Americans. As a rule of thumb, most 'trends' reported in *Time* and *Newsweek* and similar media outlets are a rediscovery of something that has always existed outside of New York, Washington, and Boston.[2]

But surely the 'moral majority' has more political clout than it used to have? When I'm asked that, I reply by asking if the questioner has ever heard of Prohibition? A surprising number either have not heard of it or do not see the point. So I have to explain that the religious right wing of our nation deprived the rest of the country of the right to consume alcoholic beverages for a decade and a half in the early part of this century. The rise of the moral majority is a falsehood on all three counts—it has not risen, it is not especially moral, and it certainly is not a majority.

To summarize what has happened to American religion during the era of social surveys (twenty-five years for most items, almost fifty for some): with the exception of some shuffling of denominational affiliation, Protestantism has not changed. Catholicism has changed, but not much, and the change is over.[3]

Most of the lines one would draw on a graph of American religious behaviour through the years are straight lines: more than 95 per cent believe in God; 77 per cent believe in the divinity of Jesus; 72 per cent believe in life after death with certainty, while another 20 per cent are unsure; 70 per cent believe in hell, 67 per cent in angels, 50 per cent in the devil; 34 per cent belong to a church-related organization; a third have had some kind of intense religious experience; half pray at least once a day and a quarter pray more than once a day; a third have a great deal of confidence in religious leadership; more than half think of themselves as very religious. Defection rates have not increased since 1960 and intermarriage rates have not changed significantly across Protestant and Catholic lines in the same time period.

Only three indicators show a decline—church attendance, financial contributions, and belief in the literal interpretation of the scripture. All three declines are limited to Catholics. The decline among Catholics in the acceptance of the literal interpretation of the Bible is limited to the young and the college-educated, and especially the young who are college-educated. Moreover, it is a decline accounted for by a change

[2] Tom Smith of the staff of NORC's General Social Survey has studied in detail the membership patterns of 'fine-tuned' denominational affiliation—the sort which distinguish, for example, among the various Baptist sub-denominations—and reports that there has been no statistically significant increase in the proportion (about 35%) of Americans in fundamentalist denominations since 1967.

[3] Andrew M. Greeley, *Religious Change in America* (Cambridge, Mass.: Harvard University Press, 1989).

to a position which is quite properly orthodox for Catholics—acceptance of the general message of the scripture as inspired without believing the literal interpretation of each word.

In 1968, 65 per cent of American Catholics attended Mass every week. Seven years later, 1975, that proportion had fallen to 50 per cent. In the ensuing thirteen years there has been no further decline. In 1960, 12 per cent of those born Catholic no longer described themselves as Catholic. By 1987 that proportion had increased, age composition taken into account, to 13 per cent. The traumatic change of the quarter-century had led to an increase of 1 per cent in the Catholic 'defection' rate—leading one to observe that there is probably nothing more that the clergy, the hierarchy, and the Vatican could do that would drive American Catholics out of the church.

In 1960 Protestants contributed 2.2 per cent of their income to their churches. In 1985 they continued to contribute the same 2.2 per cent. In 1960 Catholics also gave 2.2 per cent. In 1985 this proportion had declined to 1.1 per cent, costing the Catholic Church six billion dollars in lost income. Both the decline in Mass attendance and in financial contribution can be accounted for (statistically) by lay anger over the encyclical on birth control. Moreover, this anger affected different segments of the Catholic population differently. Church attendance declined only six percentage points among Catholics who described themselves as 'strong' Democrats or Republicans and thirty percentage points among those who described themselves as 'pure' political independents. Loyalty to the party and loyalty to the church, in other words, correlated with one another.

Michael Hout of the University of California and I subjected the correlation to a stringent statistical analysis developed by the Swiss psychometrician George Rasch to determine whether there was a latent variable linking the two, one that responded to certain precise constraints.[4] There did indeed seem to be such a relationship which we dubbed 'loyalty', a variable which resisted the negative impact of the birth control encyclical. This finding is, I believe, central to the American religious phenomenon: denominational heritages have a strong grip on Americans. They are given up only reluctantly because they are so integral to the specific forms of American pluralism. One is constrained to be loyal to that which defines what one is.

In addition to measuring simple change from survey to survey, it is

[4] Michael Hout and Andrew M. Greeley, 'The Center Doesn't Hold: Church Attendance in the United States, 1940–1984', *American Sociological Review*, 52 (June 1987), 325–45.

possible, if one has enough measures at different points in time, to analyse the relationship between age and cohort to determine if more recent age cohorts are less religious than their predecessors when the latter were the same age. Many European sociologists use an age relationship (religious variables correlating negatively with age) to prove a decline of religion. They forget that young people are less likely than older people to have made definite choices about career, job, party affiliation, place of residence, and permanent sexual partner. There is no reason to assume on a priori grounds that religion would be an exception to this pattern. That the more recent cohorts are less religious than their predecessors cannot be assumed, but remains to be proven.

In the cohort analysis in which Hout and I have engaged, the four following findings have emerged:

1. There is relationship between age and religion which affects most religious measures. Religious behaviour declines sharply between 18 and 25, begins to climb again in the late 20s and increases sharply in the 30s and 40s, then tapers off in the 50s. In general, this curve fits the most recent cohorts as well as the cohorts born in the 1920s.

2. Moreover, since the intercepts of the various cohorts (the rate of religious behaviour at which they enter the 'system' in their late teens) do not differ significantly, it is possible to simulate models which project church attendance rates till the year 2000. The most recent cohorts (born in the 1960s) will be as likely as their parents to attend church weekly: when the former reach their 40s, some three-fifths will be weekly church-goers.

3. There is, as noted briefly above, a shift of denominational affiliation occurring among Protestants, away from the 'main line' churches and towards the more conservative churches. Especially hard hit are the Methodists who were 22 per cent of Protestants born in the 1920s and only 11 per cent of those born in the 1960s. However, this 'realignment' has not involved any change in doctrinal position (including views on the literal interpretation of the Bible), church attendance, or political and social and moral positions.

4. When age is taken into account, there is a marginally significant relationship (.03) between cohort and denominational affiliation ('Protestant', 'Catholic', 'Jew', or 'other'). At present, some 3 per cent of Americans over 50 have no denominational affiliation. That will increase in years to come, we project, to 6 per cent. This increase is entirely explained by the later age at marriage and the proportion of the population never marrying. Both the change in marriage patterns and in

denominational affiliation were phenomena of the 1970s. Since 1980,
neither have changed.

The power of cohort analysis as a tool is enormous because it can
demonstrate whether there are signs of deviation from the life-cycle path
of religious behaviour in cohorts that were born forty years apart. Almost
no such deviations are to be found among Americans. Indeed, among
Catholics the decline in Mass attendance in response to the birth control
encyclical was evenly distributed in all age cohorts and not limited
merely to the younger generations. Thus my two sentences stand. With
the exception of denominational rearrangements, American Protestantism has not changed. Catholicism has changed, but the change seems
to have stopped.

Yet those two sentences of summary seem absurd. Protestantism has
experienced the rise and fall of Neo-orthodoxy, the death and rebirth of
the Social Gospel, migration from farm and small town to the city, the
appearance of the electronic evangelist, the 'surge' (or rediscovery)
of fundamentalism and evangelicalism, the musical chairs of various
denominational mergers, social and political conflict between activist
clergy and conservative laity, the clerically launched and led Civil Rights
Movement, renewed controversy between literalist and non-literalist
interpretation of scripture, and the endless battle between science and
religion.

Catholicism has experienced the twin transformation of the embour-
geoisement of the children of the immigrant and the *aggiornomento* of
the Second Vatican Council. Its people have moved from the immigrant
city to the professional suburbs, from unquestioning loyalty to frequently
contentious independence, from Latin to English, from the Counter-
reformation to the ecumenical age, from pious and docile nuns to strident
supporters of the ordination of women, from the Baltimore Catechism
to the Charismatic Renewal. Priests and nuns have left the active ministry
by the thousands, others have become involved in radical political and
social movements, sometimes with Marxist tones, still others have
doffed distinctive garb, insist on being called by first names, and instead
of pretending that they have no personal problems, insist that their
problems become the topic of constant conversation. Non-Catholic
students flock to parochial grammar schools, Liberation Theology is
taught in Catholic high schools, professed atheists hold chairs of theology in Catholic universities.

How can I possibly argue that there has been no change in Protestantism and only minor change in Catholicism? There are two answers to

the question. The first is to question whether there is as much change as meets the eye in the descriptions of the previous paragraphs and to wonder how much the actual changes affect the daily religious life and faith of ordinary Catholic and Protestant laity. Is not the 'changing church' a concern of the clergy, the lay élites, and the denominational journals of opinion rather than of the typical congregants? Is not the 'changing church' model an example of the 'Future Shock' fallacy, the utterly gratuitous assumption that changes in technology and environment must, without any need for proof, cause a change in fundamental dimensions of human life? Have not church members through the years shown remarkable skill in drawing from their faith what they want and need regardless of what the current organizational and theological fashions might be among their élites?

Priests on picket lines are news. But as dramatic as TV clips of such activity may be, is there any reason to think that such clips have any but peripheral effects on the religious life of Catholics? The protests of Catholic activists during the Vietnam War are frequently alleged to have turned the Catholic laity from hawks to doves. But survey data show that Catholics were always more dovish than typical white Americans, that their turn against the war antedated the Catholic Peace Movement, and that after each major public anti-war demonstration, there was an increase in support for the Nixon administration's conduct of the war.

Are Catholics more likely than Protestants to oppose nuclear arms because of a pastoral letter by the American hierarchy? Or is the letter itself a result of lay concern? The survey data show that Catholics were more likely to think that too much money was being spent on weapons ten years ago, long before the pastoral letter. In other words, the ecclesiastical changes which the mass media note may have little effect on the religious life of individuals, families, and local communities. Such effect needs to be proven, not assumed.

A second response is to concede the fact and the importance of the changes in American Christianity, and then add that social indicator research cannot hope to describe all the aspects of a phenomenon but only those for which there exist time-series data. Social indicators are at best a skeleton of a body politic or a body religious, an incomplete trajectory, an outline, a sketch. They represent truth as far as they go, but not surely the whole truth. The ingenious reader will perceive that the second argument is merely a less contentious version of the first. A little less explicitly than the first it hints, 'alright, give us an operational measure of religious change and we'll try to find data to test it. Till then we stand by the data we have: The null hypothesis cannot be rejected!'

Catholic church attendance rates fell sharply from 1969 to 1975 but the decline stopped in 1975 and a new level of stability has been in effect since then. The decline was caused by the birth control encyclical, the stability by an underlying loyalty to the church. Bible reading has increased over the last century; prayer may have increased in the last fifteen years; certainly the willingness to admit to ecstatic and paranormal experiences has gone up.

There has been no discernible change in belief in God, the divinity of Jesus, life after death, the existence of heaven, and divine influence on the Bible. The pattern of denominational affiliations has not changed (save for a decline in Methodism) nor has propensity to become a church 'member' and to belong to a church-affiliated voluntary organization (which organizations still have the largest claim on American organizational membership). The self-professed 'strength' of religious affiliation has not changed and this 'strength' is proven by the fact that even among the most unreligious age group—those in their early 20s—half the Christians in the United States are inside a church at least once a month.

Basic doctrines, church attendance, prayer, organizational affiliation and activity, religious experience, location on the political spectrum—are not these indicators, as superficial and as naïve as they might seem, at least a rough measure of the basic condition of religion in America? If they have not changed, is there not reason to assert that there is a certain long-term stability in American religious behaviour, whatever important changes might also be occurring? If the null hypothesis—no change in American religious behaviour— is to be rejected, must not support for such rejection be found in data other than survey data? And where is such data to be found?

Theodore Caplow and his colleagues in their study of the religion of 'Middletown' (Muncie, Indiana, first studied by Robert and Helen Lynd in 1924) note that in the late 1970s and early 1980s Middletown's religion had not changed on eleven major indicators for which there were measures at the beginning and the end of the sixty-year period:

If secularization is a shrinkage of the religious sector in relation to other sectors of society . . . then it ought to produce some or all of the following indications: (1) a decline in the number of churches per capita of the population, (2) a decline in proportion of the population attending church services, (3) a decline in the proportion of rites of passage held under religious auspices (for example, declining ratios of religious to civil marriages and of religious to secular funerals), (4) a decline in religious endogamy, (5) a decline in the proportion of the labor force engaged in religious activity, (6) a decline in the proportion of income devoted to the support of religion, (7) a decline in the ratio of religious to non-religious literature, (8) a decline in the attention given to religion in the mass media, (9) a drift toward less emotional forms of participation in religious services, (10) a dwindling of new sects and of new movements in existing churches, and (11) an increase in attention paid to secular topics in sermons and liturgy.[5]

While admitting that religion has changed greatly in Middletown since the 1920s, Caplow found no support for any of the eleven hypotheses. Muncie, Indiana, is the nation described in the present essay writ small, a place of remarkable continuity in religious behaviour.

In certain academic, journalistic, and religious circles, the response to the obvious fact of the sustained religiousness of the American people in comparison with the behaviour of Western Europeans is to dismiss the American religious 'phenomenon' as 'not authentic'. American devotion, we are told, is to 'the American way of life' and not to God. It is a 'civil religion', a 'culture religion', a reinforcement of patriotism and political conservatism, a 'religion in general' without specific doctrinal challenge or content, a materialistic creed supporting American 'consumerism' (a favourite phrase of Pope John Paul II).

Why, it is often asked by those who are prepared to accept the data that researchers like Caplow have gathered, is the United States so different from Europe, where 'secularization' is so much further advanced? The tone of voice in which the question is asked seems to imply that it is a mark of inferiority to lag behind Europe in a matter so important as religion. I shall leave to others the question of how secularized Europe actually is and merely suggest that, if it is indeed secularized, then a consideration of the rest of the world suggests not that North America is unique, but that Europe is. Religion has lost none of its power in the Third World, despite the energies which we group under the label 'modernization'. Is Iran secularized? Brazil with its powerful syncretistic cults? Is Poland? Or Croatia? Indeed the non-Western religions all seem to be undergoing dramatic revivals—not that Judaism and Christianity can properly be called 'Western'. The apparent failure of Christianity in some countries in Europe is the deviant case if one takes a world perspective, not the norm, a fact which orthodox sociology—based as it is on the work of three great theorists of 'secularization', Marx, Durkheim, and Weber—is most reluctant to admit.

---

[5] Theodore Caplow *et al., All Faithful People: Change and Continuity in Middletown's Religion* (Minneapolis: University of Minnesota Press, 1983), 34–45.

Our European counterparts, those who advance the civil religion argument seem to imply, may not be devout but at least they are hard-headed and not hypocritical. The proponents of a 'civil religion' interpretation in effect argue that there has been a notable change in American religion but that survey indicators cannot measure the phenomenon because the change—in the direction of secularization—is masked by the 'civil religion', the religion of 'the American Way of Life', of American patriotism.

The most sophisticated supporters of the theory of 'civil religion'—a term introduced into the discussion by the sociologist, Robert Bellah, in an article analysing not the religious behaviour of Americans but presidential inauguration addresses—cite the French sociologist, Emile Durkheim (along with the German, Max Weber, one of the two founding fathers of modern sociology) as the theorist behind their position. Durkheim argued that religion originates in the feelings of 'effervescence' by which society becomes conscious of itself in moments of enthusiasm during collective ritual. The American 'civil religion' is a religion of enthusiasm for the American political and social culture.

The trouble with applying Durkheim's model to contemporary Western society is that one is still faced with the question of why collective effervescence produces religious devotion in the most advanced industrialized nation in the world and not in Europe. *Qui nimis probat, nihil probat*: if you prove too much, you prove nothing. In fact, if one tries to test the 'civil religion' theory, one is hard put to find any support. Thus if one tries to find correlations between regular church attendance and militaristic attitudes (a demand for more money spent on the military and weapons), no such relationship emerges. Civil religion has flourished as a theory for more than twenty years without any substantial statistical support. Such findings are dismissed by the 'civil religion' theorists as being naïve and unsophisticated.

If a social change, a major trend in religious attitudes and behaviours, is too subtle to measure save by the wise men and women who do not need empirical data to establish trends, then it might well be true, but it is not a scientific proposition. Rather, it is an exercise in prophecy. Thus the available survey evidence cannot refute the null hypothesis that American religion continues substantially unchanged over the last three to five decades and seems likely to continue at the same levels into the third millennium of Christian history.

European scholars frequently argue that 'secularization' is the result of 'urbanization and industrialization'. That this is the case in some countries seems to be unarguable. Yet it did not happen in the United States, so the explanation is obviously inadequate. Scholars would be much better advised to put aside arguments based on such sweeping and irresistible historical trends and engage in cross-national research that asks why the migration to the cities in England (for the sake of an example) led to a decline in religious practice when the same migration in the United States and Canada did not produce similar results. Indeed, Finke and Stark have demonstrated that, in the United States at the turn of the present century, urbanization actually led to an increase in religious mobilization.[6]

There are a number of areas of explanation for the failure to replicate European trends in America. America lacks a history of feudalism, monarchy, and an established church. Thus religion in America has never been identified with any particular side in class struggles in the way it has been in Europe. 'Clericalism', in so far as it exists at all, is not perceived of as 'the enemy', as it was and is in France and has therefore not generated a virulent 'anticlericalism' (save in certain minute portions of the population) which views religion as the enemy of freedom and progress. It is not necessary today, not even in most liberal academic circles, to break with religion in order to establish one's credentials as an opponent of obscurantism, privilege, and reaction.

Moreover, on the positive side, the deliberately self-conscious pluralism which is both the official and unofficial policy of American society, has created a situation in which one's self-definition and social location have become an important part of one's personal identity. If religion is about believing and belonging, if it provides a community to which one can belong and find explanation and reinforcement for the ultimate values (symbols) one shares with other members of that community, then there is little in American experience to persuade most Americans that they should avoid such community and much to persuade them that they should join and be active in religious communities—to ask not why be religious, but rather to ask why not be religious.

Unintentionally, perhaps, American life seems to reinforce the loyalty factor which Hout and I found latent in both political affiliation and church attendance. The factor is both discrete and continuous. There is a threshold of loyalty that a person apparently elects to cross or not to cross in the late teens or early 20s. Once one chooses to be a religious

---

[6] Roger Finke and Rodney Stark, 'Religious Economies and Sacred Canopies: Religious Mobilization in American Cities, 1906', *American Sociological Review* 53 (Feb. 1988), 41–9.

and/or political alienate at that threshold, one is likely to remain in that social location for the rest of one's life. On the other hand, if one crosses the threshold, even to the extent of identifying with a party by reporting that one is an independent 'leaning' towards one party or the other or by attending church at least once a year, then one has embarked on a path which is likely to 'slide' upward politically and/or religiously as life continues.

Why this slide upward in political and religious affiliation, once one has elected to find some of one's social location in party and church? Perhaps age makes one more conservative and more in need of firm guidelines. Or perhaps with the passage of time one becomes more aware of the complexity of human existence, and hence more tolerant of the imperfections of one's church and one's party and more in need of clearly marked guideposts along the path. Or perhaps one wants to be able to pass on such useful guideposts to one's children, so that they can chart a safe and happy path through life's confusions. Or perhaps all of these three explanations come to the same thing: some guideposts, and some community to set up the posts and maintain the signs on them, are better than none; one's party and one's church may not be much, but, it turns out, they are all one has.

These possible explanations can be converted into operational measures; but social scientists will only begin to work on such measures when they are convinced that religion is not losing its importance in American life and hence is still worth studying as a major component of social structure and of the glue which holds the society, however precariously at times, together.

I am not equating religion with the social and structural characteristics which seem to facilitate it in some societies and impede it in others. I do not want to slip into a crude form of societal reductionism. I am merely suggesting that in some societies it is easy to be religious and in other societies it is easy to be non-religious. If a propensity to seek transcendental meanings for life is part of the human condition because humans are both conscious of their own mortality and apparently incurably hopeful that death is not the end, then the form and style in which individuals respond to such a propensity is likely to be shaped by the structure and culture of the given society in which individuals live.

It is possible, under these conditions, to develop a 'rational choice' theory which explains the persistence of religion in America. In American society a further 30 per cent of the population does consciously decide between their twenty-fifth birthday and their fortieth birthday to become regular church-goers (this increase from 30 to 60 per cent being an estimate based on age/cohort analysis). An additional 10 per cent of the population also decide to move (back in most cases) from religious non-identification to religious identification. Perhaps many more make decisions, in their early and middle 20s, about *continuing* their original religious identification and the devotional levels of their middle teens.

In the United States, more than 80 per cent of those who are born Catholic and more than 90 per cent of those who are born Protestant or Jewish eventually opt for their own religious heritage. Why? I would suggest that the reason for this is that, in the calculus of benefits, the choice of one's own religion seems to most Americans, finally, to confer the most benefits. You have to be something. For example, you don't want to be Jewish or Protestant because such a choice seems strange to you. So, perhaps reluctantly and perhaps with a sigh of resignation, you end up (on the average) being Catholic just as your parents were.

The choice of the religion of one's parents may suggest a certain 'addiction', a propensity to choose the familiar because so much has been invested in the familiar, perhaps a phenomenon not unlike the decision to remain with one's original word-processing programme even if other programmes promise more benefits, because (quite rationally) it is calculated that the advantages of Word Perfect over Microsoft Word are not worth the investment of start-up time required to obtain skill in the programme.

Stigler and Becker propose a theory of 'addiction' or 'consumption capital' that may be pertinent here.[7] To paraphrase the authors (on the subject of 'addiction' to classical music), an alternative way to state the same analysis is that the marginal utility of time allocated to a given denomination is increased by an increase in the stock of religious capital. Thus the consumption of a given religious heritage could be said to rise with exposure to the heritage because the marginal utility of time spent on the heritage rose with exposure. Could one be said to be 'addicted' to one's religious (or word-processing) heritage because one has acquired consumption capital in that heritage?

It's hard enough to learn one religion—its rituals, its protocols, its doctrines. Why bother learning another when the extra benefit does not seem all that great? Most Americans (we need not debate about how many exceptions there might be) are born into a religious heritage. Quite

---

[7] George J. Stigler and Gary S. Becker, 'De Gustibus Non Est Disputandum', *American Economic Review*, 67 (Mar. 1977), 76–90.

likely one could extend the assertion to say that most people in the world are born into some religious or quasi-religious heritage. There are five components of that heritage which may be conveniently considered:

(i) A set of symbols which, *pace* Clifford Geertz, purport to explain uniquely the real, to provide answers to problems of injustice, suffering, and death.

(ii) A set of rituals which activate these symbols at crucial life-cycle turning-points and inculcate the paradigms which the symbols can contain.

(iii) A community which is constituted by and transmits these symbols and rituals.

(iv) A heritage to pass on, should one wish, to one's children.

(v) A differentiation, thick or thin, from those who are not born inside the heritage.

Let us consider the schedule of benefits a person faces (for the sake of this presentation in her/his middle 20s) when considering a religious decision. First of all, the community provides a pool of preferred role opposites, friends, marital partners, perhaps business or professional colleagues. Secondly, it offers familiar rituals for crucial turning-points in one's life. Thirdly, it offers symbols, usually absorbed very early in childhood, which express meaning when one is in a situation which requires meaning. Fourthly, it offers social and organizational activities which confer advantages of various sorts on its members.[8]

In each of the cases, there will be considerable cost in giving up these utilities. Other role opposites may not respond to the most familiar interactive cues. One may lose valuable relationship networks. One may have to learn new symbols and integrate them into one's personality orientations, not an easy task in adulthood, perhaps for many not even a possible task. One may have to engage in ritual behaviours with which one is not familiar and which one might even find distasteful. One may have to find new organizational activities with relative strangers. Or one may have to live without symbols, rituals, and community. Or to try to do so.

What are the alternative benefits on the schedule of options which would attract a person to choose a heritage other than one's own or, if it be possible, no heritage at all?

---

[8] I note here that the more actively one engages in religious activities—up to a certain point, perhaps—the more available these resources may become. There may also be a law of diminishing returns: Sunday Mass attendance may find you a spouse; daily Mass may not notably enhance the chances of finding one.

1. One attractive possibility is that such a choice would punish parents and church leaders with whom one is angry.

2. Another attraction is upward social mobility. If one is not a Catholic or a Jew one might have access to élite social positions or more esteem in élite circles. It was only in the last two decades, for example, that Catholics and Jews earned access to college presidencies.

3. One might also win freedom for oneself from what one takes to be the restraints, the superstitions, the repressions, and the tyrannies that are inherent in one's heritage and community. One can, for example, eat bacon for breakfast or, in the old days, meat on Friday. One can use the birth-control pill with a clear conscience. One need not take seriously what the local pastor or priest has to say. One can ignore the Pope and refuse to be worried about Israel.

4. One is free to engage with a clear conscience in pleasurable practices on which one's religious heritage seems to frown or to embrace social and ethical concerns which do not preoccupy one's religious leaders—when was the last time the Catholic Church launched a campaign for good government?

5. By rejecting one's religious heritage one may obtain access to particularly desired role opposites—a potential spouse in most cases—who would otherwise not be available.

How does one deal with the loss of such benefits if one chooses to stay within the heritage in which one is raised (since in the concrete, this option—leave or remain—is the usual contact for religious choice)? One may choose to ignore the restraints and the liabilities that the tradition seems to impose. One can remain Catholic, devoutly Catholic in one's own estimate, and still practice birth control because one is able to appeal from a church leadership, which does not understand, to a God that does. (I presume that such behaviour would be called 'free-riding' by economists—a phenomenon which marks all religions, even Catholicism in the days since the decline of the Inquisition.)

This is the ordinary strategy in religious choice, I submit, since most Americans do indeed elect to remain in their own heritage. The choice becomes more desirable and hence more rational to the extent to which one is able, one way or another, to diminish the costs of the choice. In sum, the 'familiarity' factor (or religious consumption capital)—broadly understood—explains why it seems rational, finally, for most people in the United States to opt for their own heritage.

It is worth nothing here that there are differences in both the way the religious choice is made and the degree of religious intensity that is chosen. For some, the choice is merely a drift in the direction of least resistance—towards a renewal, not necessarily enthusiastic, of the religious identification of their childhood (or of their spouse's childhood identification, as in the case of most religious changers in America). For others, the decision is more conscious and perhaps leads to greater religious intensity. In most of the various solutions that are reached, however, the decisions are sociological in the strict sense of that word. They are the result, I suggest, of patterns of interaction with parents, spouse, friends, neighbourhood, and perhaps children, and not the result of pressures of the so-called 'mass society'.

Religious choice is more likely to be 'intimate' (that is to say, to result from interaction with close role opposites) than political choice and less likely to be intimate than marital choice. This 'intimate' nature of religious choice may be hard for scholars from other countries to comprehend because they are more familiar with religious indifference, that is to say, situations in which religion does not play an important role in identity formation.

One is forced to say to such scholars that religion is more important in this respect in America than it is in other countries and ask that they not dismiss this fact by begging the question with an assertion that such importance merely proves that Americans are not very enlightened. Such a position betrays the powerful theological assumption that religion *ought* to be unimportant, an assumption which has no place in social science discourse.

Why, then, is it rational for Americans to be more devout than the English or the French? Why is it rational for the Irish to be even more devout than Americans? (They are, be it noted, less likely to describe themselves as 'very religious', an option which, in my convert's zeal for rational choice, I think can be said to be quite rational too.) There are two possible paths to follow: one may note, with Avis, that a 'minority' religion, that is to say, one that is not established or quasi-established, is likely to try harder. It may offer more services (one thinks of parochial schools in the United Kingdom) to attract and hold its members. It thus becomes increasingly rational to stay in your tradition and reap the extra benefits that the tradition confers because of its 'minority' status—in America all religions are 'minority' as the word is being used here. Moreover, there may well be a relationship between the degree of religious devotion and activity in which you engage and the services which the institution (in the interests of its own self-preservation) will make available to you: if you are not a devout Catholic, you may not be able to take advantage of the parochial schools. In the 'minority' or pluralistic situation, the church may go out of its way to help find you a presentable marriage partner, more out of its way than it would in a situation where it has a near-monopoly on available spouses. It is rational to take advantage of such a situation. But the variety and quality of the pool may depend to some extent on your willingness to engage in high levels of religious behaviour.

This essay is not the place to discuss at length the question of why large numbers of 'minority' group members (in the usual sense of that word) do not desert their group when there seem to be ample benefits in doing so. I merely want to note that it seems to be true that for many within the minority group, the fact of being in a disadvantaged group merely intensifies the identification. Why such an 'identity' is a benefit is an interesting question but beyond my concerns at the present. That it is a benefit in a pluralistic society seems obvious enough. ('Yes, I'm Jewish and proud of it.') That which strengthens identity is often estimated to be worth the cost.

So I propose that the combination of symbol, ritual, and community provides a partial 'identity', a useful response to the question 'what are you?', an answer often stated with pride and even defiance. Such an answer signals to others (and to oneself) one's symbolic and ritual orientation and one's potential pool of preferred role opposites.

I finally propose by way of summary that a religion attracts loyalty and devotion from its members in proportion to the thickness of the differentiation and that for two reasons: (a) Ordinarily the religion will offer more services when its membership is sharply distinguished over and against the rest of society, and hence perhaps in jeopardy of defection. (b) Paradoxically, and despite the fears of religious leaders of the risk of defection, the distinction is a benefit itself; hence the more loyal one is to one's heritage, the stronger the distinction and the more proudly it is professed.

If your church does not perceive itself as threatened and your membership in it adds little to the identity into which you are born as a member of a society, if it does not differentiate you sharply from the rest of society, then there are lower costs and lower benefits in making your choice, and hence less pay-off for you in engaging in actions or professing beliefs which would link you more closely to your church. Concretely, in one-religion societies (either *de facto* or in the case of established churches *de jure*) the differentiation is thin indeed and the efforts the church perceives as necessary to attract and hold members are minimal. Hence it is less rational to commit oneself to higher levels of religious behaviour.

As a rule of thumb, I hypothesize, if you are born into a religion almost by the fact of birth in a society, then religion adds rather little to your identity and makes little demands on your behaviour to sustain that identity. On the other hand, if you are born into a pluralistic society where there is no official or quasi-offical religion, then your religious choice (even if it is to remain in the denomination of your parents) helps notably to define who you are. In such circumstances, higher levels of devotional and organizational behaviour are important to maintain your self-definition (on the average, of course).

In Great Britain, I would suggest as a hypothesis to be considered, being an Anglican adds little to the identity of being British (or English, if that word is more appropriate) and hence the affiliation can be maintained without substantial devotional activity. On the other hand, if you choose to belong to one of the 'non-established' churches, for one reason or another (including birth), then such a choice becomes an important norm in defining yourself over against the rest of British (or English) society and imposes on you constraints for devotional and organizational behaviour not unlike those experienced by your counter-parts in other (English-speaking) societies.

This would lead one to hypothesize that those identifying in England with non-Anglican denominations, whether Catholic or Protestant, would be as likely as Americans to believe, for example, in the existence of God and life after death and to attend church regularly. To put it a little differently, the difference between the United States and England, the fact of British exceptionalism, would be essentially an Anglican difference, an Anglican exceptionalism.

In point of fact, this is precisely the case: 81 per cent of the population of Great Britain believes in God as opposed to 96 per cent in the United States; 14 per cent of the people of Great Britain attend church every week (23 per cent at least once a month) as opposed to 44 per cent in the United States; 57 per cent of Britons believe in life after death as opposed to 70 per cent of Americans. But there is no difference between Roman Catholics in the United States and Roman Catholics in Great Britain and between Protestants in the United States and (non-Anglican) Protestants in Great Britain in belief in God and life after death and in church attendance. Forty-two per cent of the Protestants in both countries go to church every week, as do 50 per cent of the Catholics. Approxi-mately 70 per cent of both religious groups in both countries believe in life after death. Ninety-eight per cent of the Catholics in both countries believe in God, 94 per cent of the Protestants. The percentages in English-speaking Canada are virtually the same as in the United States: 94 per cent believe in God, 70 per cent in life after death, 44 per cent attend church regularly. (The numbers for francophones are virtually the same.)

The lower levels of religiousness in England are purely an Anglican phenomenon. Among the four English-speaking nations of the North Atlantic, then, the exception in levels of religious practice is to be found only among British Anglicans.

It is interesting to note in passing that in Australia and New Zealand, the percentages on these three items are even lower among Protestants and Catholics then they are in the English-speaking countries of the North Atlantic. The exceptions, then, in the six English-speaking countries are the inhabitants of the countries in the South Pacific and the British Anglicans. Why those from the South Pacific are exceptions is a fascinating question, indeed, but obviously beyond the scope of this exercise.

By way of conclusion, there are many differences in religion between the United States and the United Kingdom. But the point here is that, in basic essentials, the difference seems to be the result of the different identity-conferring role of religion in a society with an established (or quasi-established religion) and in a society without such an established church.

Who's exceptional, then? Australia, not America. Why did immigration and pluralism produce higher levels of religious behaviour in the latter than in the former? This is the pertinent question. It will be asked seriously, I suspect, only when scholars who study or pontificate about religion are willing to put aside their myths about broad, uni-dimensional, and uni-directional social changes (as have demographic historians) and focus on comparisons which ask why religious practice has declined in some countries and not in other very similar countries. Monopoly, official or unofficial, does not seem to help religion. Poland, however, is a clear exception. Pluralism does seem to help religion. Australia is a clear exception. Scholarship requires more than an expression of personal opinion about the reasons why.

5

Resolved, that Individualism and Egalitarianism be made Compatible in America: Political–Cultural Roots of Exceptionalism

Aaron Wildavsky

Only in America. Everyone who studies American politics (at least everyone I know) comes away feeling that it is special in some significant way without quite being able to specify precisely what that is. Me too. All who wander through American political history share the disconcerting feeling that there is a common, unifying but mysterious element that would make sense of what happens or, at least, of what does not. Many reach for the brass ring only to find themselves clutching at thin air. Many theories are called forth, as we know, but few, to our dismay, are chosen. Here is another hostage to fortune.

I. Exceptionalism in Cultural Context

Why, we ask, is there no socialism, or at least no sizeable socialist party, in America? Why have trade unions been weak compared to other democracies? Why is the United States a 'welfare laggard'? Why has it had a meliorative two-party system, instead of multi-party system with radical parties? Why, I might add, is its budgetary process unlike any other, from the primacy of its legislature to the belief in balance? The most common answer, stemming from Louis Hartz and others, is that the United States, having no feudalism, knew no hereditary hierarchy. Yet exceptions abound. How about abundant and cheap land? Other places manage that without looking the least like America. Besides, all that was long ago. What has sustained whatever American exceptionalism consists of?

Attention is paid to the separation of powers and federalism. Both sets of institutions are said to weaken central government, thus making it difficult to engage in radical transformation or to enact consistent policies.[1] Both institutional arrangements not only fragment power but also create incentives for people placed in different centres to disagree. Or so *The Federalist* says. One difficulty here is inability to determine whether these institutions are causes or consequences of behaviour deemed exceptional. Thus socialism might be harder under federal arrangements, though Australia and Germany manage quite a bit of welfare policy together with a federal structure. There might be a kind of functional explanation in which consequences of federal institutions become causes of their perpetuation. In some sense this must be so, for otherwise it would be impossible to explain why any organization persists. Yet federal structure has not notably impeded war-time arrangements or social security. Nor has separation of powers stopped vast environmental legislation.

Then there are the people. Special qualities are often attributed to them, from unusual moderation to 'creedal passion'.[2] Unfortunately, these characterizations, all of which find supporting evidence someplace, are left in mid-air, suspended without a social base. Is it the clash of passions that leads to moderation or moderation that enrages people who then become passionate? Everything one says about America and Americans is true somewhere. Unless we are to turn to cyclical theories, which only restate the questions—who is passionate, when, and why?— flesh has to be put on the bones of human or institutional nature in these United States. Are we referring to adherents of small, exclusive hierarchies, or radical egalitarians, or warrior-like individualists?

Could it be that Americans have been brainwashed or indoctrinated or otherwise fooled into believing some things and rejecting others? Could this account for their peculiar behaviour?[3] Would America be more like Europe if its people were less gullible? And, if true, does this thesis imply that other nations that have taken different paths have seen through a glass clearly? If they see differently, then that is what must be explained.

Enter the corporation and the state. Was all well in our American

---

[1] Theodore J. Lowi, 'Why Is There No Socialism in the United States? A Federal Analysis', in Robert T. Golembiewski and Aaron Wildavsky, eds., *The Costs of Federalism* (New Brunswick, NJ: Transaction Books, 1984), 37–54.

[2] Samuel Huntington, *American Politics: The Promise of Disharmony* (Cambridge, Mass.: Belknap Press of Harvard University Press, 1981).

[3] See Charles E. Lindblom's circularity hypothesis in his *Politics and Markets* (New York: Basic Books, 1977).

garden until corporate capitalism introduced such vast inequalities, buying government, schools, churches, the media, conscience itself, until no dissent could be heard or accepted? A troublesome feature of this serpent-in-the-garden theory is that the characteristics it was supposed to have caused—weak central government, a preference for *laissez-faire*, state protection of private property, and features like a powerful Congress and a predilection for balanced budgets—were part of American exceptionalism long before the industrial revolution.

My view is that all these theories have merit but are insufficient by themselves. The weakness of hierarchical forces is a perennial feature of American political life, never more so than now. The existence of large numbers of small enterprises (which is what early American farmers were) is bound to influence ideas about desirable public policy. So is abundant land. And no set of relationships among people could last unless it contained mechanisms for reproducing themselves.

What is missing, I believe, is conflict, context, and culture. Instead of seeking the Holy Grail of a single distinctive American value, we have to look for conflict among people with different and opposing values, values that are not suspended in mid-air but serve to justify the different ways of life we call cultures. Only then can we see what combination of politically charged values distinguishes America from the rest of the democratic West. Cultures are composed of people sharing values that justify different kinds of social relationships. It is the cultural context— how strong the different cultures are in relation to each other—that matters. Weak hierarchy, by itself, is one thing; combined with strong individualism, on the one hand, as in America, or strong egalitarianism, as under the Khmer Rouge in Cambodia, on the other, it is quite something else.[4]

Whatever explains American exceptionalism, moreover, must also explain European uniformity, i.e. why other Western democracies are more like each other than they are like America. One reason why theories of exceptionalism are difficult is that they must simultaneously show how both American and European contexts differ. The same variables that purport to explain why America is exceptional must show why Europe is not.

My hypothesis is that what makes America special is the deeply embedded belief, accompanied by supporting institutions, that liberty

[4] Karl D. Jackson, *Rendezvous With Death: Democratic Kampuchea, 1975–1978* (forthcoming); and Pin Yathay, *L'Utopie meurtrière* (Paris: Robert Laffont, 1980) and review article of this book by Ferenc Feher in *Telos*, 56 (Summer 1983), 193–205.

and equality, the cultures of individualism and egalitarianism, are (or can be) mutually reinforcing. In America, if not elsewhere, equal opportunity and equal results may be made compatible. Where in other Western democracies egalitarians ally with hierarchy to reduce inequality, in America egalitarians have historically allied themselves with individualism. The second section explains what I mean by cultural theory and why it is relevant to the problem of American exceptionalism. The third section exemplifies this hypothesis through a brief reconsideration of several early episodes in American history. The fourth section considers exceptionalism as specific promises. The fifth reviews the rise of egalitarianism in the last thirty years. The sixth section asks whether America will continue to be exceptional and, if so, whether it will continue to be exceptional in the same way. For if egalitarians will no longer join with individualists and hierarchy becomes ever weaker, can egalitarians, with their rejection of followership as inequality, rule by themselves?.

II. Exceptionalism in Political Culture

Political cultures are solutions people craft as they jointly form institutions to solve the problem of how human beings should live with each other. Their answers to questions of social order—Who am I? What shall I do? With whom?—are provided by their cultures. The values people hold, the social relations they prefer, and their beliefs about the world are woven together through their cultures. The dimensions of cultural theory are the strength of group boundaries and degree of social prescription.[5] Strong groups with numerous prescriptions combine to form hierarchical collectivism. Strong group boundaries with few prescriptions form a political culture of egalitarian collectivism. Competitive individualism joins few prescriptions with weak group boundaries, thereby encouraging endless new combinations through which self-regulation reduces the need for external authority. When boundaries are weak and prescriptions strong, so that decisions are made by people outside the group, its controlled culture is fatalistic.

Context counts: as the cultural parts make up the societal whole, the

[5] Mary Douglas, *Natural Symbols, Explorations in Cosmology* (Harmondsworth: Penguin, 1970); idem, 'Cultural Bias', in *In the Active Voice* (London: Routledge Kegan Paul, 1982); Mary Douglas and Aaron Wildavsky, *Risk and Culture* (Berkeley: University of California Press, 1982); and Michael Thompson, Richard Ellis, and Aaron Wildavsky, *Cultural Theory* (Denver: Westview Press, 1990).

ways in which they are combined—who allies with or opposes whom, the relative strengths of the contending cultures—is of great political importance. The combination of hierarchy and egalitarianism is what I call social democracy, after the European nations who add a strong egalitarian element to the sacrificial ethic of hierarchy, in which the individual parts are expected to aid the collective whole. Where egalitarianism and individualism combine, so that equality of opportunity is believed to be compatible with equality of results, as in the Jacksonian era of American political history, I call the mixture 'American individualism'. Extreme individualism in concert with the dominion of authoritarianism brings forth state capitalism. Authoritarianism together with hierarchy breeds totalitarianism. The alliance of hierarchy and individualism can go by its colloquial name, the establishment.

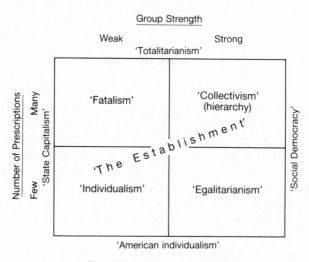

FIG. 5.1 Models of Cultures

The social ideal of individualistic cultures is self-regulation. Bidding and bargaining substitute for authority. Hierarchy is institutionalized authority. It justifies inequality on the grounds that specialization and division of labour enable people to live together with greater harmony and effectiveness than do alternative arrangements. Committed to a life of purely voluntary association, egalitarian cultures can live a life without coercion or authority only by greater equality of condition. The best indicator of egalitarian practices, therefore, is the attempt to reduce differences—between races, or income levels, or sexes, etc.[6] I should add that egalitarians are also against leadership because it involves inequality of power.[7]

The policy preferences of people in political cultures follow from the desire to reinforce their way of life and to destabilize their opponents'. Their intentions—supporting, opposing, or minimizing authority; increasing, decreasing, or maintaining economic differences—remain constant, but their ideas about what will be efficacious vary according to the conditions of the times.

For present purposes, two hybrid regimes—social democracy and American individualism—are crucial. Following a hypothesis that cannot be examined here—change tends towards the dominant culture[8]—strong hierarchies attract weaker egalitarianism in Europe while strong individualism attracts egalitarianism in America. This difference in cultural contexts, I claim, explains why America and Europe are different. European regimes are characterized by strong hierarchy, medium egalitarianism, and weak individualism, for instance, while the American regime is one of strong individualism, weak hierarchy, and medium-strength egalitarianism. Thus the same explanation (if true, of course) accounts for Western European and American divergence. It takes two to differ.

What is exceptional is the alliance between egalitarianism and individualism. Try scanning your memory banks of European regimes to find something similar; I come up empty. What made this combination possible in the United States? Historical study is necessary in order to trace the transmission of ideas and their institutional embodiment.

The cultural hybrid here called American individualism was possible because of historical circumstances that made alliance with hierarchy far less desirable than in Europe. For many (though not all) Americans, hierarchy faced a 'double whammy': Americans not only fought a revolutionary war against a hierarchy, they also took their politics from the struggles within England to limit the efforts of the Crown to subordinate republican government.

I have explained why many (but, obviously, not all) individualists

[6] For a more substantial version, see my 'Frames of Reference Come From Cultures: A Predictive Theory', in Morris Freilich *et al.*, *The Relevance of Culture* (Granby, Mass.: Bergin and Garvey, 1989).

[7] See my 'A Cultural Theory of Leadership', in Bryan D. Jones, ed., *Leadership and Politics: New Perspectives in Political Science* (Lawrence, Kan.: University Press of Kansas, 1989).

[8] See my 'Change in Political Culture', *Politics*, Journal of the Australian Political Science Association, 20 (Nov. 1985), 95–102.

opposed hierarchy (as the Federalist Party proves, an alliance between individualism and hierarchy also was possible). But how were individualists able to come to terms with egalitarians who could conceivably have wished to redistribute their property? And how were egalitarians able to join individualists whose personal networks were based on achieving more than others?

What remains is to restate what has already been said in different terms. Because egalitarians were consumed by the struggle against the English hierarchy, and were especially sensitive to monarchical efforts to undermine self-rule, they identified the central government as a cause of inequality. Hence both egalitarians and individualists could join in severely limiting the size and scope of central government. In a nation of small farmers, moreover, property was viewed as part of equality. How would large landowners be countered if not by spreading the holding of property? Rights in property, therefore, were commonly held to be essential to the defence of individual welfare.

Now we are on our way to an understanding of how the institutions that helped maintain American individualism—the separation of powers, federalism, and mass parties—were themselves reinforced by this compound of egalitarian and individualistic cultures. Federalism and separation of powers were partly carry-overs of past practice during colonial times, partly chosen to help secure small central government, and partly maintained to join egalitarianism with individualism. Where European egalitarians accept the greater coerciveness of hierarchy in order to reduce inequalities, American egalitarians chose to trade less equality for even less coerciveness. Smaller, i.e. federal government, was more beautiful to them. Roads and canals and economic development in general at the state level were supported by the cultural hybrid of American individualism. For it was not government *per se* but its purported inegalitarian character to which egalitarians objected.

To be there at the beginning is not necessarily to last. The separation of powers is given life by the identification of the different branches with stronger and weaker central government. Defending the institution then becomes equivalent to defending one's culture or way of life. Opposition to perceived inegalitarian measures taken by central governments also helped sustain federalism, while providing a home for opponents of central power. If central power corrupts, one would wish to oppose it even when one's own people were in office.

My emphasis upon the cultural union of egalitarianism and individualism, producing a belief that equal outcomes and equal opportunity can be mutually reinforcing, is strengthened by the great American political invention—mass parties. There are not just parties as an undifferentiated mass but specific Jeffersonian and Jacksonian parties organized to limit government severely. Andrew Jackson was the genius who created the president who acts publicly as a tribune of the people in order to diminish the size and scope of government.

Suppose, however, that the central government eventually became the source of equality and not the reverse. What would happen to American individualism? Before speculating about that, let us assay a preliminary test of this cultural hypothesis by briefly reviewing key episodes concerning political economy in early American history.

III. Selected Problems of Political Economy in the Early American Republic

Imagine that today's left-liberals were opposed to the growth of government and to its regulation of business and that today's right-wing conservatives supported larger government actively intervening in the economy. That supposition would provide a much better guide to the struggles over the structure of the political economy from the founding of the Republic to the Civil War than transposing current preferences into the past. Reading back current attitudes to public policy turns early political economy on its head. For the anti-federalists, the Jeffersonians and the Jacksonians, believed that central government was the source of artificial inequality that threatened republican government. Once that is engraved on our consciousness—the political forces that we would now call progressive, left, or anti-establishment then identified central government with inequality—we are in a position to understand better the conflicts over Hamilton's funding of the debt, Jackson's opposition to the Bank of the United States, and Henry Clay's American System organized around internal improvements. And from these great struggles we will come to an understanding of the cultural context of exceptionalism.

Banks and Corruption

The opposition to central funding of the debt, to a national bank, and to internal improvements was not opposition to business or to private markets *per se*. On the contrary, most families were engaged in farming and most farmers thought of themselves as engaged in business, buying and selling land as well as produce. Market competition was in high repute, provided only that it was truly competitive, i.e. uncontaminated by artificial restraints imposed by the central government. Nor was government *per se* the object of vilification. State governments were encouraged to do the very thing denied to the central government. Why this enmity to central government?

'This measure', Jefferson wrote in *The Anas*, referring to federal assumption of state debts, 'produced the most bitter and angry contest ever known in Congress before or since the Union of the States'.[9] This was so, he argued, because the debt acted 'as a machine for the corruption of the legislature'. Now by 'corruption' Jefferson and his supporters did not mean financial dishonesty; he knew Hamilton to be personally honest. Rather, drawing on their fears of the re-establishment of monarchy (read 'hierarchy') in America, they meant the perversion of judgement caused by giving men with a financial stake in the debt a special interest in and an enhanced capacity for undermining the independent judgement of Congress. This political corruption, this fear of the decay of the foundations of disinterestedness required by republican government, is traced in Lance Banning's reconstruction of the contemporary struggles between the party of the King and the party of the country in England.

Ministers could . . . call upon additional inducements in the form of governmental offices or pensions for their parliamentary supporters. Patronage and governmental influence in elections . . . made it possible for ministries to exercise a certain measure of executive control of Parliament . . . Court money was employed in parliamentary elections, purchasing the representatives and debasing the electors: 'the little beggarly boroughs' were 'pools of corruption'.[10]

The source of this power, according to Bolingbroke's description of his quarrel with Walpole, was, in Banning's words, that

Growing revenues and higher taxes make it possible for ministers to create a horde of officers, who fill the Parliament and exercise a rising influence in elections. The civil list provides vast funds for the corruption of Parliament, and the practice of anticipating revenues creates supplies. In fact, the means available to ministers have grown to such a great extent in recent years that the

[9] Adrienne Koch and William Peder, *The Life and Selected Writings of Thomas Jefferson* (New York: Modern Library, 1944), 123.

[10] Lance Banning, *The Jeffersonian Persuasion* (Ithaca, NY: Cornell University Press, 1978), 43, 56.

crown has now, through influence, powers just as great as it once had by prerogative. The fate of English liberty depends on a union of good men against the progress of corruption.[11]

This, just this, is what Jefferson meant when he charged that 'Hamilton was not only a monarchist, but for a monarchy bottomed on corruption.'[12]

Commerce and agriculture and artisanship, yes, but large-scale industry, no. James Savage sums it up:

Jefferson's great fear was that a central government burdened by deficits and debts would undermine its republican and constitutional foundations while promoting widespread social and economic inequality. This inequity would emerge through two simultaneously occurring events. First, speculators, bankers, and the moneyed aristocracy could gain the financial leverage and profits derived from financing the national debt. Second, the government itself would spend its added revenues by promoting an industrialized economy through Hamiltonian policies resembling those of mercantilist and corrupted England. Once again, England served as the model to be avoided, for just as its government was corrupted in no small way due to its enormous debt, English society and its moral values were also corrupted by a system of manufacturing and industry that created vast social and economic divisions.[13]

All this was to be undone by keeping the central government small, by paying off its debts, and by preventing the Hamiltonian machine from being driven by the engine of a national bank.

Republican thought, memorialized in writings of anti-federalists,[14] considered substantial inequality of resources and a large-scale government to be incompatible with personal liberty. Their egalitarian views called for small agricultural communities in which an educated electorate, not far from one another in economic status and geographic distance, would handle their affairs on a face-to-face basis.

By President Andrew Jackson's time, commerce had developed, the industrial revolution had begun, and banking was considerably more important than it heretofore had been. Jacksonians faced certain choices: if they controlled markets, thereby preventing inequality from growing, they risked losing personal liberty and gaining unwanted governmental growth; if they tried to remove impediments to markets, thus allowing

[11] Ibid. 59.

[12] Koch and Peder, *Life and Writings of Jefferson*, p. 126.

[13] James D. Savage, *Balanced Budgets and American Politics* (Ithaca, NY: Cornell University Press, 1988).

[14] Herbert J. Storing, *What the Anti-Federalists Were For* (Chicago: University of Chicago Press, 1981).

more people to compete, the end result might be enduring inequality with its pernicious consequences for democratic life. In the end, they denied there was any conflict between economic competition and political equality.

The widespread belief among those who theorized about Jacksonian democracy in his times, a belief apparently shared by their supporters in the citizenry as well, was that equality of opportunity, meticulously followed, would lead to an approximation of equality of result. The operation of economic markets, unimpeded by the federal government, would eventually approximate real equality of condition—as closely as innate differences in human ability permitted. At the very least, central government would not add artificial to natural inequality, and this proscription would thereby preserve representative government. It is this belief—not in equality undefined, or in just one kind of equality, but in the *mutual reinforcement of opportunity and result*—that made America truly exceptional.

Individuals would be allowed, indeed encouraged, to keep all gain that resulted from the unfettered use of their own talents. But everything artificial and unnatural, everything government imposed on man in his free state, such as charters, franchises, banks, and other monopolies, became anathema. If every man could not be his own government, he could (and many Jacksonians advocated he should) become his own banker. As William M. Gouge argued in discussing money and banking, 'A man has . . . a natural right to . . . profits', but the distribution of wealth depends on a nations's institutions. Once the granting by government of 'peculiar commercial privileges' lays the 'foundation of the artificial inequality of fortune', therefore, 'all the subsequent operations of society tend to increase the difference in the condition of different classes in the community'.[15] 'Every corporate grant', as Theodore Sedgwick, jun., put it, 'is directly in the teeth of the doctrine of equal rights, for it gives to one set of men the exercise of privileges which the main body can never enjoy'.[16] The remedy was clear: abolish the 'monster' bank.

If you believe that banks chartered by the central government produce 'artificial inequality',[17] you would also agree with Jackson's Attorney-General, Roger Taney, that the Bank of the United States should not be

---

[15] Joseph L. Blau, ed,, *Social Theories of Jacksonian Democracy* (Indianapolis: Bobbs Merrill, 1954), 25–8.
[16] Ibid. 227.
[17] Ibid. 196.

rechartered because of 'its corrupting influence . . . its patronage greater than that of the Government . . . its power to embarrass the operations of the Government—and to influence elections'.[18] You would also understand why Jackson pledged that if he became president he would pay off the national debt 'to prevent a monied aristocracy from growing up around our administration that must bend it to its views, and ultimately destroy the liberty of our country'.[19] No wonder Jackson celebrated, in his own words, his 'glorious triumph' when he 'put to death, that mamouth of corruption and power, the Bank of the United States'.[20]

Once inequality was laid at the door of central government, competitive markets could be reconciled with egalitarian outcomes, equality of opportunity with equality of result, by claiming that an attack on hierarchy (i.e. central government) could increase equality of opportunity, which would then, once artificial fetters were removed, naturally lead to tolerable equality of result. If, in hearing about American equality, the citizen cannot tell whether the word refers to opportunity or result, and if, in regard to American 'individualism', the citizen remains unaware of whether the culture referred to is individualist or egalitarian, that is the idea. The disagreement over meaning is the price of agreement on the term.

IV. The Promise of Exceptionalism: Equal Opportunity and Equal Condition are Compatible

Is the proof that America is exceptional, one may well ask, exemption from history? Has the abundance of the land, its dazzling array of resources, the conditions of its settlement, or the blessing of providence, made America invulnerable? Daniel Bell summarizes this notion of exceptionalism as

the idea that, having been 'born free', America would, in the trials of history, get off 'scot free'. Having a common political faith from the start, it would escape the ideological vicissitudes and divisive passions of the European polity, and, being entirely a middle-class society, without aristocracy or *bohème*, it would not become 'decadent', as had every other society in history. As a liberal society providing individual opportunity, safeguarding liberties, and expanding the

---

[18] Roberrt Remini, *Andrew Jackson and the Course of American Freedom, 1822–1832*, ii (New York: Harper & Row, 1981), 44.

[19] Ibid. 34.

[20] Ibid. 166.

standard of living, it would escape the disaffection of the intelligentsia, the resentment of the poor, the frustrations of the young—which, historically, had been the signs of disintegration, if not the beginning of revolution, in other societies. In this view, too, the United States, in becoming a world power, a paramount power, a hegemonic power, would, because it was democratic, be different in the exercise of that power than previous world empires.[21]

Disagreeing with this conception, I do not believe that, as Bell continues, 'Today, the belief in American exceptionalism has vanished with the end of empire, the weakening of power, the loss of faith in the nation's future.'[22] For the promise is not external but internal, a promise about how Americans might live with one another, not a promise of power over strangers. What, I ask by way of summary, is the faith reflected in American exceptionalism?

America is about possibilities, not certainties. You can (but you don't have to) get rich. America is about promises. Here class divisions do exist but they don't have to matter. Because, in America, competition can be compatible with equality, there is the promise of classlessness. Exceptionalism is the doctrine that justifies the promise.

The promise is of two kinds. One, the promise of entry, is that competition will be possible. Entry is not equality. On the contrary, it is the promise that despite inequalities of all kinds—in formal education, literacy, ethnicity, status, wealth, etc.—advancement will still be possible. The related promise is that failure, when it occurs, will not be permanent. Robert Dahl's notion of 'cumulative inequalities' tells us what America promises not to permit, i.e. that whatever inequalities exist will not grow so far in a single direction as to preclude the possibility of self-government. Thus the second part of the promise is that, if artificial is not added to natural inequality, we-the-people can still run our own lives.

When the doctrine of exceptionalism holds that equal opportunity may be made compatible with sufficiently equal results so as to make self-government possible, it both justifies inequality and seeks to prevent its institutionalization. The critical importance of balance in American political life is that it is meant to check cumulative inequalities by dividing power. Hence the importance of federalism and the separation of powers. The redundancy that results—multiple institutions for doing practically anything, uncertainty over who is

[21] Daniel Bell, 'The End of American Exceptionalism', *The Public Interest*, 41 (Fall 1975), 193–224, quote on p. 197.
[22] Ibid. Bell cites Daniel Boorstein, Alexis De Tocqueville, and Richard Hofstadter as contributing to this version of exceptionalism.

supposed to do what—is part of the price paid for keeping the promise. Redundancy adds to reliability, which helps keep the faith.[23]

When the argument goes beyond the prevention of cumulative inequalities to claim that inequality *per se* is incompatible with self-government, so that substantive equality must be achieved before equal opportunity (and hence the political system itself) may be deemed legitimate, exceptionalism American-style is over. For then egalitarianism becomes incompatible with individualism. Indeed, individualism has first to surrender its desire for differences before it can be accepted as legitimate. Social democracy, the European alliance of egalitarianism with hierarchy, becomes the remaining alternative. Or does it?

Among Lincoln's greatest achievements was the development of a Republican Party in which individualism was the dominant force, with hierarchy subordinate, thus reversing the cultural context of the Whig party. Never before had there been a party within which individualism was supreme. How, then, after the Civil War, did the heirs of Jefferson and Jackson slowly alter their heritage so as to give a greater role to government? How was 'corruption' taken from central government and placed on corporate capitalism as the source of inequality? How did 'states' rights' give way to national power as the preferred mechanism for equalization? How did Populists, the heirs of Jackson, shake off his time-honoured view of the inherent corruption of government and change it into one in which central government became a force for equality? And how did the Progressives, heirs of the Whigs, get away from the party's self-denying ordinance on executive power (a reaction to their fear of 'King Andrew' as a charismatic leader who would overturn the system)? If we knew the answers to these questions, we would know more about how America remained exceptional through depressions and wars.

And now, with the contemporary revival of egalitarianism in the form of feminism, gay rights, civil rights, animal rights, environmentalism, and the rest, we must ask whether American exceptionalism has or will soon come to an end. Will egalitarians return to their historic alliance with individualism, seeking to make opportunity serve autonomy, or will they go the European way towards hierarchy? Will egalitarians, in other words, embrace state power, accepting some coerciveness in order to gain greater equality? Or will egalitarians attempt the wholly unprecedented by ruling alone?

[23] See Martin Landau, 'Redundancy, Rationality, and the Problem of Duplication and Overlap', *Public Administration Review* 29 (July–Aug. 1969), 346–58.

V. The Misleading Decade, the Last Thirty Years

Thirty years ago, in the 1950s, there were no homeless people; there were only bums, drunks, psychos, and transients. The difference is that way back then people without homes were characterized in ways that made it clear that they and not society were responsible for the ills that befell them. 'Homeless' sounds like everybody else was given their fair portion but some, through no fault of their own, got left out. If people are homeless, presumably the remedy is for those who have neglected them to make them home-full, i.e. to provide public housing.

Perhaps, as in the case of the homeless, it is as well to begin comparing the 1950s to the 1980s with other categories of people who certainly existed then, sometimes in shocking conditions, but whose political presence was minor if not miniscule. In the 1950s (as distinguished from today), most people hardly noticed or talked about women's rights, gay rights, children's rights, or grey power. What the groups acting under these rubrics have in common is a belief in 'rights' conceived as greater equality of condition. All—yes, even animal rights—are committed to reducing differences among people. Of course, everyone you ask denies wanting everyone to be the same; on the contrary, they feel that their way will lead to a renaissance of true individuality based on personal, not social or economic, differences. Nevertheless, given the usual array of differences, they will think these are too large and ought to be reduced.

I left out civil rights so as to accentuate its importance. It was known and discussed in the 1950s. But how different that discussion was. The civil rights issue was conceived to be equal opportunity, not equal condition. Wouldn't it be wonderful if racial bias, which gave preference to whites, were overcome so black people could vote and learn and work without discrimination? It would have been unthinkable for any group of distinguished people, let alone two former presidents, as Ford and Carter did recently, to hold up equality of condition as the norm for judging achievement. Ford and Carter are able to say that conditions are getting worse for black people because they have not, as a whole, caught up with whites, though most are doing considerably better. In earlier times, they would have, as the song says, accentuated the positive.

The 1950s journalist was cynical but supportive. American institutions were good; the more the pity, then, that public officials did not always live up to them. Reporters—recall the frenzy at the Iran–Contra press conference—were not yet *paparazzi*. Imagine, in the 1980s, a President Kennedy, contrite over the Bay of Pigs, not only telling the

American people that the whole thing was so bad he was not going to talk about it again, but getting away with it. Or think back to a President Eisenhower confronting a Soviet Party Secretary Khruschev over the U-2 incident and not getting savaged by the media for duplicity. The tolerance for error, the point is, has grossly diminished. John F. Kennedy's extra-marital affairs were kept out of public view, while poor Jimmy Carter's mental temptations became headline news and Gary Hart's political career was ruined. Both survey evidence and analysis of media content reveal that the major media have an egalitarian bent.[24]

The reader possibly has been given sufficient background—a rise in system blame, a decline in system support—to appreciate a quality of the 1950s that occasions much difference of opinion. Talk to a Hungarian refugee or anyone whose main political memories date from that time, and you will find a near-idyllic America. Stability, amicability, and consensus were the bywords. After the demise of McCarthyism, no major movement appeared to threaten the tranquility of American life. Not so, a few radicals cried, pointing to poverty, racism, militarism, and other sources of discontent which they assumed to be seething beneath the surface. Asked to put up or shut up, it appeared that their voices could find no popular echo.

I think both sides were right; there was tranquility, *then;* there were also people and issues waiting to be born *later.* So what else is new? Change is part of life. True, but not so true if one takes the 1950s as the standard against which to measure other times. Looked at through the lenses of the decades before and after, the 1950s were a lot less turbulent. It may be that unexpected prosperity after the Second World War created a wave of optimism that, for a time, dampened conflict. The awakening to world-wide responsibilities, reluctantly but adventurously pursued, may have focused conflict outwards. Whatever the reasons, support for the status quo was stronger and for change was weaker than it had been or would be.

Think of America's churches. In the 1950s, Protestant fundamentalists were not active in politics. It took Supreme Court decisions permitting abortion and forbidding prayer in public schools to do that. The World Council of Churches was an international do-good organization, supporting the United Nations, foreign aid, and, along the way, American foreign policy. Nowadays, while retaining its internationalism, the WCC

[24] See my 'The Media's "American Egalitarians" ', *The Public Interest*, 88 (Summer 1987), 94–104.

has directed it towards opposing the foreign policy of the United States.
The WCC's posture is egalitarian, i.e. supporting the Third World
against the first. As for the Catholic Church, its bishops were largely
conservative, a posture ameliorated by traditional social doctrine,
which called on the better-off to help the worse-off, and the identification of many of its ethnic parishioners with the Democratic Party.
Nowadays the Catholic bishops' conference has become egalitarian.
Their pastoral letter on the economy (aside from valuing distribution
above creation) speaks of poverty not as insufficiency but as having less
than others.[25] What a long way from the more-reactionary-than-thou
Cardinal Spellman of my youth. Unless memory plays me more than its
usual tricks, I recall him breaking a strike of not-too-well-paid grave-
diggers in Catholic cemeteries by using labour recruited from the young
men of a seminary. No chance of something like that happening in our
time.

Worrying whether the United States would become addicted to
excessive force in the international system, toppling regimes in the
Dominican Republic and Iran, as in the 1950s, is quite different from
wondering if its people would support a two-week war (one week longer
than Granada, the longest 'war' conducted by the Reagan administration). It is apparent that support for armed intervention has declined
greatly. It is also apparent that there is far more disposition to challenge
government than there was thirty years ago. Against this view it
could be said that there was considerable conflict over foreign policy
in the 1950s. True but, again, misleading. True, the war in Korea became unpopular; true, also, that questions like 'Who lost China to the
communists' and (if I am permitted a year's advance) slogans about the
'missile gap' were prevalent. The point, however, is that those were
conflicts over means—how best to defend against communism—not
about the justness of the cause. The moral tone today is much different
from that of thirty years ago.

Any way you look at it, the 1950s was a misleading decade. The
question was whether McCarthyism would win, that is, whether basic
liberties would be preserved from forces wrapping themselves up in the
flag, not whether the flag would escape burning. When I became active
in a local college chapter of the American Civil Liberties Union, for
instance, I assumed it had always been (and, likely, would always be)
what it was in the late 1950s: a guardian of civil liberties, literally and

---

[25] See my 'Idolatry and "The Poor" ', *Catholicism in Crisis*, 3 (July 1985), 42–4.

conventionally conceived. Nothing could have been more wrong. In the 1920s and 1930s, the ACLU was basically a defender of trade unions. From the 1960s until today, it has become a defender of groups devoted to equality of condition. What happened in the 1950s was that conditions were perceived to be so harsh that, in order to preserve itself, the ACLU national leadership not only accommodated itself to government security demands but also retreated to core principles of civil liberties, principles so basic they were not effectively subject to attack.[26] Whichever direction one looks, back to the American past or forward to the last thirty years, the 1950s gives a distorting impression.

The most distorting impression left by the 1950s, one which colours American politics in the wrong hues even today, concerns the nation's two major political parties. Party policies and presidential candidates are still viewed, so it seems to me, as if they were the same or similar to those we saw in the 1950s—conservative, pragmatic, centrist—and made more so by competing for the same moderate non-ideological electorate. Of the mass electorate, this description may have more validity, but of their party activists and office-holders nothing could be more mistaken.

The activists who dominate the major parties and the public officials who represent them have undergone a radical transformation in the last thirty years. The Democratic Party of Hubert Humphrey and Henry Jackson is no more. Which of today's leaders carries on their belief in a strong welfare policy coupled with a strong defence? It is hard to think of a single one. (Senator Bradley, for instance, the only current nominee, is not nearly so enamored of welfare programmes.) From a boisterous, conflict-ridden, heterogeneous coalition of Northern liberals, Southern conservatives, Midwestern populists, and a sprinkling of other assorted types, 'Democrat' and 'liberal' have become nearly synonymous.

What is more, the meaning of liberal has dramatically expanded. Where it designated a belief in modestly more welfare protection, perhaps a Fair Employment Practices Commission to ward off the worst discrimination, and that was all, to be a liberal now signifies that one subscribes to most all of the following positions: more welfare, less defence, less prayer in public schools, more women's rights (including the right to abortion), more environmental protection, fewer property rights, and discrimination in favour of designated groups. In short, the

[26] See William Donohue's *The Politics of the ACLU* (New Brunswick, NJ: Transaction Press, 1984), my Introduction to it, and a revised version which appears as 'The "Reverse Sequence" in Civil Liberties', *The Public Interest*, 78 (Winter 1985), 32–42.

Democratic Party is now under the control of activists who believe generally in greater equality of condition.

The Republican Party of President Eisenhower (with a possible reprieve to be discussed) is no more. As Republicans have moved south and conservative Southern Democrats have converted to the Republican Party, each party has become more like its main tendency. Among Republicans, this means Northern and Western liberals are a vanishing breed. Republican activists now come in two kinds: free market conservatives and hierarchical–patriarchcal conservatives, popularly known as economic and social conservatives. The influx of Protestant fundamentalists may portend that the partriarchal wing will become stronger, thus challenging the so-far dominant free marketers.

Thus even a supposedly 'issue-less' or 'centrist' contest like that of 1988, I conclude, promises policy results a lot more radical right or left than is commonly understood. There will be a big difference, egalitarian versus individualist, in the judges appointed, administrators selected, the entire ethos of government. The days when *le homme bourgeois* could sleep well before the election, knowing that whichever party won wouldn't matter that much, are over. It remains only for contemporary opinion to catch up with the last thirty years.

VI. Will America Continue to be Exceptional?

Nowadays, hierarchy has grown still weaker. Every large-scale integrative institution, from parties to unions to churches, is weaker than it was. Individualism remains strong but is being challenged by egalitarianism.[27] Empathy for (and sympathy with) capitalism has declined, whether it be from Catholic bishops or Democratic Party activists[28] or public interest lobbyists[29] or major journalists[30] or academics who, like Lindblom, refer to 'The Market As Prison'.[31] There

[27] See my 'The Three Cultures', *The Public Interest*, 69 (Fall 1982), 45–58.

[28] Warren E. Miller and M. Kent Jennings, *Parties in Transition: A Longitudinal Study of Party Elites and Party Supporters* (New York: Russell Sage Foundation, 1986).

[29] Jeffrey N. Berry, *Lobbying for the People: The Political Behavior of Public Interest Groups* (Princeton, NJ: Princeton University Press, 1977); and Jack Walker, 'The Origins and Maintenance of Interest Groups in America', *American Political Science Review*, 77 (June 1983), 390–406.

[30] See S. Robert Lichter, Stanley Rothman, and Linda S. Lichter, *The Media Elite* (Bethesda, Md.: Adler & Adler, 1986); and Shanto Iyengar and Donald R. Kinder, *News That Matters: Television and American Opinion* (Chicago: University of Chicago Press, 1987).

[31] Charles E. Lindblom, 'The Market As Prison', *Journal of Politics*, 44 (May 1982), 324–36.

is still a sneaking admiration for capitalism but not, among egalitarians, positive moral support.

Democratic Party activists, the most radical segment of the party, are egalitarians.[32] They see government as a vastly expanded compensatory mechanism whose purpose it is to make up for past inequalities. Their cultural forebears, at the dawn of the American republic, saw central government as engaging in reverse redistribution. When these old exceptionalists blamed 'the system', they had in mind central government acting in ways it should not, which is what made their alliance with individualists possible. When today's left-liberal Democrats blame the system for inequality, they want government to do things it is not now doing or to do more of what it is doing, mostly through higher taxes, which leads individualists to oppose them. By the system that is blameworthy, the new egalitarians no longer mean central government but market individualism. By contrast, people like John Taylor of Carolina, who epitomized the old egalitarian view, believed that central government had to be corrupt. For such people, it was alliance with individualism or nothing.

Who, if anyone, will today's egalitarians ally themselves with? The use of central government to redistribute resources suggests that modern-day egalitarians are willing to ally themselves with hierarchical forces. The centralizing principle is there—we all see that—but the centralizers are not. Egalitarians appear hostile to social no less than economic conservatives; hierarchists appear too weak to be worth allying with. Can egalitarians rule by themselves?

The only effort to organize a uni-cultural regime, so far as I know, was President John Tyler's ('His Accidency') in 1840. It failed. The only effort at cultural fusion, combining the three cultures, was President James Monroe's, during the so-called 'Era of Good Feelings'. It lasted a few years before party conflict took over. The only other regimes with significant egalitarian content, Jefferson's and Jackson's, had large (some historians would say dominant) individualist influence.[33] That there appears to be no American historical precedent for an egalitarian–hierarchical coalition makes the next Democratic administration especially worth watching.

Is their call for equalization a last effort on the part of egalitarians to

[32] For evidence, see Sidney Verba and Gary R. Orren, *Equality in America: The View From the Top* (Cambridge, Mass.: Harvard University Press, 1985); and Miller and Jennings, *Parties in Transition*.

[33] See Richard Ellis and Aaron Wildavsky, *Dilemmas of Presidential Leadership: From Washington Through Lincoln* (New Brunswick, NJ: Transaction Press, 1989).

keep America exceptional by making liberty compatible with equality, or to convert America into a largely egalitarian society? Requiring 'substantive equal opportunity'—more equal resources before there can be genuine equal opportunity—is a call not to perfect but to replace equal opportunity with equal result.

In sum, I agree with those who see in the strength of individualism and the weakness of hierarchy clues to historic American exceptionalism. I agree also with those who see in American institutions, its land, and its people, further clues to what makes America special. I have argued not that these insights are mistaken but that they need to be combined through the analysis of conflicting cultures so that there are not ideas without people or social relations without justifications but all are seen together in cultural context.

Why has there been no socialism, no successful socialist party, no intense class conflict in America? The short answer is that Americans institutionalized beliefs that worked against such developments. The strength of individualism and the weakness of hierarchy, to start where agreement is greatest, mean that nationalization of industry is widely regarded as threatening. Not only large corporations and small businesses, who help make individualism powerful, but egalitarians of all stripes reject that solution. Instead they hope to make equal opportunity contribute to equality by depriving it of special privilege. Before the Civil War, that meant keeping central government small and weak. After the Civil War, that increasingly has come to mean using the central government to regulate big business. Though the tactics differ according to the conditions of the time, the purpose remains the same: making liberty and equality compatible.

One can (and some do) look upon this belief as naïve, foolish, or, worse, a justification of exploitation. One can also, as I do, look upon it as worthy, heroic, even romantic, a part of the world's endangered political species, of which, when gone, there may be no more. However one looks upon that hybrid cultural alliance, American individualism, it does serve to mitigate class conflict. People of different incomes need not be at loggerheads, American individualists believe, provided that government (the early view) or industry (the later view) are prevented from engaging in rigged or otherwise unfair competition. Even those who take what is called a positive view of government look at it as performing negative functions—countering private abuses or making up for private ill-fortune rather than running things itself.

Until I see more parsimonious and powerful explanations, I will continue to claim that European differences from America, and vice versa, from the Founding through the 1960s, are best explained by the differences between social democratic and American individualistic cultures. Nowadays, by contrast, the ideas and institutions leading to the extraordinary vision that liberty and equality, competition and fair-shares, are compatible with each other and with democracy may well no longer distinguish America from its other-country cousins. Or at least, contemporary egalitarians have managed to set the tone of public debate,[34] and their militant and consistent refusal to legitimate the nation's institutions until they believe there is a good deal more equality of condition may signify, for the time being at least, an end to exceptionalism as we have known it.

[34] See Aaron Wildavsky, *The Rise of Radical Egalitarianism* (Washington, DC: American University Press, 1991).

6

American Higher Education: 'Exceptional' or just Different?

Martin Trow

The Exceptionalism of American Higher Education

In this chapter I would like to discuss some differences between the systems of higher education in the United States and those of other advanced industrial societies. Obviously, there are great difficulties in generalizing to the whole of western Europe and Japan. (I exclude discussion of East European countries since their assumptions regarding the role and functions of education have until recently been fundamentally different from those in the West.) And any generalization to the educational systems of societies as different as Sweden and Japan, Italy and Great Britain, are necessarily very broad and inevitably distort the picture of any particular system. Nevertheless, taken together, the higher education systems of Western Europe and their outposts elsewhere in the world (including Japan) differ enough from that of the United States to throw into bold relief the 'exceptionalism', the uniqueness, of the American system.

Differences between the United States and other countries in their forms and structures of higher education are obscured by the fact that we tend to call elements of our systems by similar names. We all have professors and lecturers, colleges and universities, research institutes and laboratories; we all award academic degrees that resemble one another, if they are not identical. In addition, our differences are not only obscured but diminished by the international scope of science and scholarship. The fundamental building blocks of teaching and learning in colleges and universities throughout the world are academic disciplines which have an international presence. A sociologist in the United States speaks easily to one in Paris or Stockholm or Tokyo; they read the same books and deal with the same problems. And that is true, on the whole, for physicists and philosophers and economists as well. There are national characteristics that mark the work of any scholarly community, but these bear much the same relation to a discipline as it exists internationally as a regional dialect bears to the common language of a nation. Thus, to describe and understand some of the activities of academic life, particularly the development of modern science and learning, the products of research and scholarship, it is possible to subordinate (if not wholly ignore) the differences between national systems, and the unique social and historical circumstances out of which those differences arise.

Nevertheless, for many purposes the differences between American and European systems are very large, and cannot be ignored. I will look briefly at ten ways in which American higher education differs from most other systems of higher education.

1. *Attitudes Regarding Higher Education*

First there is the American belief in education for its own sake. We have a broad national commitment to education for everybody for as long as people can be persuaded to attend formal institutions of education. Our youngsters are constantly being warned about the costs and dangers of dropping out of high school, and are encouraged over television and on the backs of matchbooks to attend college, 'the college of their choice'. Americans have an almost religious belief in the desirability and efficacy of post-secondary education for almost everybody; no other nation in the world makes that commitment or holds that belief. We back that belief with the provision of post-secondary schooling somewhere for everyone who wants an education beyond higher school, most notably in a broad system of community colleges which admit students without reference to their high school performance, and in many places without even the requirement of a high school diploma.

The United States made its commitment to mass higher education, and created the structures that would permit its growth to its present size, long before large numbers were enrolled. By 1900, when only 4 per cent of Americans of college age were attending college, we already had in place almost all of the central structural characteristics of American higher education: the lay board of trustees, the strong president and his administrative staff, the well-defined structure of faculty ranks, and, in the selective institutions, promotion through academic reputation linked to publication and a readiness to move from institution to institution in pursuit of a career. On the side of the curriculum, the elective system, the modular course, credit accumulation and transfer based on the

transcript of grades, all were in place by 1900, as were the academic
departments covering all known spheres of knowledge, and some not so
well known. Underpinning all was the spirit of competition, institutional
diversity, responsiveness to markets (and especially to the market for
students), and institutional autonomy marked by strong leadership and
a diversity of sources of support. The United States already had the
organizational and structural framework for a system of mass higher
education long before it had mass enrolments. All that was needed was
growth.

What has happened since to American higher education? Of course,
there has been growth—an enormous expansion in the numbers of
students, institutions, staff, research support, and everything else. But
apart from expansion and growth, the most important structural change
in American higher education in this century has been the development of the community college system, and the way that has tied the
four-year institutions and their degrees to the world of continuing and
vocational education. Academic freedom is more firmly and broadly
protected than at the turn of the century, thanks in part to the American
Association of University Professors (AAUP). In addition, there is now
broad federal support for student aid in the form of grants and loans,
and this has supplemented rather than replaced other and earlier forms
of student aid. Federal agencies support university-based research at a
level that could hardly have been imagined ninety, or even fifty,
years ago. The machinery of fund-raising, the organization of alumni,
and the associated development of big-time sports has gone further than
one would have imagined, though their roots were already in place at
the turn of the century. And there are faculty unions in some hundreds
of colleges and universities, though not in the leading research universities. But what is impressive about American higher education at the
end of the 1980s is not how much it differs from the system that existed
at the turn of the century, but how similar it is in basic structure, diversity,
mission, governance and finance.

The question may be raised of how it came to be that a century ago
the United State created a preternaturally precocious system of higher
education with an enormous capacity for expansion without fundamental
structural change. Part of the answer lies in the weakness of central
government in America throughout the nineteenth century, and a federal
constitution which gave to the states the primary responsibility for the
provision of education. This translated into the absence of a national
academic standard, which elsewhere has prevented the rapid expansion

of higher education by preventing the creating of new institutions which could not meet that standard. By contrast, the many colleges and universities which have been established in this country since the Revolution were granted charters by the states without having to meet high academic standards. As a result, a few decades after the Civil War, England was serving a population of twenty-three million with four universities; the state of Ohio, with three million inhabitants, already boasted thirty-seven institutions of higher education.[1] By 1910, the United States had already established nearly 1,000 colleges and universities, with a third of a million students, at a time when sixteen universities in France enrolled altogether about 40,000 students, a number nearly equalled by the number of faculty members in American colleges and universities.

In most European countries, including England, enrolment rates in higher education just after the Second World War ran from 3 to 5 per cent of the age grade. With the exception of the United Kingdom, the four decades after the Second World War saw a growth in enrolment rates in Western Europe to somewhere between 25 and 35 per cent, depending on the country and how one counts. Britain enrols about 14 per cent of the age grade in degree-granting institutions or courses, a figure roughly stable for the past decade. The enormous post-war growth in higher education in every European country was of course initiated and planned by government; there is almost no private higher education in Europe—some church-related universities and a few linked to the business community are relatively small and do not affect overall national policy. Throughout Europe, central governments provide most of the funds for the support of higher education, both for teaching and research.

The sources of the post-war growth in Europe were many, but private initiative was not one of them. Throughout Western Europe, the end of the Second World War saw a broad growth of democratic sentiment, reflected (among other things) in demands for a wider access to both secondary and higher education. The expansion of secondary education and the growth of the welfare state both increased the demand for people with some kind of post-secondary education. Moreover, European governments came increasingly to believe in the contribution of education, and especially of higher education, to economic development and thus to military strength. This led in many of these countries to forms

[1] Frederick Rudolph, *The American College and University: A History* (New York: Alfred A. Knopf, 1962).

of planning which depended heavily on investment in higher education.

Despite the post-war growth of higher education throughout the world, the American system remains much larger and more diverse than any European system. Its 3,400 accredited colleges and universities and 13.5 million enrolled students represent about 50 per cent of the 'college-age' cohort; since opportunities for continuing education are widely available, the proportion of Americans who ultimately take degree-credit post-secondary study is over 50 per cent.[2] The size of American higher education is not determined by central government planning or policy, but by the demand for post-secondary education in the society at large, and by decisions regarding admissions standards and tuition costs made by or for the institutions of post-secondary education.

2. *Public and Private Sectors*

America's colleges and universities are a mixture of public and private institutions with the privately supported institutions present at every level of excellence and in every category of function.While it is true that nearly four out of five of our students are currently (1989) enrolled in public institutions, the private sector remains enormously important as a model for the public sector. For example, of the ten leading research universities, eight are private; of the top twenty re-search universities, fifteen are private institutions. And the best undergraduate four-year colleges are also part of the private sector. Many private institutions are regional and more modest in their as-pirations, but at all levels of selectivity there is easy movement of students and faculty, and ideas about teaching and learning, between the public and private institutions. This relationship is almost unique in the world of advanced industrial societies. (Japan is a partial excep-tion among industrial societies, in having a very large private sector of higher education, though with the state-supported 'national'—formerly 'Imperial'—universities at the top of the hierarchy.) By contrast, for a

[2] It is hard to estimate the proportion of the college-age cohort who go on to some form of post-secondary education, since so much of higher education is also 'continuing education', available all through life. About 75 per cent of young Americans finish high school. In a follow-up of the high school graduation class of 1972, roughly two-thirds of those graduates reported having had some exposure to higher education seven years later (which would mean about 47 per cent of the cohort), and about 35 per cent had earned a bachelor's degree by 1984. Clifford Adelman, 'A Basic Statistical Portrait of American Higher Education', paper prepared for The Second Anglo-American Dialogue on Higher Education, Princeton, NJ, Sept. 1987, p. 31, Table 11.

variety of political and historical reasons, European countries discourage private institutions of higher education by withholding charters, support, and institutional autonomy or discretion. Currently, although in a number of European countries support is being sought for higher education in the private sector, less than 5 per cent of operating costs in European higher education comes from private sources.[3]

Perhaps the crucial difference in the United States is not the existence of a large and prestigious private sector, but rather the multiplicity and diversity of funding sources for both private and leading public institutions. Overall, American higher education currently (1988–9) spends about $135 billion in operating expenses, roughly 2.7 per cent of the gross national product.[4] Government at all levels together provides nearly half of all current revenues for American higher education, not including federal aid given directly to students, which shows up for the most part in tuition and fees. The federal government provides only about 13 per cent of the total funds for higher education, including its support for research and development in the universities, but excluding the aid it provides directly to students, currently running at about $10 billion in a combination of student grants and loans. State and local governments (mostly state) provide one-third of the funds for higher education. Students provide another one-third of the funds for higher education, including federal aid they have received, and the institutions themselves about 15 per cent from their endowments and other sources. If federal aid to students is counted as federal support, it increases the federal contribution to about 23 per cent of the total, and reduces the student contribution to about the same percentage. About 6 per cent is provided by individuals, foundations, and private business firms in the form of gifts, grants, and contracts.[5]

These proportions differ between public and private colleges and universities, of course, though it must be stressed that all American colleges and universities are supported by a mixture of public and private

---

[3] Roger L. Geiger, 'The Limits of Higher Education: A Comparative Analysis of Factors Affecting Enrolment Levels in Belgium, France, Japan, and the United States', Working Paper of the Higher Education Research Group, Yale University, New Haven, Conn., 1980, p. 18. Roger L. Geiger, *Private Sectors in Higher Education* (Ann Arbor, Mich.: University of Michigan Press, 1986).

[4] US Dept. of Education, National Center for Education Statistics, *Digest of Education Statistics* (Washington: US Government Printing Office, 1988).

[5] Martin Trow, 'American Higher Education: Past, Present, and Future', *Educational Researcher* 17/3 (1988), 19.

funds. For example, while in 1985–6 public colleges and universities got 45 per cent of their operating budgets from state governments, private institutions got less than 2 per cent of theirs from state sources. (On the other hand, private colleges got a larger proportion of their support funds from the federal government than did public four-year institutions, 17 per cent versus 11 per cent.) Another big difference between public and private institutions lies in the much greater importance of student tuition, fees, and payments for services (monthly room and board) in private schools: they account for less than one-third of the revenues of public institutions but nearly two-thirds of the support for private institutions.[6] These proportions differ sharply among even finer categories of colleges and universities—for example, as between public re search universities and public four-year colleges.

But even in the public sector, among the leading research universities like Berkeley, state support may be only half or less of operating expenses, the rest coming from federal grants, gifts, endowment income, fees and tuition, and payment for services, as, for example, from patients in university-operated hospitals.[7]

In the United States, the diversity of funding sources has increased in past decades, with federal aid to students, tuition payments, and private gifts all growing rapidly. During the same period, since the Second World War, the diversity of funding sources in the United Kingdom has until very recently been decreasing, as central government has taken over tuition payments and student support. Where central government in the United Kingdom provided only about a third of operating expenses for the universities just before the Second World War, and about two-thirds just after it, that figure grew to about 90 per cent by the mid-1960s.[8]

3. *'General Education' as Part of the Curriculum*

American higher education is marked by a commitment to the idea of a 'liberal' or 'general' education for all (or at least most) undergraduates. Elsewhere, with few exceptions, a broad liberal education in our sense of the word is gained, by the minority who get it, in the upper secondary schools which prepare for universities; and beyond that,

---

[6] US Dept. of Education, National Center for Education Statistics, *Digest of Education Statistics*, p. 140.

[7] University of California, 'The Last Five U. C. Budgets', *UC Focus*, 2/1. (Sept 1987), 2.

[8] Thomas William Heyck, 'The Idea of a University in Britain, 1870–1970', *History of European Ideas*, 8 (1987), 205–19. Peter G. Moore, 'University Financing 1979–1986', *Higher Education Quarterly*, 41 (1987), 25–41.

outside of the formal curriculum altogether. Higher education in Europe is for the most part highly specialized and oriented towards professional or pre-professional training. American colleges and universities provide a good deal of 'general education' that elsewhere is done in the upper secondary schools, in part because of the broad comprehensive nature, and (in European terms) consequent academic weakness, of our secondary schools, which are designed to bring as many young people as possible to the end of secondary schooling so that they can qualify for entry to higher education. Currently, about 75 per cent of American students finish high school and are qualified for entry to some kind of college or university. By contrast, about 30 per cent of the age group in France are qualified to enter higher education, and in England the proportion is under 20 per cent. The proportions of the age grade who actually do enter some form of higher education are, of course, lower— in Britain currently around 14 per cent, in France about 25 per cent, as compared with roughly 50 per cent in the United States.

4. *The Elective System, the Modular Course, and the Unit Credit as Academic Currency*

Another unique characteristic of American higher education is the phenomenon of the modular course with its attached 'credits', and the definition of the requirements for a degree in terms of the accumulation of course credits rather than, as elsewhere, through success on an examination or the presentation of a thesis.[9] The unit credit is the currency of American higher education. Credits which can be accumulated over time and transferred between institutions and between different major fields of study within colleges and universities make it relatively easy for students to 'stop out' and return at a later date, with their past work not wasted but safely 'banked' on their transcripts. In addition, the credit system greatly facilitates the transfer of students from one institution to another, and makes possible links between continuing education and earlier studies. But while this kind of academic currency introduces enormous flexibility into our system and allows students to change their institution or fields of study two or three or more times before earning their degrees or credentials, it also tends to reduce the socializing impact of a concentrated period of study in a single university.

[9] Sheldon Rothblatt, 'Modular Systems: (United States)' paper prepared for the *Anglo-American Conference on Higher Education*, Princeton, NJ. Sept. 1987.

5. *The Academic Profession*

There are marked differences between the academic profession in the
United States and that of most other countries. In Europe, on the whole,
academic departments have been characterized by a single professor and
many assistants. In the traditional European university, from the early
or middle nineteenth century until the Second World War, the central
figure was the chairholder. In Germany the *ordinarius* professor represented his discipline in his university, and in his several roles he
not only taught, directed, and carried on research, but together with
other chairholders also governed his own faculty, and the university
through the election of a rector from among their midst. Since the
Second World War, and especially since the middle 1960s, the 'junior'
(non-professorial) teaching staff in European universities have gained
more power along with the students in the governance of departments
and universities. This governance system is formalized in various boards
and committees on which are found representatives of the professors,
junior faculty, students, and sometimes non-academic 'staff', each
elected by the 'estate' which its members represent. In many European
societies these elections are contested along the lines of the national
political parties and are thus deeply politicized; the political divisions
within the society are thus brought directly into the heart of the academic
institutions.

In Britain, the professor did not have quite the same overwhelming
power and authority as did his counterparts on the Continent, largely due
to the power of the college fellows in Oxford and Cambridge who
actually govern the colleges which were (and are) the units of those
ancient universities. While professors have been much stronger in the
University of London and in the provincial universities than in Oxbridge,
the tradition of 'a democracy of gentlemen' impeded the emergence of
a professorial oligarchy of the kind found in other European universities.
In the United Kingdom, as on the Continent, professors still comprise
only a fraction (in the UK about 10 per cent) of all university teachers,
and the rank is not normally the terminal career-grade of the academic
profession. The United States is almost alone in having a relatively
flat academic hierarchy: the ranks of lecturer, assistant professor, and
associate professor are understood to be stepping stones to the final
career-grade of full professor. Since all (young) entering assistant professors can expect to become full professors in time, they tend not to
see their interests as opposed to those of the full professors, but
acquire the values of their seniors in the course of becoming pro-

fessors themselves. And thus they are not represented in university government as a special interest group—the 'non-professorial staff'—as in most Continental countries. Moreover, American departments are more egalitarian both in the autonomy given to assistant and associate professors and in the parts they play in departmental and university decisions. (See also below.)

6. *Governance Structures*

There are basic differences in the governance of American colleges and universities as compared with their counterparts in Britain and on the Continent. Except in the United Kingdom, a ministry of education or its equivalent plays a central role in (*a*) the appointment of academic staff, especially professors; (*b*) the allocation of budget among and within universities; (*c*) the criteria for access to universities; and (*d*) the determination of the standards—the examinations or theses—required to earn a degree. In most cases, this ministry is located in central government; in Germany, the state governments have primary responsibility for higher education, with some powers, especially for the support of research, reserved to the federal ministry in Bonn. As a result, the administrative staffs for higher education are typically located in the ministry rather than in the institution itself. By contrast, in the United States, there is no federal ministry of education. Our Department of Education plays a very small role in relation to higher education, apart from administering substantial programmes of student grants and loans. In American private colleges and universities, the whole of the administrative apparatus is located within the institution and is an arm of the university president. In public institutions, most of the administrators also serve the president, though some decisions are held in the hands of a state department or commission (and this varies among the states and between different classes of institutions). Whether the administrative staff lies inside or outside the university has great consequences for the kinds of decisions it can take, and thus for its autonomy.

7. *Academic Leadership*

In the United States, the president of a college or university is both the head of 'the administration' and also the academic leader. He serves by appointment of a lay board of trustees and is responsible only to them. So long as he has their confidence and support, the American college president has a very high degree of power and authority within his own institution. By contrast, European institutions (again Britain aside) have no lay boards of governors, and ordinarily their chief academic officer is a weak rector, formerly elected by the full professors, and more commonly now by a vote of the various estates of the university. The rector (by whatever name) ordinarily is only the chairman of the various governing committees and serves a relatively short period of time, returning thereafter to his professorial chair. On the Continent, he has alongside him a permanent administrative official appointed by the ministry and responsible for the finances and most of the internal administrative decisions. This administrative officer—the *Kurator* in Germany—is a civil servant on long-term appointment, and commonly comes to exercise a very large amount of authority and power within the university. The weak rector cannot make decisions, as American college presidents can, about the internal allocation of funds, most academic matters, or ultimate decisions on academic personnel.

8. *The Lay Board*

The American college or university invariably has a lay board, which at once ensures its ultimate accountability to its local, regional, or national constituencies in the broader society, but also insulates it from the direct management and intervention of the government of the day. Such boards oridinarily have the ultimate legal authority over the institution, and come to identify with it and its interests, even though appointed, in the case of most public institutions, by the governor of the state. In European countries, the direct accountability of the institution to the broader society is ensured by the authority of the ministry and its officials over the institution. The autonomy of European universities is a function of traditional restraints on government from interfering directly in academic affairs, thus permitting a high measure of academic freedom, discussion, and debate within the walls of the institution. Apart from the freedom to teach and to learn, the university rarely has much authority to manage its own size and shape, its entry or exit requirements, or its broad character and functions. As in many other respects, the United Kindgom stands somewhere between the United States and the Continental countries in this respect. British universities, with the exception of Oxford and Cambridge, do have lay boards, but they are weaker than their American counterparts, and the instruments of central government, the Department of Education and Science and the newly created statutory funding bodies, increasingly play, or threaten to play, a more *dirigiste* role, similar to their counterparts in France and Germany.

9. *'Vocational' and 'Technical' Studies and Continuing Education*

Almost every European country has created a variety of non-degree-granting post-secondary institutions, largely committed to vocational and technical education. These 'post-secondary' institutions are very often not included in the category of 'higher education'; access to them is through different routes than to the universities, and there is almost no movement of students from those institutions to the institutions of higher education, since they provide shorter courses and do not offer the same degrees as the universities and their counterparts. Most of these institutions have been created since the Second World War to provide easier access to forms of post-secondary education that are responsive to local and regional interests, and to offer technical and vocational studies that have difficulty in expanding within the traditional universities, or are not offered there at all.

In the United States, many of the functions of these institutions are provided by community colleges, with the big difference that the community colleges are understood there to be part of the broad system of higher education. Credits within them are transferable to degree-granting institutions, and their faculty members are trained in the four-year colleges and research universities. Community colleges in the United States, and many four-year colleges and universities, both public and private, also provide a good deal of 'continuing education' for adults seeking to keep up with their fields, or to change them, or to extend their education in directions that are not vocationally oriented. In Europe, the continuing education of adults has not on the whole been provided in the traditional institutions, but in other institutions which ordinarily have few links with the traditional institutions of higher education.

10. *Service to the Society, as well as to the State*

Alongside its commitments to research and to teaching, American higher education has a broad commitment to service to almost any organized interest that asks for it, and can pay for it. This is necessarily so, since American colleges and universities are supported by the society broadly and not just by the state. They need student tuition, private gifts, and public and private research support, as well as subventions directly by the state to state-aided institutions. By contrast, European universities do not have this same kind of general commitment to serve society; they are creatures of the state and do what the state asks them to do in return for full funding (or near it) by state agencies. From the early nineteenth century until very recently, European universities have been largely (though not exclusively) engaged in the preparation of graduates for public service of various kinds (including teaching and, in Protestant countries, the established churches). And student numbers have on the whole been constrained by the limited demand for state employees. As recently as 1976–8, in West Germany, between two-thirds and three-quarters of jobs open to graduates were in the public sector; in Sweden and Denmark, about two-thirds; in France, three-quarters of the arts graduates and 60 per cent of the science graduates went into the public sector and only 17 per cent into the private sector. In 1978 in Great Britain, 44 per cent of the graduates went into public administration, teaching, or the nationalized industries, while 45 per cent took further course work, did research, or continued in academic careers.[10] Even in Italy, with its enormously inflated university enrolments, public service was and is the goal of most graduates. But in recent years, the sharp decline in the number of positions available in the public sector, and especially in teaching and research, together with the democratization and expansion of European higher education, have greatly attenuated that link between the universities and public service, and have forced graduates to look elsewhere than to the civil service for employment; in some countries this has accelerated the professionalization of business management.

But since their conceptions of service have been so dominated by their relations to the state, European universities have not been highly responsive to the emergence of new needs and interests in society that are not yet reflected in public policy or in the directives of ministries. Moreover, their full funding has given them less incentive to be responsive to local and regional interests, particularly in business and industry. In the past few years, some European nations have shown considerable interest in encouraging their institutions of higher education to develop closer ties with industry, with varying degrees of success. In some cases, governments, as in the United Kingdom, have cut the budgets of the universities so as to force them to seek support from business and

[10] Henry Wasser, 'Instrumental versus Disciplinary Curricula: A Comparative Perspective', *European Journal of Education*, 20/1 (1985), 69.

industry. This has been dramatically 'successful' in some universities (e.g. Salford) where the cuts were very deep. But it is an ineffective strategy where the university does not have the resources to serve local interests, or where it has not built up links of service and attitudes of responsiveness over decades.

There are, of course, many exceptions to this generalization, and more all the time; the 'Americanization' of European higher education reflects itself not so much in broader access or a less specialized curriculum as in a growing sensitivity to the needs of business and industry in return for increasing levels of support by the business community. This is clearest in some British universities and polytechnics, in the 'petits grandes écoles' in France, which are often directly sponsored by local chambers of commerce, and in such institutions as the University of Turin, known colloquially as 'Fiat University' for its close links to that large firm.

This is by no means an exhaustive inventory of unique characteristics of American higher education. Other features of the system flow from those cited above. For example, the relative youth of American students, the great distances that so many have had to travel to college from home, and the early and continuing religious ties of so many colleges and universities, all have led American colleges and universities to accept a greater responsibility for their students' physical and moral welfare, *in loco parentis*, than most European universities. This in turn has led to the growth of very large and highly professionalized student services in such areas as health, counselling, halls of residence, and intramural sports, among others, staffed for the most part by non-academic professionals. These large staffs are directly responsible to the college or university president, and give him direct control over resources, of people and money, that his European counterparts do not have.

Or to take another example of the way unique characteristics generate others: the large measure of institutional autonomy in American higher education, the modular course, and the absence of national examinations together make it relatively easy to create new courses, new departments and professional fields, interdisciplinary courses, and educational innovations of all kinds.

This last point suggests a broader or more general way of looking at the specific differences that I have enumerated above. This more general perspective pivots around the distinction among 'élite', 'mass', and 'universal access' systems of higher education.[11] On the whole, until

[11] Martin Trow, 'Problems in the Transition from Elite to Mass Higher Education', *Policies for Higher Education*, from the General Report on the Conference on Future

the Second World War, European systems of higher education supported élite systems of higher education, offering access to no more than 3–5 per cent of the university age grade. Since the Second World War, all European systems of higher education have expanded very considerably, moving towards structures which allow the entry 15, 25 and even 35 per cent of the age grade. This transformation from an élite to a mass system involves not merely the expansion of small institutions into bigger ones, or the creation of many new colleges and universities. It involves profound changes in attitudes towards higher education on the part of students and teachers; in its organization, finance, and governance; in the structure of secondary education; in the criteria for admission to higher education; in the recruitment and education of faculty; in curriculum, physical planning, and much else. But the history of European higher education since the Second World War has been the story of efforts to grow in size and in functions without radically transforming institutional structures, and of the ensuing difficulties all European systems have encountered in trying to accommodate mass numbers and mass functions within structures designed for élite higher education.

These efforts have been marked by very great strains and difficulties, and have been only partially suc-cessful. The difficulties became especially pronounced when most European systems began, some fifteen years ago, to accept more than 15 per cent of the age grade in degree-granting institutions of higher education. (The British have held their proportion to just under 15 per cent, in an effort to preserve the forms, structures, and standards of élite higher education in all their degree-granting institutions.) By contrast, the organizational structure of mass higher education in the United States was already in place 100 years ago. American higher education has many problems of its own, arising directly out of its broad access and relaxed standards—the recurrent discussions about the quality of undergraduate education are a case in point.[12] But on the whole we have a precocious system, without many of the problems, and weak solutions, that mark contemporary European higher education. How we have come to develop such a unique, and uniquely adaptive and responsive, system is the subject of the next section, in which the question is raised in the context of a comparison

Structures of Post-Secondary Education (Paris: Organisation for Economic Co-operation and Development, 1974), 35–101.

[12] Ernest L. Boyer, *College: The Undergraduate Experience in America* (New York: Harper and Row, 1987). Allan Bloom, *The Closing of the American Mind* (New York: Simon and Schuster, 1987).

with the history and organization of higher education in the United Kingdom. Many, but not all, the comparisons made in that section would apply to Continental countries as well. But Britain has its own forms of 'exceptionalism'; American higher education differs in different ways from the higher educational systems of different countries.

The United States–United Kingdom Comparison:
Contrasting Sequences

It is common knowledge that Harvard College was created on the model of a college of Cambridge University. But we know also that almost from the first moment, American forms of higher education began to diverge from the English model—and that divergence has continued apace over three and a half centuries. Already by the time of the American Revolution, the Colonies had eight institutions of higher learning, while two were still adequate for the much richer and more populous mother country. And by the Civil War, the United States had hundreds of colleges and universities, while four—the two ancient universities plus Durham and London—were all that England had chartered. The divergence has continued, so that today England has a relatively small system of degree-granting institutions (universities, polytechnics, and colleges) with relatively high and common standards for the first degree and low rates of attrition, enrolling the smallest proportion of the age grade of any modern industrial society, while the United States has the largest and most diverse system in the world—enrolling some 13.5 million students in some 3,400 institutions, earning credits toward degrees, working at every level of academic standard.

That quantitative comparison, of course, is 'unfair' to the United Kingdom in that it excludes the whole of its further education sector, with its 1.3 million students, while it includes the American community colleges, a large part of whose work is in 'vocational' studies that are not of degree standard in England (or in the United States), and much else which is at or below the standard of English sixth-form work. (On the other hand, the American figures also exclude an enormous amount of post-secondary continuing education that is not pursued in degree-credit courses.) But even if we are not making invidious quantitative comparisons, it is of some considerable importance for other reasons that in the United Kingdom the institutions of further education are not part of higher education, whereas in the United States the community colleges are. And that is only one of many significant differences between these two national systems, differences whose nature and origins challenge our understanding.

Why is it that these two systems, starting from common assumptions and models, evolved in such sharply different directions over the centuries? Or, put differently, how can we explain the fact that the United States has developed a large and diverse system of colleges and universities with near-universal access to students of all abilities, ages, and interests, where 'any student can study any subject', while by contrast the United Kingdom has created a system of universities, polytechnics, and colleges for academically gifted students, enrolling altogether a much smaller proportion of the post-secondary-school age grade, a system marked also by high academic standards, low rates of attrition, deep and close attention to teaching, and distinguished levels of scholarship and research carried on within the universities themselves?

If we place the historical development of two great systems of higher education over two centuries side by side, and perhaps in no other way, we may discover a number of occasions in which the sequences of development in the two societies have differed. Moreover, these differing sequences have their roots in the characteristics of the larger societies and in a broad range of ramified consequences for those societies. Sequences, for the chronicler of a single society, almost never excite special notice or attention: it is simply the way things occurred in time, the way history happened. But there is surprise, and questions arise, when one places two chronologies side by side and discovers that the sequences which seem to be the 'normal' progression in one society did not occur that way in the other. And the questions that arise out of that recognition take a familiar set of forms:

(i) Are the phenomena themselves, whose sequences we are chronicling, the 'same' phenomena in the two societies, or if similar, how do they differ?

(ii) Why do these sequences occur differently in these two societies—how do we account for those differences?

(iii) What consequences flow from the fact that these sequences differ?

I want to point to five of these 'sequence reversals'—though there are others in the comparative modern histories of these two societies and their educational systems—to suggest their importance both as sources of subsequent differences between the two systems, and as reflections of prior differences in the basic character and development of the two societies.

1. In America, in Louis Hartz's vivid phrase, the market preceded the society and its institutions of higher education. In the United Kingdom, Oxford and Cambridge, the powerful models for all subsequent higher education, were created in the medieval world before market forces came to dominate social and institutional relations.[13]

2. In America, the presidents of our colleges and universities were present before the creation of a body of teachers and scholars which later became the faculty and even later the academic profession. In the United Kingdom, a class of learned men preceded the creation of the university and its leadership; their coming together in fact created Oxford and Cambridge, and over time they came to elect or choose their own institutional leaders.[14] Put somewhat differently, in the United Kingdom the academic guilds preceded the modern university; in America the university, initially only the lay board, a president, and a few assistants, came over time to create the academic guilds.

3. In America, for the most part, colleges and universities developed before the emergence of a broad system of upper secondary schooling.[15] In the United Kingdom, by contrast, while mass secondary schooling was also a late development, of the late nineteenth and twentieth centuries, the schools that prepared students for university (when they were not tutored privately at home) were in place all through the modern period, and indeed changes in the leading secondary schools—the public schools—stimulated change and reform in the ancient universities in the second half of the nineteenth century.

4. In America, the professional guilds have been relatively weak compared with professional education in the universities; on the whole, professional education has created the professions and still gives them leadership. Professional schools and colleges (as we all know) are enormously strong in American universities *and* colleges. In the United Kingdom, by contrast, professional education was largely excluded from the universities. There the professional guilds have dominated professional education, often providing the bulk of it themselves through a form of apprenticeship as in law and, to a large degree, in engineering.

[13] Louis Hartz, *The Liberal Tradition in America: An Interpretation of American Political Thought Since the Revolution* (New York: Harcourt Brace, 1955).

[14] Alan B. Cobban, *The Medieval English Universities: Oxford and Cambridge to c.1500* (Berkeley: University of California Press, 1988), pp. 49–50.

[15] Rudolph, *American College and University*, p. 281 ff.

Even where they do not provide it all themselves, the professions and their organizations continue to be strong in relation to university-based professional education.

5. In the United Kingdom in the nineteenth and twentieth centuries, the college as a teaching institution, and the federation of colleges as modelled on Oxford and Cambridge and as embodied in London and Victoria Universities and in the provincial colleges, preceded the emergence of the university, which granted degrees. Indeed, the 'university' in the United Kingdom was and is the degree-granting body, as opposed to the colleges which have been the agencies for teaching. In Britain, the authority to grant degrees is jealously guarded and is associated with the granting of a royal charter, but only to institutions which can demonstrate that they can teach and examine to high and common academic standards; it is thus an instrument for quality control of undergraduate education. In the United States, 'university' came to mean an institution which offered higher degrees, and especially the doctorate, by contrast with a 'college' which offered only the bachelors degree. In the United Kingdom the crucial issue was which body taught and which body examined and awarded degrees; in the United States these functions were carried out in the same institution, whether college or university. The crucial distinction here was whether an institution was concerned primarily with the transmission of knowledge, or at least equally with the creation of knowledge. The idea of the university as the locus and agency for the creation of knowledge came later in the United Kingdom and, it can be argued, did not achieve full equality with the teaching function until after the Second World War, and even then only in a handful of universities, and was centred on the professors. This helps account for the quite different weight and importance attached in the two countries to postgraduate education as compared with education for the first degree. Let us look at three of these issues a little more closely.

1. *A Temporal Order for Market* vs. *Society*

America has been, almost since its earliest settlements, a liberal society, whose reliance on free markets and mistrust of central government is built deeply into our structures of society and government, for example, in our constitutional separation of powers, in our federalism and the continuing power of the states, and in our Bill of Rights. We are not embarrassed by the enormous role of markets—and of commercial considerations—at the very heart of our institutions. Indeed, land speculation has been a significant motive in the creation of colleges and universities throughout American history.

By contrast, while the United Kingdom has had a stronger liberal tradition than most European societies, it never accepted the hegemony of the market over the sphere of high culture. If we set aside the Dissenting academies (which collapsed at the end of the eighteenth century, probably because they could not get charters to give degrees), there was a brief window of liberal—that is, of private local—initiative in British higher education in the nineteenth century, taking the form first of the creation of University College (London) and then of the University of London, but showing greater life in the second half of the nineteenth century with the creation of the provincial universities (Owens College, Manchester, and the subsequent federation in 1880 of Owens, Leeds, and Liverpool in the short-lived Victoria University). There were also colleges created in Newcastle, Birmingham, and Bristol in the last decades of the nineteenth century, but most of the old civic universities did not gain charters as independent universities—that is, the right to award their own degrees—until the first decade of this century.

The creation of the English provincial universities in the late nineteenth and early twentieth centuries can be seen as a response to local initiatives and demands arising in the market for graduates for local business and industry as well as for increased access to universities for local youth. But universities in England were, and continue to be, bedevilled by a conflict among different ideas of the university: the university as an instrument for the transmission of high culture and the cultivation of the sensibilities and character of young gentlemen; the German and later American conception of the university as a locus of research and the creation of knowledge; and a third conception of universities, now regaining strength under severe cuts and pressures from central government, as places for practical, even vocational, studies, and service to local business and industry.

The English provincial universities of the late nineteenth century were established by local notables and interests in part to provide trained graduates and services for local needs, though, as always, motives were mixed. But no British university could be established without the enormous weight of Oxford and Cambridge, as models and mentors, having a profound influence on their subsequent development. Indeed, the creation of the provincial universities coincided with reforms at Oxbridge, which led to their improving the quality of their teaching and a gradual raising of their academic standards.[16] These reforms made Oxford and Cambridge even weightier as models for the new institutions. But, above all, Oxford and Cambridge were where England's national élites were educated, and for the provincial universities to seek academic distinction and social status meant moving out of their local orbits and the provision of services for local needs towards Oxford and Cambridge's standards and values, in the process becoming less local institutions and more and more part of a national system with common entry standards, common standards for the honours degree, a common academic salary scale, and above all a commitment to national rather than local service.

This national system only developed slowly; the creation of the University Grants Committee in 1919 as the agency for the development of a common state budget request and the allocation of the block grant from the Treasury was an important milestone, but the national system had already begun to develop before that, and did not fully crystallize until after the Second World War.[17] Nevertheless, it can be said that, for the provincial universities, useful practical studies were inherently linked to local ties, local support, and the kind of responsiveness to the market for graduates and services that marks the college and university in a liberal society. There was every motive for these new provincial colleges and universities to forgo those ties to their local origins, to flee from their dependence on the market, to find a greater nobility of mission and function (as they saw it) in becoming linked to national public service and the old professions, coming under the benevolent wing of the Treasury and then of the University Grants Committee and its provision of public funds from central government.

Indeed, the increasing dependency on the state has been dramatic over the past sixty years, and especially since the Second World War. In 1920, taking all British universities together, only about a third of their total income came on a direct grant from central government. Between 1939 and 1949 that went up to nearly two-thirds, and by 1989 it was roughly three-quarters.[18] For British universities, to gain support from central

[16] Sheldon Rothblatt, *The Revolution of the Dons: Cambridge and Society in Victorian England* (Cambridge: Cambridge University Press, 1968). A. J. Engel, *From Clergyman to Don: The Rise of the Academic Profession in Nineteenth Century Oxford* (Cambridge, Mass.: Harvard University Press, 1982).

[17] Martin Trow, 'Comparative Perspectives on Higher Education Policy in the U.K. and the U.S.', *Oxford Review of Education*, 14/1 (1988), 81–96.

[18] Michael Shattock, '*The Last Days of the University Grants Committee*', *Minerva*, 4/25 (Winter 1987), 471–85. Heyck, 'Idea of a University'.

government was a liberation from the petty demands and ignoble interests of local government and local trade; we see the very same process occurring today, as the polytechnics, created with strong local ties in ways very similar to the creation of the provincial universities, welcome the severance of their remaining dependence on local government and local industry as central government assumes their whole direct support.[19]

The American contrast is well known: dependence almost from the beginning on markets of various kinds, and the need to provide services and products for those markets, have shaped every aspect of the subsequent development of our system of higher education. This is a force whose importance can hardly be exaggerated. We can look at this orientation to the market in two ways. On one hand, the absence of stable and assured support for our colleges and universities from the State or an established church has forced them to look for support from a multiplicity of other sources, notably student tuition and fees, contributions from alumni and other friends, and especially from wealthy benefactors and institutions. A constant concern for financial survival and resources for development and growth engendered a steady sensitivity to the needs and interests of this varied support community, reflected in the enormous diversity of activities and services that our institutions have provided. The other side of the coin shows the relative autonomy of our colleges and universities, even formally 'public' institutions, from direct control and management by agents of state or central government.

The force of markets on American colleges and universities has also greatly increased the power of the student as consumer, and that in turn has driven the curriculum to meet the interests of the students, which in turn often reflect the interests of the job market. It also forces the colleges and universities to shape their curriculum to the realities of the primary and secondary schools, whose preparation the students bring with them. If our colleges and universities, for example, were to try to maintain a high and common standard for entry, as in the United Kingdom, many of them would have no students at all. So the great diversity of entry standards, of curricular offerings, and of standards for

[19] It was not until the late 1970s and 1980s that British universities began to have second thoughts about their near-total dependence on central government grants, and only under the most severe financial pressures and constraints have these universities, or at least some of them, begun to cultivate anew their local ties, and seek out local missions and services in the hope of gaining local financial support. There is, under duress, what may be a rebirth of liberal perspectives in the British universities.

the degree are all indirectly related to the need to attract students who ultimately support the institution in large part through their fees or to generate support from state authorities by way of enrolment-based budgetary formulas.

If entry into markets implies sensitivity to the preferences of the buyers, it also suggests competition among the providers. Most American colleges and universities (though not all) were relatively poor at their founding (and some for long periods thereafter), and could only survive by finding ways to serve various constituencies which provided their support—students, benefactors, religious denominations, state and local governments, more recently business organizations and federal governmental agencies, in various combinations. But the habits of service do not disappear with affluence and security. And that is because our colleges and universities are also competitive with each other for distinction and prestige—nationally, regionally, or in some functional category. Moreover, in the pursuit of distinction and relative status, affluence provides no security. A college or university—even the richest—always needs more: another science building, higher faculty salaries, another chair in a new subject, more residence halls, and so on. So even our wealthiest colleges and universities act as if they were poor, always engaged in fund-raising, continually cultivating new friends and supporters, public and private, seeking always to find new ways of serving old and new constituencies in a constant exchange of service for support.

The forms of service, as of support, are many and various, and the connections between them are often subtle, indirect, and delayed (though equally often simple and direct, through the cash nexus). But our richest colleges and universities act, in this respect, as if they were poor. In the United Kingdom it is the most desperate university, Salford, whose budget was cut most deeply in 1981–2, which has been most energetic and successful in raising private funds. In the United States, the most successful fund-raisers are the richest universities—Harvard, Stanford, Princeton, MIT—and among the colleges, their counterparts— Amherst, Swarthmore, and the like. They raise money so as to compete academically, and they also compete in how much money they can raise. And all with no embarrassment. That too is of long standing.

But however strong these market forces may be, they are not all-powerful, and part of the history of American higher education has been of the tension between the 'popular' functions of these institutions, the services they perform for other institutions in society and for the vocational interests of students and their future employers, on the one hand, and the 'autonomous' functions, those that arise out of the intellectual life of the subjects that are taught and studied in the colleges and universities, on the other.[20] Some colleges and universities have been able to provide a measure of resistance to the powerful demands of the market, asserting their own inherent logic and integrity, refusing to be pressed into some kinds of public service or subordinating 'liberal' to 'vocational' studies in their curriculum. Most successful in this have been the private colleges and universities with large endowments, those state institutions that have been able to count on substantial private support, and all institutions which have a multiplicity of financial support sources so that student fees are not the dominant or overwhelming element.

All of those factors reduce the direct influence of student preferences and give the autonomous functions of the institution a measure of room to survive and in some places even to flourish. So institutional autonomy, the ability of an institution to defend its own character and mission, is, I suggest, a function less of sheer wealth than of the multiplicity of sources of support. This can be shown over time in the United States, and events in the United Kingdom since the Second World War, and especially since 1970, also support this thesis.[21] But there the direct intervention of central government into the private life of the universities—what they teach and study—has had to overcome the traditions of autonomy rooted in the models of Oxford and Cambridge and their centuries of self-governing and endowed colleges. Those traditions were institutionalized in 1919 in the University Grants Committee, which the present government has replaced with another body called the University Funding Council, directly responsive to central state policy. But the process is still underway there, and the outcomes uncertain.

2. *The Relationship between Higher and Secondary Education*

I have said that in the United States, for the most part, colleges and universities developed before the emergence of a system of public secondary schooling. One consequence was that our colleges and universities all through their history have had to do considerable remedial work to bring students even up to the not-very-demanding

[20] Martin Trow, 'The Public and Private Lives of Higher Education', *Daedalus*, 2 (Winter 1975), 113–27.

[21] Martin Trow, 'Comparative Perspectives'.

standards that they have imposed. The continuing weakness of their links to the secondary schools has meant that most American colleges and universities have not been able to assume any general standard of accomplishment, and have had to teach students of widely varying ability and preparation. That has had consequences for their curriculum, methods of instruction, and requirements for the degree.

One result of the emergence of higher education before secondary schooling over the greater part of the United States, and the scarcity of what Europeans would call upper secondary education even to this day, is that throughout our history much of what colleges and universities do would seem to Europeans (and the British) to be appropriate to the upper secondary schools. The whole idea of general education—the non-specialized introduction to the main branches of learning which characterizes the first two years of almost all American higher education—is in Europe completed in secondary school, and indeed in the United Kingdom at age 16, before entry into the upper secondary school, the sixth form. In addition, there is the enormous variety of student services provided by our colleges and universities—health centres, centres for remedial studies, for academic counselling, psychological counselling, career counselling, learning centres, and many more—all staffed by professionals employed directly by the university. The elaborate facilities for sports and games, both intramural and inter-collegiate, also staffed by professionals, again remind Europeans of the spirit of schools rather than of university, as do the many staff who look after student residence halls. Everywhere we find counsellors and older students providing a certain measure of adult—and institutional—presence in situations where students in the Universities of Paris, Stockholm, or Rome, or the British universities, would be astonished to find it.

This psychological climate of prolonged immature dependency, that is to say, the climate of the school, was more pronounced in American colleges and universities twenty-five years ago than it is today. Political and legal challenges to the concept of the college standing *in loco parentis* have reduced the weight of institutional authority in the extra-curricular life of American students. But the universities' presence in extracurricular life is still large, and indeed has grown over these past two decades as student service staffs have become more highly profes-sionalized and have spun off subspecialties, professional associations, annual meetings, journals, and special postgraduate degrees that have become new professional credentials. All this activity now falls under the rubric of student services. No longer retaining the authoritarian overtones of a dean of students enforcing rules, representing the college or university *in loco parentis*, it has assumed the character of technical services rather than moral guidance. But these services inevitably have a moral dimension, and link the student to the institution more closely than is common in Europe.

In the United Kingdom, by contrast, public and grammar schools had co-existed for centuries with Oxbridge, though many upper-class students had been tutored privately for the universities, a much rarer pattern in the United States. But in the crucial middle years of the nineteenth century, the Arnoldian reforms in the leading public schools had an impact on the universities through their graduates, the moral force of their headmasters, and the establishment of close links between the sixth forms in these public schools and the universities, which made that avenue almost the only way into higher education, an avenue marked by many tied scholarships and strengthened by the Oxford and Cambridge entrance examinations.[22]

In important respects, the secondary schools in the United States have been extensions of primary education upwards, in their forms of teacher training and credentialing, in their structure, governance, and finance, and in the status and qualifications of the secondary school teachers. By contrast, in the United Kingdom as in most other European countries, upper secondary education, both public and private, has been an extension of the universities downwards, both in the character (and in the United Kingdom, the specialization) of studies and teaching and in the origins and education of the sixth-form teachers, university-trained scholars who might, in more expansive times, have held university posts. Again the exceptions in the United States are illuminating: one thinks of the significant role of the selective preparatory high schools and streams in the public sector in the 1920s and 1930s, with Ph.D.s as department heads, before the great post-war expansion drew such people out of the high schools and into the colleges and universities.

It is hard to think of any fundamental ways in which American secondary schools have influenced American colleges and universities, except by the weakness of their curriculum and teaching, or, as in most of our history before the turn of this century, their near-total absence. There is of course one outpost of the schools in our colleges and universities, the departments and professional schools of education. But

[22] Rothblatt, *Revolution of the Dons.*

that linkage has inhibited the integration of schools of education into the university and prevented them from gaining the relatively strong and independent status of other professional schools. As Burton Clark has suggested, the fundamental organizational, political, and normative characteristics of public secondary schools in America have a strong 'bias toward mediocrity',[23] and are in this aspect fundamentally different from the organizational characteristics of American colleges and universities.[24]

Indeed, one important characteristic of the educational system of the United States is the enormous contrast between its public secondary schools, which are arguably among the least effective major institutions in society, and its colleges and universities, which are among its most successful and effective. The differences in organization, character, and quality between American secondary schools, which are largely insulated from market forces, and its colleges and universities have many consequences for both the schools and the colleges. Burton Clark finds the sources of this inherent bias against academic excellence in certain structural characteristics of American secondary education. Looked at from a comparative perspective, the characteristics that he points to comprise a unique cluster that distinguishes American secondary education from that of other countries. One of those characteristics is the commitment of American secondary schools to universal participation, and thus to a great diversity in the school population.

School persistence rates for the various age groups in the U.S. have been double those of European schoolchildren. Virtually all U.S. students enter the first year of high school . . . and, in 1980, about 75% of the age group graduated from high school. Thus, in our extremely heterogeneous society, the secondary school system has to cope with youngsters from a variety of social and cultural backgrounds. The system has been compelled to accommodate the deprived and the disaffected, as well as the advantaged and the highly motivated—to accomodate those for whom the school diploma is a terminal credential, as well as those bound for higher education (a roughly 50–50 split in recent years).[25]

Another structural source of bias toward mediocrity in American secondary education, in Clark's view, is the relative absence of differentiation between and within schools. 'The advantages of special-

---

[23] Burton R. Clark, 'The High School and the University: What Went Wrong in America, Part I', *Phi Delta Kappan*, 66/6 (1985), 391–7.

[24] National Commission on Excellence in Education, *A Nation at Risk: The Imperative for Educational Reform* (Washington: US Dept. of Education, Apr. 1983). Martin Trow, 'The National Reports on Higher Education: A Skeptical View', *Educational Policy*, 1/4 (1987).

[25] Clark, 'High School and University', p. 392.

ization—and especially of distinctiveness—are largely lost ; instead, educational purpose has been dulled, and communities that share common interests have been dispersed.'[26] Without differentiation, any particular school cannot sustain a marked sense of its own character and distinctiveness, and without that sense there cannot be a strong commitment to excellence. (Although lack of differentiation still characterizes much of American secondary education, the situation in this respect may now be changing in response to the growth in the number of 'magnet schools' which differ in important respects from the standard American comprehensive high schools.)

A third feature of the American secondary school is its closer ties with primary education than with higher education. In other countries, upper secondary schools are closely linked to the universities for which they prepare. But mass secondary education in the United States developed around the turn of the century as a terminal system, one that in its comprehensiveness and emphasis on 'education for life' simply carries further the education of the elementary school of which it was an outgrowth.[27] There have always been exceptions: academically selective high schools were established in many cities in the nineteenth and early twentieth centuries, and some comprehensive high schools have en-couraged and sustained strong academic streams, often against populist and anti-intellectual pressures. But on the whole, American secondary schools have been linked both philosophically and organizationally with primary schools; their governance and finance, their staff recruitment, training, and conditions of work are all much more like those of primary schools than like those of colleges and universities.

A fourth feature of American secondary schools is the element of local and political control. Their part-time elected lay school boards, their big administrative staffs, and increasingly active parents groups all have a large influence on the working lives of secondary school teachers, an influence tending to undermine their commitment to high academic purpose. 'All of these factors adversely affect the professional autonomy of U.S. teachers, and a malaise born of powerlessness becomes widespread. To a degree not widely recognized by Americans, the pattern of local control over secondary education contributes to a "deprofessionalization" of teaching.'[28]

[26] Ibid. 393.

[27] Martin Trow, 'The Second Transformation of American Secondary Education', *International Journal of Comparative Sociology*, 2/2 (Sept. 1961), 144–66.

[28] Clark, 'High School and University', p. 394.

Finally, public secondary schools have a near-monopoly over the educational services available to students in a given geographic area. Private schools are few and expensive, and thus 'we have diminished the amount of choice left to parents and students, virtually eliminated competition among schools for enrolment, and rendered scholastic comparisons among schools operationally harmless'.[29] These characteristics that give most American high schools their distinctive character— universal secondary education, comprehensive school organization, close links with primary schools, local control, elected lay boards, big bureaucratic staffs, and the local monopoly—all tend to weaken the academic and intellectual role of those schools, and thus their links with higher education.

By contrast, American colleges and universities have structural advantages precisely to the extent that their characteristics differ from those of the high school. One crucial difference is that enrolment in higher education is voluntary. While it is a mass system, it is not a universal system; less capable and less highly motivated students do not make the transition to college or university. Moreover, colleges and universities are highly differentiated among themselves, and the larger ones are differentiated internally.[30] They can and do cultivate distinctive images, purposes, and missions, and they can recruit and motivate faculty and students around those distinctive images. They have thus the enormous advantage for intellectual life that arises out of academic differentiation.

In addition, higher education even at the undergraduate level is pulled towards new knowledge, towards graduate education and research, and towards professional practice, both by its faculty and by the job and career orientations of its students. Colleges and universities differ from secondary schools further in their higher degree of autonomy in relation to government and their own boards of trustees. This autonomy, especially marked in the leading research universities, is rooted in the monopoly of expertise that academics have in the subjects they teach and study. Even in more modest institutions, faculty members not at the frontiers of their fields, who do little or no research, borrow their claim to autonomy from academics in the more prestigious institutions which provide the models for all of academic life.

[29] Clark, 'High School and University', p. 394.
[30] Martin Trow, 'Elite Higher Education: An Endangered Species?', *Minerva*, 14/3 (Autumn 1976), 355–76.

Unlike secondary schools, American colleges and universities compete actively for students, for financial support, and for prestige. And these kinds of competition make them responsive to a wide range of trends and forces in American life, some of them economic and demographic, others intellectual. As a result, American higher education exhibits an enormously dynamic character, both as a system and in its component institutions. We see this in many ways, among them the ability of many private American colleges to survive in circumstances that many observers have predicted would lead to their closure.[31]

This is all very much by contrast with the United Kingdom and other European societies where, as I have suggested, the preparatory upper-secondary schools have over time become extensions of the universities downwards into the schools. But that has allowed the maintenance of high and common entry standards, which replaced money and social status as the chief constraint on the expansion and democratization of access to British universities as they slowly became meritocratic in this century. By contrast, the looseness of the articulation of our schools and colleges, the weakness and variability of secondary education in the United States, all contributed to the ease of access to the latter since no general level of secondary school achievement could be either expected or examined. That meant in turn that admissions criteria (beyond, in this century, a high school diploma) would be for most American colleges and universities almost wholly lacking, and for others highly variable.

Indeed, it also helps to explain the continued variability of achievement and ability among the entering class within any specific college or university, even those thought to be 'selective'. And this variability of preparation, and the extraordinary diversity of ability, achievement, and motivation among the entering students, all have tended to force on the colleges and universities the virtues of the elective curriculum, and that in turn depended on the primacy of the autonomous modular course, taught and examined by the same college or university instructor at whatever level of standard he could achieve or his students allow. This modular course structure which began to be introduced into American higher education after the Civil War is a crucial structural characteristic of the American organization of teach-

---

[31] Earl F. Cheit, *The New Depression in Higher Education* (New York: McGraw-Hill Book Company, 1971). Idem, *The New Depression in Higher Education: Two Years Later* (Berkeley: Carnegie Commission on Higher Education, 1973).

ing and instruction, with a broad range of implications for other aspects of the life of our institutions and the curriculum.

3. *The Academic Profession and the University*

I have been pointing to a series of questions which, I suggest, arise with special force and clarity from a comparative and historical study of inverted sequences in the development of our systems of higher education. Another such question is why the professorship—the chair—never assumed the overwhelming importance either in the United Kingdom or in the United States that it did on the Continent, and particularly in Germany and German-influenced systems. The chaired professor, often also directing his own research institute, was, until the major 'reforms' of the 1960s, the central figure in most European universities, in both the Humboldtian and Napoleonic systems. Indeed, in a sense the professors *were* the university; they dominated its intellectual and scholarly life, they elected its deans and rectors, and they shared with politicians and officials in the ministries the governance and direction of the university. Remnants of this system survive to this day, diluted by the great increase in their numbers and the presence on internal governance committees of representatives of non-professorial teaching staff, students, and other staff members.

But neither the United Kingdom nor the United States have ever given the chairholding professor such enormous authority and power in their universities. The reasons for this in the two countries are quite different. In the case of the United States, the absence of a large class of learned men throughout much of our history meant that almost without exception our colleges and universities have been created by a group of laymen who selected a president to direct and manage the day-to-day life of the institution. This founding body and their successors—now the governing body, the lay board of trustees, or 'regents'—together with their chosen agent, the president, have occupied the leading positions of authority and power in American colleges and universities, and still do.[32] While the academic staff—the 'faculty'—in a few leading universities and colleges have managed to persuade their boards to delegate to them a substantial measure of authority over the academic life of the institution, that authority is almost always exercised through academic

[32] The decision of the Supreme Court in the Dartmouth College case (1819) confirmed their authority and the inviolability of their charters against challenge by state authorities. See Jurgen Herbst, *From Crisis to Crisis: American College Government 1636–1819* (Cambridge, Mass.: Harvard University Press, 1982).

bodies (usually 'Senates') consisting of all the members of the academic staff, or at least all the tenured ones, and further is actually exercised in steady consultation with the president and his senior academic staff (the academic vice-president, provosts, deans, and department chairmen). There were few great scholars present at the birth of our colleges and universities, and no room for them to exercise great powers when they finally did emerge through the development of their academic disciplines.

In the United Kingdom, the power of the professors was constrained in the ancient universities not by a lay board and powerful president, as in the United States, but by corporate bodies of academics (the fellows) who are the governing bodies of the Oxford and Cambridge colleges, and have been since their founding. These bodies have retained the egalitarian democracy (within their own élite membership) of medieval guilds of masters, and have little room for the hierarchical and authoritarian rule of professors of the traditional European universities. While the professorial chairholder has had a much more powerful position in the provincial universities than in Oxbridge, the influence of Oxford and Cambridge as models for the others, and the experience of most English professors as students or fellows in Oxbridge colleges, along with other factors, has inhibited the emergence of a dominant 'professoriate' at any English university comparable to the power of chairholders on the Continent. And the differences between professors in Oxbridge and elsewhere have been declining with the introduction of rotating and even elected headships of departments in the provinces.

The emerging shape and nature of the academic profession in the United States and United Kingdom poses an interesting contrast. Of particular interest is the emergence of an academic profession and career in the United States after the Civil War, marked by our familiar academic ranks (instructor, assistant professor, associate professor, 'full' professor) in which it came early to be assumed that the ordinary career rank would be full professor, and that every new instructor could *expect* to become a full professor *somewhere* as the predictable outcome of competent service, rather than of extraordinary scholarly achievement as in the United Kingdom and the Continental countries. There are several problems here:

(i) When did the crystallization of this academic hierarchy occur in the United States, and with what variations among different institutions?

(ii) Why did the academic profession develop in this way—as nowhere else?

(iii) What have been the consequences of this set of arrangements for academics, and for their institutions?

A tentative answer to the second question, of why the profession developed this way, can be suggested in the following terms. The relative ease with which American academics could achieve the rank of professor may be oddly related to the relative poverty of our institutions. Academics in the United States were paid in part in rank and title rather than in money, and since professors collectively did not have much power (for reasons already discussed), the existing ones did not and could not resist further diluting the status of the rank by adding to its numbers.

This raises the question of the enormously greater role of 'exit' over 'voice' in the higher levels of the academic profession in the United States, and the weakness of the guild as an instrument of 'voice' as compared to the individual exercising his own power in the academic marketplace.[33] 'Exit', of course, is a function of the market for academics, which in turn is related to the sheer number of competing institutions. 'Exit' as a threat scarcely exists as a serious way for a European academic to improve his situation in his own institution, though to be called elsewhere may be, and often is, a step in a progress upward. But that 'call' (or in our language 'offer') is rarely met by the home institution in the competitive way familiar to American colleges and universities.

One consequence of this arrangement in the United States has been to increase the importance of an individual's own scholarly distinction and reputation, and slow the development of academic unions. If one's professional fate is so much more a function of one's own research work and reputation, this greatly reduces the sense of a shared life fate in the same rank, institution, or system which is the main motivation for the development of an academic union. Not surprisingly, faculty unions in the United States are found for the most part in the non-research institutions whose faculty are least able to exercise the power or threat of exit as a way of improving their own situations. And so they turn more to 'voice' through a union as a way of strengthening their positions. This fact has clear consequences for the governance of institutions, both those full of research academics and those with non-research-oriented teaching staffs.

[33] Albert Hirschman, *Exit, Voice and Loyalty: Response to Decline in Firms* (Cambridge, Mass.: Harvard University Press, 1970).

But there are other consequences of a normal career linking instructor to full professor as well. The absence in the United States of a distinct body of junior non-professorial faculty who will never be professors, as found in the United Kingdom and on the Continent, is a factor in the anticipatory socialization of all academics in American colleges and universities to common norms. If most instructors and assistant professors see themselves as full professors in the future, they are less likely to want to reduce the power and prerogatives of that status to which they realistically aspire. (This does not apply to the growing body of part-time and 'temporary' faculty in many American institutions, excluded from the 'tenure track', a reserve army that buffers these institutions against the vicissitudes of the market.) On the Continent, of course, the changes in university governance since the mid-1960s have been marked by sharp conflicts between the professoriate and the 'junior' academic ranks. This is less visible in British universities, perhaps because British academics inherited the relatively egalitarian ethos and governance structures of Oxford and Cambridge, and perhaps also because the roughly 40 per cent of all academics currently in the 'senior' ranks (professor, reader, senior lecturer) make achievement of those ranks a reasonable expectation for most junior staff (though perhaps still a source of bitterness and resentment for the substantial minority who do not make it).

Events, Challenges, and Contrasting Patterns of Response

Such questions as the above, which arise out of a comparative perspective, can be multiplied in number and extended in treatment. But there is another level of analysis which looks toward a more comprehensive statement about the intrinsic nature of these two systems, their internal development, and their evolving relationships with other groups and institutions in their societies. Let me come back to the question of why it is that the United States, alone among modern nations and in sharp contrast with the United Kingdom, had a system of mass higher education already in place 100 years ago, before it had the numbers that we associate with mass higher education. As a result of its structural and normative precocity, the great expansions of the twentieth century have not required any fundamental change in any of the basic structural, organizational, or normative features of American higher education and its component parts; those features were already in place, ready to accept the growing numbers that would pour into them in this century, and especially rapidly since the Second World War.

It was as if the system had been created in anticipation of growth, and to some extent that seems to be true. So much in the history of the United States has been predicated on the assumptions of growth: its location of towns and cities; its infrastructure of roads, canals, and railroads; its very conception of itself.[34] But we cannot make too much of the 'intentionality' of higher educational policy; much of the premature readiness of the American system of higher education, before its movement to mass and then to universal access, was the result of the way the system was already being created and growing in the period between the Revolution and the Civil War, and some of its characteristics were foreshadowed before that. It is, I believe, possible to show the marked similarities in origins, organization, and behaviour of American colleges created in 1815, 1870, and 1960. The continuties in their character and structure are striking, even if changes in the undergraduate curriculum over time are large, and the research function almost wholly missing from the pre-Civil War colleges.

We must root this discussion in the literature of theories of American exceptionalism, theories which try to explain the large and persistent differences between the American experience and that of most other advanced industrial societies. This discussion must at least make reference to diverse approaches to this concern for exceptionalism: Louis Hartz's focus on the role of the market in American life;[35] Potter's on the role of general affluence and wealth in the American experience;[36] Turner and his critics on the influence of the moving frontier;[37] Lipset on our historical experience as 'the first new nation', and on the economic and political forces that resulted in our being the only industrial society that never developed a strong socialist movement and tradition;[38] and above all Tocqueville's classic analysis of American democracy and the enormous weight it has placed on the equality of

[34] Daniel Boorstin, *The Americans: The National Experience* (New York: Random House, 1967).

[35] Louis Hartz, *The Liberal Tradition in America: An Interpretation of American Political Thought Since the Revolution* (New York: Harcourt Brace, 1955).

[36] David M. Potter, *People of Plenty: Economic Abundance and the American Character* (Chicago: University of Chicago Press, 1954).

[37] Frederick Jackson Turner, *The Frontier in American History* (New York: Henry Holt and Co., 1920). Richard Hofstadter and S. M. Lipset, *Turner and the Sociology of the Frontier* (New York: Basic Books, 1968).

[38] S. M. Lipset, *The First New Nation: The United States in Historical and Comparative Perspective* (New York: Basic Books, 1963).

condition, on individual opportunity and achievement, and on our highly developed propensity to create and join private associations to accomplish all kinds of purposes.[39] Each of these (and other) broad perspectives on American history has its implications for the character and functions of our colleges and universities; they are by no means mutually contradictory or incompatible, and one task is to show how together they and other aspects of the American experience, and not least our experience as a country of immigrants, had consequences for our colleges and universities, which in turn have reacted back upon other aspects of American life, other American institutions.

Similarly, there is a rich literature on English 'exceptionalism'—on the unique features of its history and culture which have distinguished it not only from the United States, but from other European nations. Among these surely are the social and political consequences of its revolution in the seventeenth century, its pioneering role in the industrial revolution, the continuing social and political roles played by its aristocracy, its steady extension of the concept of citizenship, and the evolving cultural roles of its several social classes. British and American colleges and universities were affected in part by characteristics of their internal life and structure—as in the ways they were chartered, or the forms of the academic profession and career that evolved on both sides of the Atlantic. But they were also shaped by characteristics of their societies and social structures, as for example in their contrasting patterns of access, or the different provisions they have made for engineering and other technical studies within the university.

Surely one unique aspect of American higher education has been the character of the 'policy' of the federal government towards higher education over the past 200 years. One might start with the early land grants, even before the Constitution was ratified, built into the Northwest Ordinance. But five other milestones over the past two centuries define a pattern of relationship between the federal government and our colleges and universities. First came the efforts made by George Washington and his immediate successors to establish a University of the United States, and the failure of those efforts. That precluded the emergence of a 'capstone' institution able to establish national norms and standards, and thus constrain the proliferation of colleges and universities. Second, the Supreme Court decision (1819) in the case of Dartmouth College, which confirmed the right of private

---

[39] Alexis de Tocqueville, *Democracy in America*, repr., ed. J. P. Mayer (New York: Harper and Row, [1835], 1966).

groups and bodies to establish colleges and to retain control of them
in the face of efforts by state and local governments to take them over
and operate them as public institutions. This ensured the survival of the
many small private colleges which have characterized American higher
education ever since.

Third, the Land Grant (Morrill) Acts of 1862 and 1891 which provided
federal money first to the states and then to the colleges themselves for
the creation of institutions and programmes devoted to a combination
of liberal studies and the agricultural and mechanical arts, and did so
with very few administrative controls or regulations. Fourth, the GI Bill
of Rights which provided free tuition and support for over two million
veterans to attend some form of post-secondary education after the
Second World War. The GI Bill triggered the rapid expansion of
enrolments in the post-war decades; it also became the model for later
forms of federal support for student aid—in particular, the legislation
passed in 1972 providing general student support for higher education
in the form of grants and loans to individual students which they could
take to any accredited institution, rather than grants to the institutions
themselves. And, fifth, the growth of federal support for science during
the Second World War, and the establishment of the National Science
Foundation and the National Institute of Health after the war,[40] with their
support taking the form largely of direct grants to individual scientists
through peer review organized by the federal funding agency.

I might have added to that list the Hatch Act of 1887 which funded
agricultural experiment stations in the land-grant colleges directly
rather than through the states, and the federal programmes after the
Second World War that provided colleges and universities with science
buildings, instruments, and aid to libraries. In each case, the decision
or policy contributed to the diversity of American higher education, a
diversity of character, mission, academic standard, and access. In each
case, public policy tended to strengthen the competitive market in
higher education by weakening any central authority that could substitute regulations and standards for competition. It accomplished this by
driving decisions downwards and outwards, by giving more resources
and discretion to the consumers of education and the institutions most
responsive to them. It increased the power of the states in relation to the
federal government, as in the defeat of the University of the United States
and the first Morrill Act; the power of the institutions in relation to state
governments, as in the Dartmouth College case and the Hatch Act; and

---

[40] The National Institutes of Health also support a good deal of in-house research.

the power of the students in relation to their own institutions, as in the GI Bill and the Higher Education Act of 1972.

By contrast with the pattern in the United States, where decisions at the centre have tended to strengthen the principle of competition between institutions and within various markets for students, support, and faculty, the English pattern has been a continued tendency to impose constraints from the centre, and more recently to strengthen the direct role of central government in a way that begins to resemble the *dirigisme* of Continental countries in respect to their systems of higher education. We can see this from the establishment of the Universities of Durham and London in the first third of the nineteenth century. In both cases, central government exercised a tight control over the granting of their charters and the conditions under which degrees could be awarded. We also see the role of central government in the Oxbridge reforms of the 1860s and 1970s, the introduction of civil service examinations and the effects of these on the university honours degree examinations, the establishment of the provincial universities, and their slow transformation and incorporation into a national system between 1880 and 1925.

The creation of the University Grants Committee in 1919 provided an instrument for mediating the role of central government in the life of the universities where the central element of control over their establishment and of the standard of first degree had already been put in place. The British pattern was also visible in the character of the Veterans' Act of 1944 and the marked differences between that legislation and its counterpart in the United States, the GI Bill.[41] Post-war expansion in Britain took the form of the establishment of colleges of advanced technology and their incorporation in the 1960s into the university system; the creation of new 'plate-glass' universities in cathedral towns, small by American standards and only marginally different from the older provincial 'red-brick' universities; and the establishment of the polytechnics in the 1960s as a 'public sector' side by side with the universities, though maintaining at least in principle the same standards for admission and the same high level for the first degree. All of this expansion was marked by (*a*) a tight control over growth, (*b*) a strong commitment to the maintenance of high and uniform academic standards for the first degree, and (*c*) the rhetorical encouragement, and actual discouragement, of diversity in the forms and content of British higher education. Since the middle 1970s, we have seen a pattern of budget cuts by central government, a steady increase

[41] Trow, 'Comparative Perspective'.

in the influence of central government on the decisions of the individual universities, and the decline and subsequent disappearance of the UGC as a buffer between central government and the universities.

But the differences between the British and American systems of higher education go deeper than the dramatic events in the United Kingdom of the last decade, and the quite different kinds of criticism directed at American colleges and universities, and especially at undergraduate education, in the last few years.[42] A broad comparative and historical perspective may help us better understand recent developments in both countries.

Trends and Countertrends: 'The Americanization' of European Higher Education?

The issue of American exceptionalism can be looked at in a number of different ways: the nature and extent of differences between America and other countries, institution by institution, or as societies; the sources of those differences in history, geography, demography, culture, and values, or whatever; and trends towards the convergence or divergence of America and other nations in specific or general respects. In this last section I will point to what I take to be trends in most European societies toward American-style forms and structures, which I see as inherent in their move towards mass higher education. But I do not assume that these trends will result in an absolute narrowing of the differences between American and European higher education over the next few decades, for several reasons, among these the strong resistance built into European countries and their educational systems to an expansion and differentiation of higher education on the American model, and the continuing evolution of mass higher education in the United States.

In any event, I close by pointing to three broad trends in European systems of higher education *towards* American patterns, which may (or may not) narrow the differences between our systems over the next few decades.

1. *Differentiation Among Universities*

The first is the tendency in all European countries towards the further differentiation of function among institutions of higher education, a

[42] Trow, 'Comparative Perspective'.

continuing differentiation between and sometimes within institutions that reflects the increasing heterogeneity of students in their social origins, their academic preparation and abilities, their ages, their experiences while in higher education, and their future careers. This increasing differentiation is a concomitant of the move from élite to mass forms of higher education, and the consequent growth, both in the number and variety of students and what they study.

This tendency towards diversity does not proceed without resistance in some countries, especially those in which the state has a monopoly, or near-monopoly, over higher education. Diversity causes problems for central state management. It is more difficult to administer different kinds of institutions, with different costs, functions, admission policies, standards of instruction, variety of courses, etc. Moreover, with diversity inevitably comes inequalities among institutions and sectors—in student achievement, staff/student ratios, status and prestige in the larger society—inequalities which are natural concomitants of the different activities and functions of the institutions and of the kinds of people they recruit, both as students and as teachers.

But while these inequalities are inherent in diversity, they are extremely awkward when the state has a monopoly over the higher educational system. Pubic authorities are embarrassed by inequalities among institutions which formally have equal status; governments tend to try to reduce those inequalities by applying common standards for entry and for degrees, common salary schedules for staff, common funding formulas, common formulas for support of research, building, and capital investment. These central efforts are in part a response to the tendency of bureaucracy to standardize its treatment of all dependent units, but also reflect norms in almost all societies which require that states treat institutions that are dependent on them equally and 'fairly'. These tendencies towards equality, which are inherent in the nature of public authority and bureaucratic management, run contrary to the inherent tendency of diversity to generate differences which can be perceived as inequalities.

It is possible for state authorities to plan for a certain measure of diversity within the state system—as in the maintenance of three or four distinct strata of institutions of higher education. Examples are the differences between universities, polytechnics, and institutions of further education in England; in France, the sharp differences between the *grandes écoles*, the universities, and the IUTs; and in California, the differences between the University of California (with

its nine   campuses), the California State University system (on nineteen campuses), and the 120 community colleges. In each case, this formal differentiation, and the legitimation of marked differences in treatment among the sectors, is a partial response to the pressures for diversity in a system of mass higher education. But, in each case, there are strong pressures for equality between institutions *within* the same sector and, in some European nations, other pressures to reduce the differences in character, mission, and level of support *between* different segments (as, for example, between the universities and the polytechnics in the United Kingdom).

There is another reason why state authority has difficulty encouraging the emergence of a truly wide diversity of institutions, and that is the political expectation that it make decisions—and correct decisions—in the face of alternatives. It is hard for political authorities to confess that they do not know which of a variety of forms of higher education ought to be the model for future development, or to say that all of them should be encouraged. The response of their political opponents is likely to be: 'It is your responsibility to decide which of these forms of development is best and to choose it; anything else is to waste resources when resources are scarce and when such waste is reprehensible or worse.' How can a government defend itself against the charge that it is so indecisive it cannot even decide what form and shape an emerging publicly supported system of higher education should take, and continues to support some forms which almost certainly will be shown to be ineffective and inadequate?

The problem of course is that, at the time these innovative institutions or programmes are launched, it is not at all clear *which* of them are likely to be successful. But, politically, this need to assert omniscience, and to show decisiveness and a mastery of events, is almost mandatory for public authorities who face opposition and criticism. That need to appear to be strong, wise, all-knowing, and decisive forces public authorities to act with more conviction than they must feel in the design of educational systems. Or, looked at another way, if they were to support a wide diversity of institutions on public funds, it could be charged that the government was consciously supporting institutions that would probably fail. That charge would be true, except that no one at the time could know which of them would in fact fail.

Americans accept, as on the whole Europeans do not, that competition in higher education, as in other areas of organized social life, is the most

effective way of planning for an unpredictable future, on the ground that, despite the appearance of waste, it creates a diversity of institutions some of which will be better fitted for future (as yet unpredictable) conditions and demands than any that can be designed by a central state authority. One illustration of what unrestrained market forces and competition in continuing education in the United States looks like is provided by Grand Rapids, Michigan, an industrial and market city of about 250,000 population, with about 400,000 in the broader metropolitan area. It is a leading centre in the United States for the manufacture of office furniture.[43] The city is served by a strong state-supported regional college, Grand Valley State College, which offers work through the master's (but not the doctoral) degree to some 9,000 students, mainly traditional-aged and studying full-time. This college has a beautiful campus a few miles outside of town and modest facilities in Grand Rapids itself, where it currently provides some continuing education in graduate study in social welfare, education, public administration, and business studies. However, also present in Grand Rapids and also offering continuing education in all kinds of subjects, mostly in rented space, are the following institutions:

1. Michigan State University—a branch of the big land-grant state research university;
2. Western Michigan University, a regional state university;
3. Ferris State College, a regional state college, like Grand Valley;
4. Aquinas College, a private Catholic institution;
5. Davenport College, a proprietary college offering a bachelor's degree in Business Studies;
6. Jordan College, a proprietary college;
7. Grand Rapids Community College, offering degree credit courses at the level of the first two years of the baccalaureate, plus many non-credit vocational studies;
8. Calvin College, a private church-related college;
9. Grand Rapids Bapitst College, a private church-related college; and
10. Kendall School of Design, a proprietary college.

One might think that that would be provision enough. But, no, Grand Valley State College has been given $30 million by the State

---

[43] Martin Trow, 'American Higher Education: Past, Present and Future,' *Educational Researcher*, 17/3 (1988), 13–23.

of Michigan to build a large building in Grand Rapids as a facility
for a major expansion of its provision of continuing education. The
college's engineering departments will be moving there, together with
the department specializing in the study of work environments, primarily
offering degree-level and postgraduate engineering ˙programmes
to adult employed learners. Moreover, there is little planning or
co-ordination among these providers.

So, in this representative American town, we see a nearly free
market for the provision of continuing education, some of it wholly
self-supporting, some of it partly subsidized. One might ask: Why this
fierce competition? The answer seems to be that for each institution,
more students mean more money, either from their fees, or through
enrolment-driven formula budgeting from the state, or from both. In
addition, continuing education is yet another service that engenders
support for the provider in the broader community. Thus the providers
are all highly motivated to recruit students, that is, to create a learning
society, and they are all highly sensitive to the consumers' interests.
Above all, behind all this lies the assumption that 'supply creates
demand'.

To many Europeans, this picture of continuing education in America
is marked by unnecessary diversity, lack of co-ordination or central
control over quality, inefficient duplication, waste, and the absence of
continuity. The standard American answer to all these criticisms is the
answer of the market: 'We cannot be inefficient and wasteful, or we
would not be able to survive.' Such an appeal to the 'unseen hand'
reduces the need to develop a more elaborate educational, political, or
philosophical rationale; if students continue to enrol and pay, then the
provision seems evidently needed and desirable. That story, it seems to
me, illustrates five characteristics of American higher education which
are not shared in most European countries, and which help explain the
peculiar form that continuing education takes in the United States:

1. The high measure of autonomy attached to our individual
   institutions, and their ability to go into the market without seeking
   approval elsewhere, in a ministry or a regional board.
2. The broad assumption in the United States, very widely shared,
   that education is intrinsically a good thing, and that everyone
   should get as much of it as they can be persuaded to enrol for.
3. The fact that there is no cap, no upper limit to the number of
   students who can be enrolled in the state's public institutions of

higher education. There are, of course, limits on entry to specific colleges or universities, but not to some institution in the system.

4. Most public institutions and systems are funded on a per capita basis, and thus have a continuing incentive to enrol as many students as possible.

5. A substantial part of continuing education in the United States (depending on how it is defined) is supported by student fees. That means that much continuing education in the United States is not felt to be competitive with other public goods like welfare, other levels of schooling, roads, health care, and the like, but rather with the students' own private consumption. Public policy issues ordinarily arise when some decision has to be made about the allocation of scarce public resources among competitive claims for different public services. In so far as continuing education is self-supporting, or is treated as if it were, it does not have to justify expansion.

European systems have refused to go down this road of uncontrolled market-driven competition. Nevertheless, the next decades of development in higher education in many countries will be marked by strong tensions between diversifying forces within institutions and between them, tensions arising out of the growing diversity of students and the explosion of knowledge on the one hand, and the constraining forces of public authority on the other. Of all the issues in higher education policy currently being debated in Europe, there is the broadest consensus on the importance of extending access to mature students, for reasons both of social justice and of technological advancement and economic growth. Nevertheless, the resistance to continuing eduction is strong, especially in the traditional universities and faculties, which see the education of mature part-time students as very clearly not a characteristic of élite education as it was known in the nineteenth and most of the twentieth century.

It may be that continuing education in Europe will take alternative forms which will show their relative merit in their capacity to respond effectively to fast-changing and unpredictable conditions in society and industry—introducing diversity through the back door, so to speak. But, meanwhile, American higher education will continue to change during these next decades, among other things incorporating more part-time continuing education into our traditional colleges and universities, while further blurring the lines

between university and society, life and learning, as more part-
time education for degree credit is offered by business firms and the
military.[44]

2. Co-ordination between Universities and
   Other Educational Institutions

The growth and democratization of higher education leads, among other
things, to the development of closer organizational ties between
universities and various non-university forms of post-secondary education. In every country, the latter take many different forms: higher
vocational colleges, teacher training institutions, schools of music,
art, drama, nursing, agriculture and fisheries, administration and
management, and other specified vocations; extension services and
other forms of continuing education; and open universities. In many
countries, these institutions have grown up in somewhat haphazard
ways over the years in response to the efforts of a special interest or a
powerful politician; sometimes they offer certificates, sometimes an
academic degree, though usually a different one than the universities
offer. The courses that they offer often overlap both with one another
and with courses offered in university. Often these institutions, at
least those in the public sector, are under the supervision of different
ministries, sometimes with each government ministry having its own
training institution. But rarely do these institutions provide access to the
university sector; they are not, as we say, well articulated.

Governments may make efforts to rationalize this sector of post-
secondary education—at least the public institutions in it—by bringing
them into regional groupings and other administrative relationships,
as in Sweden. But again, the special interests which created these
institutions, and the ministries which sponsor them, will resist this
rationalization, usually successfully. I have noted that these institutions rarely provide access directly to the universities. That may
change. One well-documented finding of recent studies in many
countries is that people who want to continue their education as adults
are more likely to be those who already have had a lot of it.[45] Wanting

[44] N. P. Eurich, *Corporate Classrooms: The Learning Business* (Princeton, NJ: Carnegie
Foundation for the Advancement of Teaching, 1985). Stephen Kemp Bailey, *Academic
Quality Control* (Washington: American Academic Association for Higher Education,
1979).

[45] Organization for Economic Co-operation and Development, *Learning Opportunities
for Adults, General Report*, i (Paris: OECD, 1977).

more education is an acquired taste, acquired through education itself. If that is so, then the graduates of many of these non-university colleges and institutes will increasingly want to continue their higher education, and will seek higher academic degrees and the advanced study that the university offers. These opportunities exist now in most places for exceptional individuals. I anticipate that, as this demand grows, it may be made easier for mature students to 'transfer' to the university and be enabled to earn the university degree.

The increase in the number of mature students in the university—we can already see this trend in many places—will have effects of various kinds on university education itself: on the curriculum, on modes of instruction, on student financial support, on the relations between student and teacher. Resistance to this trend from the universities lies in the traditional link between élite forms of higher education and the education of young men (and more recently women) usually from upper or upper-middle class origins, at a time when their minds and characters are being shaped and formed. Mature students are often of lower social origins (and hence less likely to have gone to university directly from secondary school); they seek to increase their skills rather than to undergo character formation; they may not be interested in the university's notion of what constitutes appropriate higher education; and they tend to make a university look increasingly like a technical or polytechnical institute, with the loss of status that implies. Nevertheless, I believe that the movement of mature students, many with prior experience in non-university forms of higher education, into the university will continue, and that universities everywhere will change and adapt to this trend. Here again, private institutions (where they exist) will have the advantage of their greater adaptability to change.

3. *Reorganization within Universities*

Another trend in many European countries is towards stronger university presidents, whatever they may be called in different countries and institutions. This trend arises out of the tendency towards diversity that I have already spoken of, and also out of the rapidly changing environments in which higher educational institutions will find themselves. To turn to the last point first: where the characteristics and mission of 'the university' is clear in the society, and where all of the universities in the society are similar, except for their age and distinction, then state authorities can manage them from outside the institution in a fairly routine and predictable way. The intellectual life of the institution goes on with a certain measure of continuity, while the civil servants in the ministries manage the relatively simple administrative and financial affairs of the institution from outside. In another setting where institutions have relatively clear and stable functions, they can be governed from inside by committees of academics, as in Oxford and Cambridge, or by committees of chairholders and full professors with a weak elected rector, as in many European universities in the past. Both of those arrangements depend on slowly changing external conditions and a broad consensual agreement on what the mission of the institution is.

But as institutions of higher education become more varied in character, and as their relation to their environments changes rapidly, they have to be more responsive to new situations. And this requires the kind of decisiveness and discretionary power at the centre that we find in effective business organizations, which also have to act quickly and decisively in response to changing market and financial conditions. A strong chief institutional officer, I suggest, is the only authority who can point an institution of higher education in a new direction, who can seize opportunities when they arise and give an institution the˙leadership along various dimensions—academic, political, managerial, symbolic—that it needs for success in the competitive academic world that is emerging.[46]

I do not underestimate the very strong cultural and institutional resistance to this tendency in European systems. Neither state authorities nor the powerful academic guilds look with kindness on strong administrative officers at the head of their institutions, nor do the strong academic, staff, and student unions that have emerged as actors in the governance structures of many European institutions over the past few decades. So I am far from suggesting that the strong university president will be common outside the United States very soon, especially in the public sectors of European higher education. But we can see it already in many countries outside of Europe, especially in the private sector, where institutions have the freedom to create their own governance arrangements.[47] And I think it is one of the organizational characteristics that will give private institutions a marginal advantage over public institutions in the decades ahead. Private universities not only are able

---

[46] Martin Trow, 'Comparative Reflections on Leadership in Higher Education', *European Journal of Education*, 20/2–3 (1985), 143–59.

[47] Geiger, *Private Sectors*.

to create a strong executive at their head, but they *need* a strong executive in order to survive in a world that may not give them the guarantees and subsidies that it does to public institutions.[48] In so far as governments give publicly supported colleges and universities more autonomy and more responsibility for their own support and functions, they must also give more power and discretion to college and university presidents.

Conclusion

In this chapter I have been exploring some of the differences between American higher education and the forms it takes in other modern societies. I have also touched on some of the historical sources of our 'exceptionalism', in the course of which I have suggested some of the ways in which the peculiar characteristics of American society and government gave rise to and sustained its unique system of higher education. But a third aspect of this topic has been almost wholly neglected: the impact of American higher education on American society and on American democracy. For example, much research supports the assertion that higher education has substantial and enduring effects on the attitudes of those exposed to it.[49] Those changed attitudes in a population in turn make possible real changes in social relations, if and when they are accompanied by changes in law and institutional behaviour.

For example, in the United States, the years after the Second World War saw a steady decline in hostility toward black Americans and a growing readiness on the part of whites to give blacks equal treatment and fair access to education, housing, and jobs. These changes in attitudes were strongly correlated with exposure to higher education. I believe that the considerable progress the United States made in race relations after the Second World War was made possible by the growth of mass higher education, and the marked decline in racial prejudice that accompanied it. If that is true, then it represents a very great contribution of American higher education to the life of the society. And the 'affirmative action' policies of American colleges and univer-

[48] Though most 'private' universities on the Continent, e.g. church-related universities in Belgium and the Netherlands, are fully funded by the state, and resemble the public institutions in their governance arrangements.

[49] H. H. Hyman and C. R. Wright, *Education's Lasting Influence on Values* (Chicago: University of Chicago Press, 1979). K. A. Feldman and T. M. Newcomb, *The Impact of College on Students*, ii (San Francisco: Jossey–Bass, 1969).

sities may have helped to create and expand a black middle class, policies that could not have been pursued in a society with high national standards for university access.

But this is merely one illustrative example of the effects of American higher education on American society. An institution now so broadly and deeply implicated in so many aspects of American life must have effects on it of many kinds—political, economic, and cultural, both for good and for ill. It may be that it is those connections between higher education and the institutions of American society that are of greatest relevance to this theme of 'American exceptionalism'.

7

Is American Public Policy Exceptional?

Richard Rose

Because public policy links the activities of government with the problems of society, there are grounds on both counts for expecting America to be exceptional. Its government was founded by a constitutional compact unique in the world at that time, and American government today remains very different from the parliamentary system normal to most advanced industrial nations. The 'new' nation was a novel mixture of immigrants from different parts of Europe and of African slaves too; contemporary Latin and Asian immigration adds to the very distinctive ethnic mixture of American society.

Yet most of the problems that American government addresses are common to all modern societies. All modern governments are concerned with maintaining law and order and national security, mobilizing economic resources, and ensuring social welfare. The American economy is no different from other advanced industrial nations in that a lot of money must be spent in providing for health, education, and security in old age, and individuals and corporations are expected to pay a substantial amount of money in tax in order to finance such publicly provided collective goods as defence and public order.

There are great differences in the social sciences in the extent to which nations are expected to be exceptional. Economists, political scientists, and sociologists tend to assume that there are general or universal laws and processes that apply across national boundaries. Moreover, concerns with money, class, power, and influence are stated in terms of universalistic concepts rather than as referring to the American dollar, socio-economic status in the United States, or influence in Washington. American social scientists, when focusing exclusively upon the United States, often assume that conclusions relevant throughout the modern world can be drawn from a study of specifically American phenomena. For example, Lewis-Beck and Rice state in their analysis of government growth in America: 'We see no reason why this model of government growth, although developed out of the United States experience, would not be applicable in its essentials to other advanced capitalist democracies'.[1]

In Europe, social scientists similarly think in universalistic terms— but Europe rather than the United States is the matrix of experience. A Eurocentric view provides a universe of more than fifteen nations for comparative analysis. The number of units is smaller than the fifty American states but the potential variance is far greater. While Europeans read American books avidly, European social scientists usually exclude analysis of the United States from their field of research. The systematic comparative work of such scholars as Stein Rokkan and Peter Flora is explicitly limited to Western Europe since 1815.[2] In addition to excluding the United States, it also excludes such Mediterranean late-comers to democracy as Spain, Portugal, and Greece, along with the non-European democratic nations of Canada, New Zealand, Australia, and Japan. Eurocentric scholars treat their models, whether Marxist, philosophical or legalistic, as the norm for advanced industrial societies, and invite Americans to analyse the New World in terms devised for understanding the evolution of a mixed-economy welfare state from predemocratic and feudal origins.

Historians typically treat every country as exceptional, each being assumed to have a unique government and society. America is not the only society to invent a myth of uniqueness as part of a struggle for national independence. The founding fathers of other nations, such as Padraig Pearse in Ireland and Kwame Nkrumah in Ghana, have argued that all would be transformed by the achievement of national independence, which was viewed as not only desirable in itself but also a means to larger social ends. Yet, if every country is exceptional, there are no general rules. Many theorists of world politics have argued the opposite: they argue that the governments of nominally sovereign states are in fact subject to internationally pervasive influences, such as the logic of industrialism or pressures of world markets.

Ireland provides an instructive example of an OECD nation that has simultaneously asserted its uniqueness in revolt against England yet also demonstrated that even a fiercely and distinctively independent

[1] Michael Lewis-Beck and Tom W. Rice, 'Government Growth in the United States', *Journal of Politics*, 47 (Feb. 1985), 25. However, Rice does not try to confirm this hypothesis in 'The Determinants of Western European Government Growth:1950–1980'. *Comparative Political Studies*, 19 (July 1986), 233–58.

[2] Five volumes have been published from the HIWED (Historical Indicators of the Western European Democracies) project, which is based at the University of Mannheim.

government can have many things in common with other countries.[3] If actions of the British Parliament are taken as the norm, then Ireland is exceptional in policies on war and peace, the economy, and social welfare. But being different from one other country does not make it unique by comparison with every other country. In foreign policy Ireland has often resembled neutralist nations such as Switzerland and Sweden; in other social matters it has sometimes resembled peasant and Catholic Southern European nations; and in yet other fields, the United States. Just because a country differs from another nation with which it may be compared, it does not follow that it differs from all other nations. The evident differences in social policies between America and Sweden may reflect Swedish exceptionalism rather than American uniqueness.

In order to decide whether, under what circumstances, and to what extent America is exceptional, we must first have ground rules for defining public policies. Secondly, we need to examine empirical evidence comparing America with other OECD nations in major fields of public policy. A third section considers the dynamics of public policy: is America growing more or less like the OECD norm? The study concludes that America is not an exception to a norm of the mixed-economy welfare state; advanced industrial nations now divide into two contrasting groups. Because America is a rich nation with a not-so-big government it is actually *more representative* of the majority of people in advanced industrial societies today.

I. Defining Public Policy

Public policy is a term that can be used in a variety of ways within political science, and usages differ even more between modern nations.[4] It is here defined in terms of the programmes by which government has an impact upon society, such as defence, agriculture, health care, transportation, etc. Programmes are authorized by laws, funded by budget appropriations, carried out by public employees of government agencies, and recipients often have a statutory entitlement to benefits.[5] Public policies are more concrete than the shifting intentions of politicians, and they account for a substantial proportion of society's total resources.

[3] Richard Rose and Tom Garvin, 'The Public Policy Effects of Independence: Ireland as a Test Case', *European Journal of Political Research*, 11 (Dec. 1983), 377–97.

[4] See Arnold J. Heidenheimer, 'Comparative Public Policy at the Crossroads'. *Journal of Public Policy*, 5 (Nov. 1985), 441–66.

[5] See Richard Rose, *Understanding Big Government: The Programme Approach* (London and Beverly Hills: Sage Publications, 1984).

An historical analysis of the development of public programmes in modern states from the mid-nineteenth century onwards reveals a high degree of consistency in the stages of growth in public policy.[6] First came the creation of central departments to look after the defining, *sine qua non*, activities of government: defence, foreign affairs, finance, and justice. All four departments were in George Washington's first Cabinet as well as in the contemporary French regime of Napoleon Bonaparte; they were also found in the Roman empire. The United States is normal in having these priorities, for they are by definition the concern of every modern state.

Twentieth-century government has grown as programmes have extended beyond the minimum requirements of a nightwatchman state. Programmes to mobilize economic resources came second in the process: the post office, telephones, and telegraph; the construction of highways, canals, and railways; the encouragement of agriculture, commerce, and labour. These responsibilities were recognized by Bismarck and by Asquith, and in the Cabinets of American presidents since the time of Theodore Roosevelt.

Social welfare programmes are most recent yet largest in their claims upon public resources. Education, social security, and health care often have origins antedating the First World War, but their significance has grown greatly since 1945, as additional programmes have been introduced and established programmes expanded. The United States appears a relative late-comer in the introduction of social security and welfare services, but since the New Deal, and even more since President Johnson's war on poverty, social programmes have been a major political concern, and source of controversy.

Because social welfare programmes are prominent in contemporary public policy, they rightly receive much attention. But it is doubly misleading to reduce the study of public policy to what is called the welfare state. Social welfare is not the original or sole concern of the state. Defence, the maintenance of public order, and the payment of debt interest have been historically prior. Half of total government spending is normally devoted to non-social welfare programmes. Reducing welfare to state-provided services also has the effect of ruling out non-state sources of welfare.

---

[6] See Richard Rose, 'On the Priorities of Government'. *European Journal of Political Research*, 4 (Sept. 1976), 247–89.

Differences of Degree or Kind?

Analyses of public policy invariably focus attention upon quantities: the amount of money spent on education or agricultural subsidies; the number of people employed in health care or education; the number of people receiving social security benefits or living in public housing. By definition, quantitative comparisons involve differences of degree. As long as all countries can be ranked on a common scale, for example, from biggest-spending to lowest-spending on health care, then no country is unique; countries differ only in the extent of expenditure.

Ranking countries in terms of 'league tables' of spending is misleading if it is interpreted to imply a unilinear development in which all nations are striving to spend more and more, until they reach the top level of spending. Many studies of social welfare programmes commit this mistake. Comparisons of nations in terms of public expenditure on health care, education, or social security assume that more is better. A government that spends less than average or less than its national product would permit is classified as 'backward' or a 'welfare laggard'; this is often the way the United States is characterized. Comparisons of public spending on defence, which show the United States as ranking very high, can similarly be used to chastise European countries for being free riders in a military alliance in which the United States bears a disproportionate amount of the total defence expenditure.

Quantitative comparisons can be misleading when qualitative concerns are omitted. Comparisons of programme expenditure in East European and OECD nations may show many similarities on such indicators of public effort as spending on education as a percentage of the national product. But that does not mean that the forms and terms of education are the same in a Soviet-style system as in a liberal regime. When T. H. Marshall wrote about the evolution of citizenship a generation ago, he rightly started with the priceless criteria of civil rights and political rights; these were the political demands that gradually turned more or less authoritarian regimes into democracies. Social welfare benefits are important in a pecuniary sense, but civil and political rights are literally priceless, because they are secured by laws, not money.[7]

In comparing public policies it is not easy to decide when differences of degree are substantial enough to constitute differences in kind. The

[7] Thomas H. Marshall, *Citizenship and Social Class* (Cambridge: Cambridge University Press, 1950). For a contemporary restatement relevant to the environment, see Stephen Kelman, *What Price Incentives?* (Boston: Auburn House, 1981).

following sections provide tables that give precise measures of the difference between the United States and other OECD nations. Readers can thus judge the author's interpretation of when differences in degree become differences in kind. In so far as the United States is converging towards other countries, then any difference should be less today than yesterday, and differences should gradually disappear in the years ahead. But in so far as America is exceptional, then the degree of exceptionalism should be large and constant, or even increasing.

Alternative Hypotheses

At a high level of abstraction, theories can treat all nations as if they similarly approximated an ideal-type political system. Theories of advanced industrial societies emphasize commonalities, whether empirical or assumed, for example, class structure, or rational egoism as the motive for action. Public policies can be deduced from the axioms and assumptions of a theory, and all countries are then treated as if approximating the theory. Even if differences are noted, these theories of convergence hypothesize that countries can be expected to become increasingly like each other. Theories developed by American social scientists usually assume that this will happen through the world becoming more like America; Eurocentric theories assume convergence will lead Americans to adopt European welfare-state policies. Whether Americanization or socialization of public policy is assumed to be the wave of the future, the end result would be homogeneity not exceptionalism.

Historians usually have an implicit theory of uniqueness: the important characteristic of a society is that it is *American* public policy, or English rather than German history. A decision about the development of social security in the United States is likely to emphasize only national influences rather than ask why what happened in America occurred later than in Europe, and with less commitment.[8] There is no doubt that the origins of American government are unique in time and place. Moreover, institutions and policies can be carried forward with the force of political inertia; for example, government departments and Acts of Congress normally remain in place until repealed, and the failure of a European-style socialist party to arise early in the century in the United States has had long-lasting consequences.

Many theories of American exceptionalism are incomplete. While

[8] For an exception, see Theda Skocpol, 'A Society without a "State"? Political Organization, Social Conflict, and Welfare Provision in the United States', *Journal of Public Policy*, 7 (Oct.–Dec.1987), 349–71.

there is an assumption that America is different, little attention is given to the question: different from what? Paradoxically, American exceptionalism assumes that advanced industrial societies are like each other—for example, that they conform to an ideal-type model of a European welfare state. Thus homogeneity is assumed in Wagner's law, that public expenditure will rise with an increase in a country's gross national product.[9] Almost all nations from Portugal to Sweden can be placed somewhere along an upward-sloping regression line, according to the level of their national product per capita. The higher the national product, the greater the share claimed for public expenditure. The United States is then expected to deviate from the pattern common to most advanced industrial nations, being a wealthy nation that does not have a government claiming a large proportion of the national product to finance welfare state measures.

But what if Wagner's law does not hold, and there is no relation between the size of a country's national product and public expenditure? If advanced industrial nations differ substantially from each other, then the United States cannot be exceptional. In such circumstances, it would differ from some advanced industrial societies but be similar to others. This possibility has been given little attention. Americanists have assumed that other governments share many positive characteristics as well as the negative attribute of not being American. In a complementary fashion, Eurocentric analyses have not considered that some European countries may have more in common with the United States than with other European countries. Nor has either group come to terms with the emergence of non-American and non-European advanced industrial societies, of which Japan is the most prominent example.

II. America: A Rich Nation with a Not-So-Big Government

To test whether American public policy is exceptional, we must compare public expenditure in the United States with what is done in other advanced industrial nations, here defined as the twenty-one OECD nations. All have had free elections since the end of the Second World War, except for Greece, Spain, and Portugal, which have been democracies for at least the past decade.[10]

[9] For a good discussion of Wagner's law and related concepts, see Daniel Tarschys, 'The Growth of Public Expenditures: Nine Modes of Explanation', *Scandinavian Political Studies Yearbook* (Oslo: Universitetsforlaget No. 9, 1975), 9–31.

[10] Turkey is omitted because it has a different political history and is not yet industrialized,

Richard Rose

TABLE 7.1. *National product per capita in OECD countries 1988*

	Current		PPP adjusted	
	(US $)	%OECD mean	(US $)	%OECD mean
USA	18,338	126	18,338	149
Canada	16,019	110	17,216	140
Norway	19,756	136	15,405	125
Switzerland	25,848	177	15,838	120
Sweden	18,876	130	13,771	112
Denmark	19,730	135	13,241	108
Germany	18,280	125	13,323	108
Japan	19,437	133	13,181	107
France	15,818	109	12,803	104
Finland	17,151	125	12,838	104
Australia	11,919	82	12,612	102
United Kingdom	11,765	81	12,340	100
Netherlands	14,530	100	12,252	100
Italy	13,224	91	12,254	100
Belgium	14,071	97	11,802	96
Austria	15,470	106	11,664	95
New Zealand	10,620	73	10,680	87
Spain	7,449	51	8,681	71
Ireland	8,297	57	7,541	61
Greece	4,719	32	6,363	52
Portugal	3,761	26	6,297	51
Average	14,575		12,306	

Source: OECD in Figures (1989), 22–3

Income per Head: America First

By comparison with the median country in the United Nations, all advanced industrial societies are wealthy. This is particularly true of democratic societies, for OECD countries tend to have a more even distribution of income than oil sheikdoms, where any figure about GDP per capita will be distorted by the concentration of wealth and power in a small number of hands. Among OECD nations, the gross domestic product per capita was $14,575 in current dollars in 1988, and $12,306 after adjusting for purchasing power parity (PPP). In an era of volatile exchange rates, any cross-national comparison that relies upon

and Iceland and Luxembourg are excluded for lack of data and because they are mini-countries.

nominal money values is sensitive to fluctuations in the value of the dollar *vis-à-vis* twenty other currencies. Because we are concerned with the value of public benefits, the most appropriate control is purchasing power parity, an OECD measure that takes account of cross-national differences between the cost of living and exchange rates. The overall effect of doing this is to reduce substantially the difference between the top and bottom nations; this is reasonable, for a given sum of money will buy more in Greece or Portugal than in Tokyo or Stockholm.[11]

American society has the highest per capita income among advanced industrial nations, with a 1988 national product of $18,338 per person, 49 per cent above the OECD average. The value of American GDP is well above that of free enterprise Switzerland, and of social democratic Sweden. Even if one does not correct for differences in purchasing power, the United States ranked sixth among twenty-one nations in per capita GDP, as reckoned by the exchange rates then in use.

Public Effort in Aggregate: America both Low and High

The conventional measure of *public effort* is the proportion of the national product that government claims for public expenditure. The emphasis is upon the effort that a government makes rather than upon the money sums involved. To maintain a variety of welfare-state services for citizens, government must make much more effort than in a society where the state takes less responsibility for welfare. Whatever the level of wealth in a nation, government in a social democratic country will make a greater effort to control the national product than in a country where private enterprise is valued more highly. Total national expenditure is not the result of decisions taken by a single level of government. Washington does not decide that public spending at all levels of government in the United States should comprise *x* per cent of the national product. Because total public expenditure reflects the sum total of decisions taken by many agencies at all levels of government, it is thus a reasonable reflection of the society's support for collective public action, rather than individual choice in the market place.

Government in the United States makes much less effort than almost anywhere else in the OECD world. (Government is here defined as all levels of government: thus, the evidence for the United States includes

[11] See Derek Blades and David Roberts, 'A Note on the New OECD Benchmark Purchasing Power Parities for 1985', *OECD Economic Studies*, 9 (Autumn 1987), 184–97. As a cross-check, the calculations in this study were also run with current money values. This changes the position of countries, but the overall conclusions remain unaffected.

state and local as well as federal expenditure.[12] In the average advanced industrial society, public expenditure claimed 43.4 per cent of the national product in 1988; American government spent only 35.3 per cent. Public effort in the United States is thus 19 percentage points below the OECD mean. Only two other countries—Japan and Switzerland—make less effort to mobilize national resources for public policy (see Table 7.2.).

T ABLE 7.2. *Public expenditure as percentage of GDP and in per capita $*

	% GDP	% OECD mean	Per capita expenditure PPP $	% OECD mean
USA	35.3	81	6,473	121
Canada	42.8	99	7,368	138
Norway	48.1	111	7,410	139
Switzerland	30.1	69	4,767	89
Sweden	60.0	138	8,262	155
Denmark	55.7	128	7,375	138
Germany	43.2	99	5,755	108
Japan	27.2	63	3,585	66
France	48.4	112	6,197	116
Finland	38.2	88	4,904	92
Australia	35.0	81	4,414	83
United Kingdom	42.9	99	5,293	99
Netherlands	54.0	124	6,616	124
Italy	45.2	104	5,538	104
Belgium	50.6	117	5,972	112
Austria	47.3	109	5,517	104
New Zealand	41.9	97	4,475	84
Spain	36.1	83	3,134	59
Ireland	50.4	116	3,801	71
Greece	43.0	99	2,736	51
Portugal	37.6	87	2,368	44
Average	43.4		5,331	

Source: OECD In Figures (1989), 22–3.

Evidence of public employment similarly emphasizes that America has a not-so-big government. Public employment averages 30.5 per cent of the work force in Britain, France, Germany, Italy and Sweden.

[12] Strictly speaking, one should refer to governments in America, for there are tens of thousands of separate government organizations. The figures reported here concern *all* levels of government in federal as well as unitary systems.

However, in the United States it is two-fifths less, 18.3 per cent. American public employment is so much lower because there are few nationalized industries and there is no national health service.[13]

The level of *public benefits*, that is, public expenditure per capita, is a function of a nation's wealth as well as of its effort. A Third-World dictatorship might claim the totality of the national product, but if its country is poor, public benefits would remain small. In a reciprocal fashion, even though government in a rich country makes limited effort to mobilize resources, its national product can yield higher public benefits than a poor country can afford. We must therefore look at the absolute value of public expenditure as well as at relative effort.

Whereas the United States ranks nearly at the bottom in public effort, it ranks in the top third in terms of the cash value of its public expenditure (Table 7.2). In 1988, governments at all levels in the United States spent $6,473 per person; this was more than one-fifth above the OECD average. The value of public expenditure per American was thus above that of governments with a long history of social welfare pro- grammes, such as Germany and Britain. The value of public benefits in America is several times greater than in Mediterranean countries where democratic parties of the left are strong. For example, Spain, Greece, and Portugal make a greater public effort than the United States, but because their per capita national product is so much lower, the United States spends more than twice as much per person on public benefits.

Programme Outputs

While comparisons of public expenditure in aggregate are familiar, they can be misleading because they are aggregates combining spending on different types of programmes. Yet ordinary people are not so much interested in spending by the billions, for such totals are outside ordinary experience. People are concerned about spending upon the   particular programmes that benefit themselves and their families, such as education, health, and social security.[14] Nor are Congres- sional committees and executive branch agencies so much interested in aggregate totals as in spending on the particular programmes for which they are responsible.

[13] See Richard Rose, *Public Employment in Western Nations* (Cambridge: Cambridge University Press, 1985).
[14] Richard Rose, 'The Programme Approach to the Growth of Government'. *British Journal of Political Science*, 15 (Jan. 1985), 1–28, and Richard Rose, *Ordinary People in Public Policy* (Newbury Park, Calif., and London: Sage Publications, 1989), ch. 1.

The extent of public activity in society is, to a significant extent, the by-product of decisions about spending on particular programmes of many agencies and levels of government. Six different programmes are examined here. Two concern classic functions of government, defence and debt interest. Four social programmes affect virtually the whole population: health, education, pensions, and other social services. Altogether, these programmes account for more than three-quarters of public expenditure in the average OECD nation. Many measures that catch the headlines, such as subsidies for farmers or industry, or measures to regulate pollution or deregulate the economy, account for only a small proportion of total public effort.

The shape of public expenditure is defined by the profile produced by the way that a government allocates money between social programmes and such collective concerns as defence. By this standard, the shape as well as the size of American public policy is exceptional, for spending priorities are very different from the average OECD nation (Table 7.3). The share of America's national product devoted to defence is more than twice the average. If spending on domestic programmes in the United States were as much above the OECD average as is spending on defence, then total public expenditure would be an astronomical 95 per cent of America's gross domestic product!

TABLE 7.3. *Programme effort of American government compared to OECD average*

Programme	As % GDP			Per capita	
	USA	OECD mean	USA as % mean	USA $	As % OECD mean
Defence	6.5	3.0	217	1,192	323
Education	5.3	5.2	102	971	152
Debt interest	4.6	5.1	90	844	134
Pensions	7.2	8.8	82	1,320	122
Health	4.5	5.6	80	825	120
Other social	1.2	5.1	24	220	35
All other programmes	6.0	10.6	57	1,100	84

Sources: All social programmes: *OECD in Figures* (1989), 16-17; data normally for 1986. Debt interest: OECD, *Economic Outlook*, 36 (1984), Table 5. Defence: *SIPRI Yearbook 1986* (New York: Oxford University Press, 1986) Table 11A.5, normally for 1984.

On most major domestic programmes, American government makes less effort than the average OECD nation. It is 76 per cent below the OECD mean in spending on other social programmes, such as unemployment compensation and sickness and maternity benefits that are part of the comprehensive coverage of European welfare systems. In the absence of a national health service, public effort for health is one-fifth below the OECD mean, and for pensions it is more than one-sixth below the mean. Only public education, which has historically been valued more highly in the United States than Europe, has a level of public spending a little above average. As of the mid-1980s, debt payment as a proportion of the national product was below the mean, but its size is growing.

When attention is shifted to the money spent on benefits per citizen, a very different picture emerges (Table 7.3). Because the value of America's national product is high, government can make less effort yet spend more money. It spends substantially more money than the OECD average on the three main social welfare programmes: education, pensions, and health care. The health figure is particularly striking. By the conventional measure of public effort—spending as a proportion of the national product—British spending on health care is one-sixth greater than in America. But because the United States has a much higher income per head, the value of American public spending on health is more than one-quarter greater than in Britain. Dollars spent on debt interest and defence are also much above the OECD average.

When we ask what the scale of public policy is in America, the answer is: it depends. In terms of the conventional measure of effort, public expenditure as a percentage of the national product, American government is relatively small. When priorities among programmes are examined, American exceptionalism is emphasized, for by contrast with welfare-oriented European governments, the United States concentrates more effort on defence than on pensions and health. But if we examine how much money American government spends on its citizens, then the United States is well above average. Because the national product is well above average, even though American government makes less effort, it can still spend more on its citizens.

The wealth of American society makes it inevitable that public policy is in some sense exceptional. If public effort were the same as the average OECD nation, then the dollar value of benefits per citizen would be exceptionally high—49 per cent above the average. If the value of programme benefits were kept to the average for OECD nations, this would require a spending cut of $1,145 per person; government would need only claim 29 per cent of America's national product to match the

purchasing power value of public expenditure in the average advanced
industrial nation today.

III. The Direction of Change

The fact that government in America shows less public effort than
governments in other countries says nothing about the important dynamic question: in what direction is American government changing
relative to other nations? If we only look at change within the United
States, it is inevitable that government will appear bigger than in the
days of Calvin Coolidge or Dwight D. Eisenhower, if only as a function
of the growth of the national economy. Those in favour of an expansion
of welfare-state programmes could interpret this as evidence that America
was beginning to 'catch up', that is, moving closer to the OECD average.
But if American government grows more slowly than in other OECD
nations, then it could simultaneously be growing in relation to its own
past yet falling behind in relation to the performance of other countries.
Theories of convergence hypothesize that American government should
be growing faster than the OECD average, whereas theories of American
exceptionalism imply that it should be growing more slowly, and thus
diverging from the mean.

Social science theories normally predict that government size will
increase with wealth. Therefore, public effort should be rising. Such
events as the War on Poverty and the rising cost of Medicare, Medicaid,
and social security are often interpreted within the United States as
evidence of American government becoming more like the normal
mixed-economy welfare state. An alternative possibility is that other
OECD nations have become more 'Americanized', that is, that the
growth in wealth in economies from Japan to Europe would increasingly
be devoted to mass consumption. In so far as the growth of mixed
economy welfare states creates a reaction against high levels of taxation,
forcing government to put the brakes on spending, this would make it
easier for America to catch up in terms of public effort.

Changes Absolute and Relative

The starting point for comparing America with other countries that are
now considered advanced industrial nations is 1950. At that time, most
European countries were still recovering from the ravages of war; limited

industry and national product was sufficient for an austere rather than affluent standard of living. The United States was then truly exceptional; its gross domestic product was 263 per cent of the OECD mean. Public expenditure as a share of the national product was below the mean; the United States spent less than one-fifth of its GDP through the public sector. But because of America's wealth, per capita public spending was more than double the international average (Table 7.4).

TABLE 7.4. *Relative changes in American public policy, 1950–1988*

	1950	1960	1970	1980	1988	Change 1950–88
GDP per capita (US $*)						
USA	1,886	2,843	4,922	11,804	18,338	+16,452
OECD mean	716	1,214	2,531	10,092	12,306	+11,592
USA as %						
OECD mean	263	213	183	117	149	−114
Public expenditure as % GDP						
USA	19.9	25.0	28.1	32.4	35.3	+15.4
OECD mean	21.4	23.6	29.1	39.4	43.4	+22.0
USA as %						
OECD mean	89	103	96	82	81	−8
Public expenditure per capita (US $*)						
USA	377	722	1,457	3,824	6,473	+6,098
OECD mean	162	303	765	4,098	5,328	+5,166
USA as %						
OECD mean	233	238	190	93	121	−112

* Current dollars and exchange rates, 1950–1980. A satisfactory Purchasing Power Parity rate, developed since, is used to control for volatile exchange rates in 1988.

Source: As in Table 7.1 and *National Accounts of OECD Countries, 1950–68* (Paris, 1970), 10, 50, 54. For New Zealand and Australia, IMF, *International Financial Statistics* (appropriate years).

In 1960, when John F. Kennedy was elected president, American public expenditure as a percentage of GDP was slightly above the OECD average. In part, this reflected domestic influences: America had had a slow growth economy in the 1950s, social benefits introduced in the 1930s were beginning to mature, and the baby boom boosted spending on education. At the end of the Eisenhower administration, American public spending had risen to one-quarter of the national product, above the OECD mean, for other nations had given priority to the growth of private affluence in the 1950s.

The 1960s was an exceptional time in the United States for two reasons. There was a very great mobilization of public resources to fight the Vietnam War. In addition, the 1960s was the decade of the War on Poverty, which introduced special programmes to benefit the disadvantaged, and took a major step towards a national health system in Medicare and Medicaid. Following from Peacock and Wiseman's theory of the displacement effects of war-time taxing and spending patterns to social expenditures after a war is over,[15] social spending should have boomed in consequence, for programmes distributing popular (and costly) social benefits to tens of millions of people were in place by 1970. America's long-term domestic War on Poverty and its temporary Asian war could have resulted in steps to close the gap in public effort between the United States and other OECD nations.

Although public effort increased in the United States during the 1960s, it increased even more in European welfare states. The typical European nation devoted this decade to expanding social programmes for the mass of the population. Such broadly based programmes have a far greater potential for long-term growth and broad-based popularity than have American poverty programmes providing 'welfare' for a limited fraction of the population. As of 1970, American public effort had risen slightly in absolute terms but fallen below the average of OECD nations, where public effort showed a sharper rise.

When world recession, inflation, and oil crisis hit the international economy in the 1970s, most countries maintained a high level of public spending. By 1980, public effort in the average OECD nation was more than one-third higher than it had been a decade earlier. In the United States, however, public spending rose at less than half the average rate; public effort fell from average for advanced industrial nations to 23 per cent below average by 1977. It has remained one-fifth below the OECD average ever since. Concurrently, foreign exchange markets were destabilized, accelerating a reduction in the gap between American national product per capita and that of other advanced industrial nations. As of 1980 the national product of the United States was one-sixth above the OECD average and public effort was one-sixth below average, resulting in the current money values of public benefits temporarily falling below average (Table 7.4).

The Reagan presidency appears very different in an international perspective than when viewed solely in a domestic light. During this

---

[15] Alan Peacock and Jack Wiseman, *The Growth of Public Expenditure in the United Kingdom* (Princeton: Princeton University Press, 1961).

eight-year period, the rate of growth of the American economy was above the OECD average. Thus, after controlling for purchasing power parity, the per capita value of the national product was substantially higher in the United States in 1988 than in 1980. The claim of all levels of American government on the national product increased too. From 1980 to 1988, total public spending grew by as much as in the 'go-go' decade of the 1960s. The fact that this increase was due to changes at the state and local level is a reminder that, in a federal system, cuts at one level can be offset by increased expenditure at another level.

When we examine the particular programmes that account for relative changes in American public spending, the starting year must be 1960, the first year in which comparable data becomes available for nearly all OECD countries. The relatively high level of American public expenditure then was principally due to defence, which accounted for 8.9 per cent of the national product, compared to 3.6 per cent as the OECD average. Spending on social programmes was nearly one-fifth below the OECD mean.

In the past quarter-century American programme priorities have diverged from the OECD average. Except for education, all domestic programmes are now below average in public effort. Total spending effort on social programmes in the average OECD nation is now more than one-third greater than that of the United States, and the gap has widened in the Reagan years. While American effort on defence has fallen since the height of the Cold War in 1960, it is still more than double that of the average OECD nation, and during the Reagan years public effort on defence rose in comparison to other nations.

In absolute terms, American government has grown greatly since 1950, due to the growth in the national product, the population explosion, and inflation. In terms of public effort, growth has been very substantial too; public expenditure has increased its claim on a much enlarged national product by more than three-quarters in the past thirty-eight years. From an introverted perspective, in which American government is treated as the only government in the world, this appears to be a very substantial growth. But when viewed comparatively, it is not.

Decline into Normalcy?

In 1950, America was exceptionally wealthy and public effort was not much below that of a European society that had yet to mobilize the political or the economic resources to become committed to big-

spending welfare-state measures. American per capita income was
more than double the OECD average, and so was the value of public
expenditure per person.

Since 1950, the American political economy has declined into normalcy. America's gross national product per capita ranks first, after
adjustment is made for purchasing power parity, but the difference
between the United States and countries from Sweden and Germany to
Japan and Australia is a difference in degree, not kind. All OECD
countries now enjoy standards of living undreamt of in 1950. It is now
normal to be affluent—and in that sense, America is normal.[16]

The benefits provided by American government are momentarily
normal too. Whereas public spending per head was more than double
the OECD mean in 1950, today it is only one-fifth above the mean. The
economic boom in America in the 1980s has buoyed up public spending,
albeit financed by borrowing as well as by tax revenue from the fiscal
dividend of economic growth. Simultaneously, public effort has fallen
relative to the OECD average—and relative to the position in the world
at the end of President Eisenhower's second term of office.

Numerical normalcy is not the same as political normalcy. The
expansion of social programmes in most OECD nations has been
accompanied by a growing commitment to the values of what can
variously be described as the social democratic, the social market, or the
Christian social state. Whatever label is used, the common attribute is
a widespread belief that the state ought to make collective provision for
the social wellbeing of all the citizens, and do so to a standard satisfying
middle-class users as well as those with a below-average income.

By contrast, the growth of American public programmes was financed
by a process that Hugh Heclo has characterized as 'policy without
pain'.[17] Growth was painless as long as the economy expanded at a fast
enough rate for take-home pay to rise and government to receive a fiscal
dividend that financed increased spending on public policies. By comparison
with major European nations, the front-end load of American government—that is, the amount of economic growth required to fund the

[16] American critics argue, however, that the greater degree of inequality in income
distribution in the United States makes relative (though not necessarily absolute) deprivation
greater in the United States. This depends upon the measure used; see Michael O' Higgins,
Guenther Schmaus, and Geoffrey Stephenson, 'Income Distribution and Redistribution:
A Microdata Analysis for Seven Countries', *Review of Income and Wealth*, 35 (June 1989),
107–31.

[17] Hugh Heclo, 'Toward a New Welfare State?', In Peter Flora and Arnold J. Heidenheimer, eds., *The Development of Welfare States in Europe and America* (New Brunswick,
NJ: Transaction, 1981), 397.

average annual growth in public spending—has been below the annual rate of growth in the American economy, and far below that of 'overloaded' European economies such as Sweden.[18] Yet even though public spending and taxation were growing more slowly in America than in most countries, a tax backlash occurred in the United States—and no tax backlash has occurred in Sweden, where public spending tops the league table of OECD nations.[19]

While many European nations have retained a high level of commitment to social programmes in the 1980s, President Reagan attacked the idea that government ought to make collective provision for the wellbeing of ordinary Americans. Even though American public expenditure was below average by comparative standards, President Reagan portrayed it as far too high. Even though the 1981 Tax Act produced a massive reduction in federal taxing capacity, George Bush was elected President by campaigning with a pledge of 'No tax increases'. Whereas government in America appears to be relatively small by Europeans standards, Americans tend to perceive it as too big. This implies that America is abnormal—and that it ought to change in the future.

IV. No Exceptions Because No General Rule

America is different from the average OECD nation—but it could be argued that Spain, Switzerland, Sweden, and Japan are atypical too. American public policy can only be characterized as exceptional if other nations have lots in common. To conclude that America is exceptional, we only need to find what Wagner's law would lead us to expect, namely, that other countries with a relatively high level of GDP per capita also make a big public effort, spending a larger portion of their economic resources on public policy than countries below average in GDP per

---

[18] The 'front-end load' of government (that is, the amount of economic growth required to fund the average rate of growth in public spending) has consistently been much lower in the United States than in major European countries. See table 2.6 in Richard Rose and Terence Karran, 'Inertia or Incrementalism? A Long-Term View of the Growth of Government', in Alexander J. Groth and Larry L. Wade, eds., *Comparative Resource Allocation* (Beverly Hills: Sage Publications, 1984).

[19] Cf. Axel Hadenius, 'Citizens Strike a Balance: Discontent with Taxes, Content with Spending', *Journal of Public Policy*, 5 (Aug 1985), 349–65, and Advisory Commission on Intergovernmental Relations, *Changing Public Attitudes on Government and Taxes 1983* (Washington DC: ACIR S-12, 1983), 17, 34.

capita. Whether this is so can be tested by plotting on a graph the relationship between public effort and GDP, and calculating a least squares regression line that shows the relationship between these two characteristics. If most countries are·near the line and the United States is a deviant outlier then America is truly exceptional in public policy. But if there is no relationship between the two characteristics, then countries will be scattered all over the graph.

In fact, there is no significant relation between per capita GDP and public effort; the correlation between the two is actually slightly negative (—.07). Among advanced industrial societies, a country's wealth explains less than one per cent of the variance in public expenditure. In so far as any tendency can be said to exist, it is for public effort to decline slightly as the national product increases; that is the meaning of the downward slope of the line in Fig. 7.1. For every instance of a rich nation with a government making a big effort, such as Sweden or Denmark, a counter-example can be found, such as the United States or Switzerland. Equally striking, there are a substantial number of countries, such as Ireland and Italy, which have big governments but are not rich (Fig. 7.1).

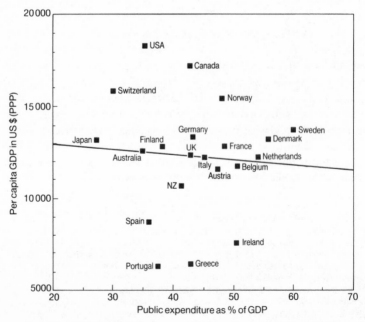

Fig. 7.1. Nil relation between national product and public spending

In the absence of a central tendency, it is impossible for America to be exceptional. Four types of political economies can be identified, according to the relationship between public expenditure as a proportion of the national product, and the per capita value of the national product (Table 7.5). Countries equal to or greater than the OECD median for each attribute are relatively rich or making a relatively big effort in public policy; those economies below the median are classified as not so rich or not showing so much public effort.[20]

As a rich nation spending not so much money on public programmes, *America is unexceptional*; five other nations are similar: Canada, Switzerland, Japan, Finland, and Australia (Table 7.5). Each has the money to provide a high level of public benefits: the mean national product per capita of these nations is actually 9 per cent higher than in big-spending welfare states. However, their governments have chosen *not* to levy taxes claiming a large proportion of the national product. Public expenditure averages 34.8 per cent of the national product in this group of nations, one-third less than the average in rich countries with big governments.

Conventional studies of the level of public spending tend to ignore rich countries that do not make a big effort. In the case of Japan, distance and cultural differences explain much of the historic neglect. Australia is distant like Japan, but Canada borders the United States and parts of Canada have strong cultural affinities with Europe. Switzerland may be ignored because it is small, and Finland is both small and the most Eastern of Nordic countries. Whatever reasons may be given for ignoring one particular country, no serious scientific study of the political economies of advanced industrial nations can justifiably ignore six countries with 428,000,000 people, accounting for more than half the population and nearly two-thirds of the total gross product of OECD nations! Ignoring similarities between America and other non-European developed countries is too high a price to pay for saving the hypothesis of American exceptionalism. Equally, to ignore differences among European countries is too high a price to pay to maintain the assumption that Europe consists of a homogeneous set of welfare states.

---

[20] Since there are 21 nations, the median nation, ranked 11th, falls on the dividing line. For GDP per capita adjusted for PPP (Table 7.1) it is Australia. Australia is assigned to the category of rich nations with not-so-big governments, since its government is well below average in size. The median nation for public effort is Greece. It is assigned to the category of no-so-rich countries with not-so-big governments, which also includes Spain and Portugal. Altering the dividing lines between the four categories would marginally change the size of groups but it would not alter the substantive conclusions presented here.

TABLE 7.5. *Political economies by wealth and size of government*

	Per capita GDP	Public Expenditure		Total Population (millions)	GDP ($ billions)
		% GDP	per cap $		
Rich, not-so-big government					
USA	18,338	35.3	6,473	243	4,805
Canada	17,216	42.8	7,368	25	440
Switzerland	15,838	30.1	4,767	7	105
Japan	13,181	27.2	3,585	122	1,608
Finland	12,838	38.2	4,904	5	63
Australia	12,612	35.0	4,414	16	202
Mean (total)	15,003	34.8	5,252	(428)	(7,223)
(% OECD nations)				(55%)	(64%)
Rich, big government					
Norway	15,405	48.1	7,410	4	65
Sweden	13,771	60.0	8,262	8	116
Germany	13,323	43.2	5,755	61	815
Denmark	13,241	55.7	7,375	5	67
France	12,803	48.4	6,197	56	712
Mean (total)	13,708	51.1	7,000	(134)	(1,765)
(% OECD nations)				(17%)	(16%)
Not-so-rich, big government					
Netherlands	12,252	54.0	6,616	15	179
Italy	12,254	45.2	5,538	57	702
Belgium	11,802	50.6	5,972	10	116
Austria	11,664	47.3	5,517	7	88
Ireland	7,541	50.4	3,801	3	26
Mean (total)	11,102	49.5	5,489	92	1,111
(% OECD nations)				(12%)	(10%)
Not-so-rich, not-so-big government					
United Kingdom	12,340	42.9	5,293	57	704
New Zealand	10,680	41.9	4,475	3	35
Spain	8,681	36.1	3,134	38	337
Greece	6,363	43.0	2,736	10	64
Portugal	6,297	37.6	2,368	10	64
Mean (total)	8,872	40.3	3,601	118	1,204
(% OECD nations)				(15%)	(11%)

The rejection of Wagner's law relating public expenditure to national product is reinforced by the size of the second deviant group, not-so-rich countries with high levels of public policy: the Netherlands, Belgium, Italy, Austria, and Ireland. Altogether they account for one-eighth of the population of OECD nations and a tenth of its GDP. These governments on average spend 49.5 per cent of the national product, two-fifths more than rich countries with not-so-big governments. But the per capita GDP of these big-spending welfare states is a quarter less than that of rich nations with not-so-big governments. In order to match the level of public spending per capita achieved in rich societies with not-so-big governments, these countries must levy taxes at a rate that claims almost half the national product. Given so high a level of taxes, it would be much easier for these countries to increase public expenditure through higher rates of economic growth than by increasing their already high level of public effort.

Many studies of contemporary political economies tend to regard European welfare states as normal in a statistical sense, as well as normatively desirable. However, intellectual hegemony should not be mistaken for political hegemony. Rich societies with big governments characterize only three Scandinavian nations plus France and Germany. The fact that Scandinavian societies can pay high taxes and receive a high level of public benefits and also enjoy a high per capita national product demonstrates that it is possible to combine a welfare state and economic prosperity. But the fact that these countries account for only one-sixth of the population in the OECD world, and one-sixth of its gross domestic product, shows that it is not a typical experience. While one can treat a Scandinavian country such as Sweden as the prototype of the social-democratic mixed-economy welfare state, it is not empirically justifiable to treat it as a leader that other countries are bound to follow. That would only be justified if there were a good fit between the level of a nation's national product and public effort; Fig. 7.1 shows there is none.

Five not-so-rich societies with not-so-big governments are the United Kingdom, New Zealand, Spain, Portugal, and Greece. The inclusion of Britain in this group is a reminder that it is possible for a Northern European country to move away from the ideal of a prosperous welfare state. In the 1970s, Britain took the first step as its economy grew so slowly that it fell below the OECD median in terms of wealth. Under Margaret Thatcher, the British government has taken the second step: slamming the brakes on the growth of public expenditure so that it is now below average in public effort too. Nor is this strategy unique to the Thatcher government; it has also been followed by a

Labour government in New Zealand, and a Socialist government in Spain. Together, the group of not-so-rich countries with not-so-big governments is larger than the group that are not-so-rich and have big governments, and is comparable in size with rich countries with big governments.

Together, the two theoretically deviant groups—rich nations with not-so-big governments and not-so-rich nations with big governments— account for 70 per cent of the population of the OECD world, and three-quarters of its total national product. If one were to infer a theory from this evidence, it would be at least as reasonable to hypothesize that as countries grow richer, they tend to allocate more of their income through the private sector rather than the public sector. In any event, Table 7.5 and Fig. 7.1 clearly reject the assumption of Wagner's law, that as national income rises, so too does public expenditure as a percentage of the national product.[21]

Accounting for Different Ways

Given the absence of any correlation between a country's standard of living and the public effort of government, a Scandinavian-style welfare state could just as easily be treated as deviant as could the United States. Analytically, the need is to identify those variables that can explain why some rich countries spend much more money through the state than do other rich countries. The Scandinavian model of the mixed-economy welfare state depends upon two important conditions: trust in the state and social solidarity. In the absence of a civic sense of trust or social solidarity, it is much less likely that a government will mobilize a high proportion of the national product in taxation to finance a high level of social benefits.

A welfare state depends upon citizens trusting the state. America has a weak sense of state;[22] the idea of the state is alien to a society founded on a rejection of European authoritarian values. Only if the state is trusted to be caring and effective does it make sense for people to put their welfare in the hands of officials armed with the power of law and the

[21] See e.g. Peter Saunders, 'Public Expenditure and Economic Performance in OECD Countries', *Journal of Public Policy*, 5 (Jan.–Mar. 1985), 1–22.

[22] See J. P. Nettl, 'The State as a Conceptual Variable', *World Politics*, 20 (July 1968), 559–92, and William Leuchtenberg, 'The Pertinence of Political History: Reflections on the Significance of the State in America', *Journal of American History*, 73 (Dec. 1986), 585–600.

resources of the fisc. Trust in public officials varies across cultures. Officials appear more fully trusted in Northern Europe than in Southern Europe. In the United States, the urban centres that might in theory mobilize working-class pressures for publicly provided welfare services are perceived as having municipal governments that are dishonest, uncaring, and ineffective. These same characteristics can also be applied to urban union locals serving the political and economic interests of officials and small numbers of members, unlike European unions that have more often been national institutions promoting collective welfare through governmental action.

Americans love their country but distrust their government. The negative image of government in America is in striking contrast with the very high level of positive pride that citizens have in America as an abstract patriotic concept. Patriotism is reflected in the very high level of public effort made on defence, just as a distrust of public services is reflected in the low level of public effort for health care. People who will fight and die for the flag may not want to be made well in a public hospital or treated by a doctor on the public payroll.[23]

Secondly, citizenship must be a social bond as well as a legal status. The universalistic European ideal of the welfare state sees society as a collective body, integrating every individual. Just as members of a family are expected to care for each other, so society is expected to make collective provision for education, health care, and income security through institutions of government.[24] Citizenship is thus a sufficient condition to qualify for public benefits. By contrast, in America, entitlement depends upon market criteria: you get what you pay for—and what you do not pay for, you cannot expect to get. While American social welfare services may not discriminate on the basis of race or sex, they can and do discriminate on the basis of income. Access to non-public services is normally determined by payment of a fee (e.g. a private school) or by membership in a non-governmental collectivity (e.g. a Blue Cross health group). Gatekeepers controlling access are often private authorities rather than elected governments.

Scandinavian high-taxing and high-spending welfare states are very homogeneous, with many face-to-face, small-scale relationships en-

[23] See Richard Rose, 'Pride in Nation', ch. 2 in Rose, *Ordinary People in Public Policy*.
[24] See e.g. Erik Allardt. 'The Civic Conception of the Welfare State in Scandinavia', in Richard Rose and Rei Shiratori, eds., *The Welfare State East and West* (New York: Oxford University Press, 1986), 107–25. Compare the contribution in the same volume by Nathan Glazer, 'Welfare and "Welfare" in America', pp. 40–63.

couraging solidarity and trust. It is arguable whether there is a solidary society in America, that is, a social system with which the great majority identifies and which encompasses blacks and whites; Asians and Latinos; Catholics, Protestants, Jews, and born-again Christians; Southerners, Northerners, Westerners, and Easterners; inner-city dwellers, suburbanites, small-town dwellers, and farmers. While each of these groups is recognizable as part of the American mosaic, each piece of the mosaic is visibly separate from others. The sum of the social segments into which Americans group themselves is not a society but an aggregate.

Social segmentation is important because many not-for-profit institutions have their origins in religious or ethnic groups that are basic reference groups with which individual Americans identify.[25] This is true of hospitals with a religious foundation. It is also true of small and inadequate denominational colleges as well as of universities such as Harvard, Yale, and Princeton. Health care funded by Blue Cross and Blue Shield is principally based upon associations at work. Primary identification with a segment of society has created a vast network of not-for-profit institutions that can provide major social services without being public agencies. Receipt of federal funds and federal regulation does not make their employees civil servants, nor does control change with each election, as would be the case of a public agency. It is characteristic of America that these institutions have *not* become public agencies, as has happened in Europe.

Reliance upon a combination of market and not-for-profit institutions in addition to public agencies can provide a high level of welfare for the average American. But it leaves a problem of access for citizens who lack the income or economic status necessary to secure benefits. The poverty problem in America is not just an economic problem or a social problem. A third critical dimension is political: there is no identification between the minority who are poor and the majority who are not. Only in war do Americans mobilize for collective action as an inclusive society joining rich and poor. In peacetime the typical form of mobilization is as an exclusive communal group. Individuals can receive collectively provided benefits by virtue of their status as employees of a large corporation, the residents of a one-class suburb, or members

---

[25] For an interpretation, see Gary Klass, 'Explaining America and the Welfare State', *British Journal of Political Science*, 15 (Oct. 1985), 427–50. For an historical background concentrating upon the lack of social solidarity in early Protestant New England, see Peter Dobkin Hall, *The Organization of American Culture, 1700–1900* (New York: New York University Press, 1984).

of a denominational church. Residents of a Standard Metropolitan Statistical Area define themselves by what is excluded from their community—as much as or even more than by what it includes.

V. A Future Prospect: Divergence Not Convergence

The important dynamic question is: in what direction is public policy heading? It is reasonable to assume that all advanced industrial societies want to become richer. But it is not empirically valid to assume that as societies grow richer, their governments must necessarily increase spending on public policies. Even though convergence has often been assumed, political economies have actually been moving apart. In 1950, the standard deviation around the mean of public expenditure as a percentage of GDP was 3.6 per cent; in 1960, 5.5 per cent; in 1970, 6.8 per cent; and by 1988, it was 8.4 per cent. The rise in the standard deviation in public effort is evidence of an increasing divergence in public effort.

Growing Apart

In 1960, a case could have been made for developments conforming to Wagner's law.[26] The correlation between GDP per capita and public expenditure as a proportion of GDP was positive, albeit not significant ($r=.21$; $r^2=4$ per cent). More importantly, twelve political economies with 75 per cent of the population of the OECD world then fitted the categories specified by Wagner's law, six being rich countries spending a relatively high proportion of their national product on public programmes, and six being not-so-rich countries without a high level of public effort. At that time, the United States was not exceptional; the only rich nations with relatively low-spending governments were Switzerland and Australia, with 3 per cent of OECD population. In 1960, the United States was representative of six rich countries spending a relatively large amount on public policies.[27]

Convergence was not an unreasonable expectation in the circumstances of three decades ago. The logic of industrialism and post-industrial society was expected to lead to greater political as well

[26] The war-ravaged state of Europe in 1950 makes 1960 a much more appropriate date as the base point for examining dynamic patterns.

[27] The six rich nations with big governments in 1960 were: the United States, Canada, Sweden, France, Britain, and New Zealand (mean per capita GDP: $1,871; public

as economic similarities.[28] In 1960, the United States and Sweden were both relatively rich with relatively big governments; theories of convergence postulated that such governments would continue to expand public effort to support the growth of the welfare state. In the Kennedy–Johnson years, America was not only a military leader but also taking positive governmental action to improve social conditions. Convergence also implied that the seven not-so-rich countries with big governments as of 1960 (Belgium, the Netherlands, Germany, Austria, Ireland, Italy, and Norway) would tend to enjoy faster rates of economic growth, as their relatively high levels of public spending yielded dividends as an investment in human capital formation.

In the quarter-century since, divergence has been the predominant characteristic of political economies. The distance between the OECD country with the highest and lowest level of public expenditure has increased from 16 per cent in 1950 (from Spain to Britain) to 33 per cent in 1988 (Japan to Sweden). The weak correlation between wealth and public spending has actually turned slightly negative (Fig. 7.1). The number of political economies that conform to the pattern predicted by Wagner's law has declined; their proportion of the population of the OECD world has fallen dramatically, from 75 per cent of the total to 32 per cent; the total size of their national product has declined dramatically too.

A high level of government spending on public policies is neither a necessary nor a permanent condition of a rich society. The United States since 1960 has demonstrated that it is possible for a nation above-average in spending to put the brakes on the growth of government. This does not mean securing an absolute reduction in public spending or cutting the proportion of the national product devoted to public expenditure. Putting on the brakes means slowing down the rate of growth of public policies. Concurrently, Japan has shown that a relatively poor agricultural society can become a wealthy nation without providing the social programmes that characterize a Scandinavian-style welfare state.

expenditure as a % of GDP, 27.9%). The six not-so-rich nations with not-so-big governments were: Spain, Portugal, Greece, Japan, Finland, and Denmark (mean per capita GDP: $662; public expenditure, 17.2%). The average GDP per capita for the two rich countries with not so big governments was $2,594, and public expenditure, 18.0% of GDP.

[28] See e.g. Daniel Bell, *The Future of Post-Industrial Society* (New York: Basic Books, 1973), and Clark Kerr, *The Future of Industrial Societies* (Cambridge, Mass.: Harvard University Press, 1983).

Common Wants but Different Means

Social scientists assume that people in all modern societies have a more or less common set of wants: health, security of income, education for themselves and their children, good housing, a buoyant economy, national security, and public order. All of these conditions are the product of social institutions, such as schools, hospitals, savings funds, and social service workers. But national security and public order are the only services that must be provided by the state. Other services can be and, to a greater or lesser extent, are available from non-state as well as public sector agencies.

If we regard people as concerned with their own and their family's welfare, then total welfare in society (TWS) reflects the sum of welfare goods and sevices produced by the state (S), market (M), charity (or in America, not-for-profit: NFP), and non-monetized household production (H). Rather than welfare being produced solely by the state or the market, there is a welfare mix.

$$TWS = S + M + NFP + H$$

While there is a welfare mix in every society, the contribution of the state and other institutions is variable cross-nationally, and can change across time. By shifting focus from the public sector to the national accounts of a society, which register the production of all goods and services that involve the payment of money, we can identify the extent to which non-government institutions substitute for or add to public spending by not-so-big governments.[29]

As soon as we consider the production of welfare in the whole of society, we realize that public policies are not the sole source of individual and family welfare. In advanced industrial societies, food and clothing are produced and allocated in the market. Transportation, affecting where a person can live or work, has been greatly expanded by the spread of automobile ownership, and this advance has been accompanied by a decline in public transport. Housing receives some public support, but it remains primarily a market activity and housing maintenance is a paradigmatic example of a non-monetized, do-it-yourself product. Personal social services are provided by members

[29] For a detailed exposition of the analytic framework invoked here, see Richard Rose, 'Common Goals but Different Roles: The State's Contribution to the Welfare Mix', in Rose and Rei Shiratori, eds., *The Welfare State East and West*, and for applications, see Rose, *Ordinary People in Public Policy*. Both these studies provide some data for non-monetized welfare production, which support the conclusions reported above.

of a household caring for each other; when this is not possible, they can be provided by friends and neighbours, not-for-profit institutions, or the market, instead of (or as well as) by a bureaucratic state. Private savings coexist with public savings for pensions in old age, and to a greater or lesser extent so does private health care and education. While many sources of welfare do not turn up in public expenditure statements, they are empirically observable, and most are registered in national income accounts, or in census data. Moreover, in societies such as the United States, where the state is not an object of trust, government can encourage non-state institutions to make substantial provision for social services.[30]

When we think in terms of society, we can understand how Americans secure their welfare in a rich society that gives a low priority to public policy. Most Americans are ready and able to use non-state agencies to provide for their social needs. Health care provides a striking example. In 1986, public expenditure on health care, as a proportion of GDP, was one-fifth below the mean for advanced industrial societies. That figure is often cited as evidence of American neglect of welfare. Yet if we think in money terms, American government with less effort spent 20 per cent more than average on health care, because the government of a wealthy nation can spend more money while simultaneously making less public effort (Table 7.6).

Examining total spending on health by all types of social institutions—government, profit-making, and not-for-profit—points to a very different conclusion than does an analysis concerned only with public spending. The average OECD society spends 7.3 per cent of its national product on health; public expenditure thus accounts for three-quarters of total spending on health in society. The United States is different: private expenditure on health care by individuals and their employers, insurance companies, and not-for-profit hospitals is greater than public expenditure. In consequence, the United States spends 10.9 per cent of its national product on health; this is nearly half again more than the average country, and one-fifth more than Sweden, which ranks second in total health spending among OECD societies.

When we look at how much money is spent per capita by all institutions in society, then the United States is exceptionally high in the priority given to health expenditure. A total of $1,999 was spent on

[30] See e.g. Lester Salamon, 'Government and the Voluntary Sector in an Era of Retrenchment', *Journal of Public Policy*, 6 (Jan–Mar. 1986), 1–20; Sheila Kamerman and Alfred Kahn, eds., *Privatization and the Welfare State* (Princeton: Princeton University Press, 1989).

TABLE 7.6. *Expenditure on health in society: America in perspective*

	USA	OECD	USA as % OECD mean
Public effort			
As % GDP	4.5	5.6	80
US $	825	689	120
Private sector health spending			
As % GDP	6.4	1.7	376
US $	1,174	209	561
Total health expenditure			
As % GDP	10.9	7.3	149
US $	1,999	898	223

Source: OECD in Figures (Paris: OECD, 1989), 16–17, and Table 7.1 above.

the care of the average American in 1988, more than double the amount in the average OECD nation. The British national health service, often held up to America as an example to emulate, makes a greater public effort to spend money on health care; 5.3 per cent of British GDP is spent on health. But a consequence of the British emphasis upon public funding for health care is that it is subject to the cash limits that affect many forms of public spending, and private expenditure is discouraged. Thus social effort on health care in Britain (that is, public plus private spending) is only 6.1 per cent of GDP, scarcely half that of the United States; in cash terms, it is only three-eighths what American society spends on health care.

Health care is extreme but not atypical of the different ways in which rich countries can allocate their wealth as between the public and the private sector. The United States also has an abnormally high proportion of students in private schools at all levels of education, from primary schools through colleges and universities. This explains its relatively low ranking in public effort on education. Employer-financed fringe benefits are likewise important in providing income security.[31]

Japan provides spectacular confirmation that there is nothing unique in American reliance upon non-state sources of welfare. In 1952, the first year for which OECD statistics are available for Japan, the country was still poor; its GDP per capita was less than one-tenth that of the United States and less than one-quarter the OECD average. When Japan was poor, public effort was 14.6 per cent of the national product, 40 per cent

[31] Cf. Martin Rein and Lee Rainwater, eds., *Public/Private Interplay in Social Protection: A Comparative Study* (Armonk, NY: M. E. Sharpe, 1986).

below the OECD average. The Japanese economy has grown enormously since then, surpassing the OECD average by 1981, and continuing to expand relative to other advanced industrial societies. But the Japanese government has not tried to catch up with the spending levels of European welfare states.

By international standards, Japan is today a rich society with a high level of social wellbeing. Education and life expectancy are well above average for OECD nations, and social security provided by the employer and family, instead of (or as well as) the state, is also high. Bonds of social solidarity are strongest in the family and other face-to-face groups in Japan; there is good reason for individuals to distrust the state. Public provision for social welfare is thus low; government in Japan spends only 16.0 per cent of its national product on social programmes, less than the United States and one-third below the OECD average. As the national product has increased, the Japanese make increasingly generous provision for themselves independently of government. For example, pupil–teacher ratios are high in secondary education but many parents compensate by paying for additional private tuition for their children. The Japanese mix of non-state and state expenditure on welfare in society is much closer to that of the United States than to Scandinavian welfare states.[32]

Two Alternatives: American Pacific and Scandinavian Models

Eurocentric studies of contemporary public policy have tended not only to assume that America was exceptional but also criticized it for being different from the Scandinavian model of welfare through the state. The foregoing shows that this conventional picture is only half-true. The Scandinavian model of a high-tax, high-public-effort, state-centred system of social welfare exists and is flourishing in Northern Europe, but it is a minority taste, characterizing only a small fraction of the OECD world. In a strictly statistical sense, it would be more appropriate to describe this group of nations as deviating from the average, for it serves only one-sixth of the population of the OECD world.

Concurrently, there has been a silent revolution: an increasing divergence between the Scandinavian model and what can be called an 'American Pacific' model of welfare in society, of which America and Japan are the prime but not the sole examples. This group of nations also

[32] See e.g. contributions to Rose and Shiratori, *The Welfare State East and West*, and Richard Rose, 'Welfare: The Lesson from Japan', *New Society*, 28 June 1985.

includes Australia, with a population equivalent to that of the three Scandinavian welfare states, and Canada, with a population equal to Belgium and the Netherlands. Whether population or national product is the criterion, rich countries with not-so-big governments are the dominant group in OECD nations today—and they have been growing in size and significance since 1960.

Political and social theorists disagree about whether the Scandinavian or the American Pacific model is more desirable. In so far as the two groups of nations are not only far apart but have been growing further apart still, the debate is of no practical significance. However, for not-so-rich countries that have yet to experience the problems of great affluence, the debate is significant—for they still have the opportunity of choice. Moreover, the choices that they make will influence the relative importance of American Pacific as against Scandinavian models of welfare in advanced industrial societies at the beginning of the twenty-first century.

As affluence increases, not-so-rich industrial nations can choose between devoting more of their rising standard of living to private or public provision of social benefits. The choice is particularly critical for nations that currently have a per capita income below $10,000 a year, but can expect their standard of living to rise above this in the foreseeable future. Mediterranean countries best represent this group.[33] Given the recent history of authoritarian rule in Spain, Portugal, and Greece, citizens there cannot identify individual welfare with state action in the way that civic solidarity underpins Scandinavian welfare states. Nor are fiscal standards and bureaucratic levels of efficiency in Mediterranean nations likely to encourage trust in fair, rational, and effective public action, another important condition of public policy provision on the scale of Scandinavia.

Among the group of American Pacific nations, the United States is too rich and remote to be an appropriate model for the industrializing nations of the Pacific Basin. Japan is the proximate model; it has grown rapidly from a poor, agrarian base. The Japanese consciously reject

---

[33] Italy also has a Mediterranean political system and per capita GDP below the average for OECD nations. The logic of analysis here predicts that it would use increased growth to reduce the proportion of the national product claimed for public expenditure, not only by social services but also by the *parastatale* and by the *parassiti*, a goal of 'clean government' parties of the left. If the economies of other not-so-rich nations, such as the Netherlands, Belgium, and Austria continue to grow and public effort remains above average too, they will progress toward the Scandinavian model—but altogether their population is less than that of Spain. Britain and New Zealand are less easy to predict, having had big governments in the past but not-so-big governments at present.

state-centred reliance upon welfare, relying upon the market, the family, and self-investment in human capital formation (that is, individual effort). A semi-official report, *Japan in the Year 2000*, has noted: 'Now that the social troubles of the West European-type welfare society are becoming clear, a society of the Western type can no longer be a model for Japan'.[34] This statement can also apply to Taiwan, Korea, and Singapore, which have yet to evolve Western-style democratic institutions; distrust of the state is even more appropriate in the precarious circumstances of Hong Kong.

The collapse of pressure from the Soviet Union gives Eastern European nations an opportunity to think of alternative models too. COME-CON nations have demonstrated that it is possible to have a welfare state without free elections or free markets. Circumstances differ greatly from one Eastern European nation to the other, but they share a common starting-point: an extraordinarily high level of dependence upon the state for social welfare. Thus the state's role as a source of welfare can hardly increase, and there is resulting scope for liberalization in polity and economy, perhaps leading to a reduced role for the state in the political economies of Eastern Europe.

As we approach the year 2000, there is less and less reason to regard the United States as exceptional in public policy.[35] This is not because the United States is catching up with Scandinavia, but for the opposite reason: it is diverging from the Northern European model. In doing so, America shows much in common with other countries that are distant from Europe, starting with Japan. The well-publicized instances of Japan-bashing in the United States may reflect antagonism, but even more they show an awareness of growing interdependence between the two societies.[36]

Among the nations of the Atlantic community, the United States is exceptional in being the only country that also has a major Pacific presence. The shift in population from frostbelt to sunbelt in the United States has, among other things, brought America closer to Japan. California is more than the biggest state in the Union; it is also a pre-

[34] Quoted in Staffan Linder, *The Pacific Century* (Stanford: Stanford University Press, 1986), 126.

[35] The chief qualification concerns America's military prominence, and its hegemonic power in the international system. On this score too, America is losing its claim to unique dominance. See e.g. Robert Gilpin, *The Political Economy of International Relations* (Princeton: Princeton University Press, 1987), and Richard Rose, *The Postmodern President: the White House Meets the World* (Chatham, NJ: Chatham House, 1991).

[36] For a wide-ranging review of the evidence, see Kent Calder, 'The Emerging Politics of the Trans-Pacific Economy', *World Policy Journal*, 2 (1985), 593–623.

mier *Pacific* state, not only in relation to New York and Detroit but even in relation to sovereign trans-Pacific countries. About one-fifth of American society is of non-European origin, and the current pattern of immigration from Latin America and Asia is increasing this share. There is thus a diminishing proportion of Americans of European ethnic background. As the twenty-first century approaches, the American political economy appears exceptional by European standards, but normal by the standards of more and more people in advanced industrial societies.

8

What is the American Way?
Four Themes in Search of Their
Next Incarnation

Byron E. Shafer

What is the American model? What has happened to this model during, specifically, the last thirty years? What is, finally and in that light, the apparent fate of 'American exceptionalism'? The essays in this volume have pursued these questions through a focus on major sectors of American life. In this pursuit, four grand aspects of the larger society—government, the economy, religion, and culture—have been singled out for special treatment. So has the applied realm which is perhaps most commonly offered in our time as practical evidence for a continuing exceptionalism—namely, education—and so has the wider realm of public policy, which emerges out of all the preceding. Such an approach to the three questions opening this chapter is, most fundamentally, an attempt to give these questions a concrete and pointed reality, by embedding them in a precise and specifiable (an empirical) social context.

At the same time, by pursuing an entire social sector—or even more, as in Seymour Martin Lipset's magisterial overview—these essays have attempted to escape from a focus on simple distinctiveness of detail, in order to isolate an integrating pattern, which may or may not itself be distinctive. Yet even the cursory reader will have noted not just the range of topics covered, but the range of conclusions drawn by their authors about developments within these realms. Indeed, even the simplest summary question, about the fate of American exceptionalism as an organizing notion, draws tremendously varied responses here: it never was; it once was, but is no more; new versions have substituted for old; it continues on, unchanged in its essence. In that light, can anything general—anything central and consistently integrating—be said about the realms described and analysed within these essays?

Again, the initial response would appear to be no. In fact, it only further emphasizes a superficial variety to return to the question which formed the most immediate reason for holding a conference and producing a volume: what has been the influence of the last thirty years? I shall myself return to that question and survey the available answers in the first part of this final chapter. Yet in spite of this variety (an almost-excessive richness of definitions, analyses, conclusions, and, behind them all, social phenomena) it also appears, at least to these eyes, that there are four continuing themes which emerge within and cut across every one of these essays. *Populism* and *individualism* at the personal level, *democratization* and *market-making* at the institutional level—if anything can constitute an 'American model', it must be the interaction of these four putatively integrating themes. The bulk of this closing essay will, accordingly, centre on them.

Yet, at the outset, and perhaps in the nature of continuities elicited through such a historically problematic notion, it must also be noted that these themes are not simple and straightforward, and hence easily extrapolated. Indeed, the larger integrating concerns which emerge from these essays would conventionally be seen as tensions, rather than just as tendencies: populism *versus* individualism, democratization *versus* market-making. As a result, it is the simultaneous coexistence, even the effective reinforcement, of these apparently tension-producing themes which is their most distinctive quality—and which most fundamentally characterizes the American experience. By extension, it is the continuing interaction of these four grand themes which promises not just to shape the next incarnation of any American model, but to determine the practical fate of any 'American exceptionalism'. The final sections of this essay thus examine the cumulative influence of these themes on the current 'American model', and their cumulative implications for its future.

No individual author within this volume, nor any subset of authors collectively, need subscribe to (any of) these alleged larger themes. The substance of their individual essays was intended to be large enough for each to be able to stand on its own, and their authors do insist (most successfully) on the integrity of their individual efforts. Nevertheless, even the *arguments among* these various authors at the conference where early versions of these papers were presented—again, at least according to these ears—contained certain recurring questions and responses. If those questions and responses can in fact be converted into a small set of integrating themes, then the next concrete embodiment of those themes should certainly provide the next answer to the question of the status—and fate—of American exceptionalism.

The Influence of the Last Thirty Years

Before that, however, it is worth returning to the issue of the latest, the most recent, embodiment of these tendencies, especially since the authors of these essays come to such widely varying conclusions about the impact of the last thirty years on the reality of American exceptionalism. Daniel Bell underlines the *end* of one large argument about exceptionalism, from American political life, revolving around the allegation that the United States was the sole developed nation characterized by a near-absence of a national 'state'. This argument, in his view, is no longer tenable, and a major, alleged, American exceptionalism has died with it. The New Deal, the Second World War, the institutionalized welfare state, and the institutionalized Cold War—these produced a focusing of power in the national government, buttressed by a large standing army and a larger domestic bureaucracy. The United States may still be lower down this continuum (as Richard Rose argues in his look at public policies), but it is now only quantitatively, not qualitatively, different.

On the other hand, a reconsideration of the character of the American governmental world, before and after the emergence of this state, produces, perhaps surprisingly, a much more open-ended prognosis. For such a review highlights the larger development, at an even higher level of abstraction, which may ultimately be seen as the great American contribution to the realm of politics and governance. Because the essence of political life in the 'before' era (before the emergence of a stereotypical state) was provided by the presence of a 'civil society', and because the main lineaments of that society continue unimpeached, it may well be the next incarnation of this civil society which affirms the distinctively American model. An era of governmental retrenchment, especially if it is coupled with the winding down of the Cold War, only emphasizes this possibility.

In fact, it may well be the civil society—social relations quite distinct from governmental activity, relations which themselves assume responsibility for dealing with societal problems rather than assigning them to a 'state'—which becomes the larger and more continuing contribution of American politics to *world* models of government. In his oral defence of the notion, as empirical category and as symbolic beacon, Bell summarized it as

a society which develops outside the State, which rejects the State, which has a government instead of a State and does not justify the nature of power in respect to the idea of the State . . . The underlying philosophical theme is the theme of *rights*, rights which inhere as inalienable rights endowed naturally in individuals. To that extent, therefore, inevitably, the *society* becomes a social contract, a contract especially between people and *rights*.[1]

Attending to economic rather than political life, Peter Temin comes to noticeably different conclusions. He, too, locates major shaping factors which, being themselves distinctive, produced a model of economic development which deserves to be called exceptional. Yet in this case, the last thirty years have seen the dilution of that model, to the point where American economic exceptionalism must be described, in Temin's words, as 'fading like an old photograph'. Free land and federalism, as his title indicates, more than purely economic forms and forces, kept American economic development distinctive for much of the life of the nation. From one side, however, the last thirty years have seen the severe *attenuation* not just of free land but even of federalism as distinctive economic underpinnings, while from the other side, those years have seen the *adoption* of the most distinctive products of those two factors by many other nations.

Together, free land and federalism originally prevented the creation of an indigenous economic or status hierarchy to replace the feudal hierarchy from which early American settlers had escaped, though this ultimately had to be guaranteed through a bloody civil war. Yet free land and federalism had already provided the background to development of the 'American System' of manufacturing, with its emphasis on labour-saving devices and on the interchangeability of parts, and it was this, as much as anything else, which determined the *outcome* of that war. Moreover, free land and federalism combined again afterwards to foster the creation and spread of the modern corporate form of organization, that is, the modern business enterprise, the large-scale, vertically integrated firm. What looked by the early 1950s to be uniquely successful, however, to the point where it appeared that

[1] In his comments which began discussion of this paper at the conference itself, Richard Hodder-Williams touched on a notion that would recur in other papers and at other points in the discussion—namely, that in questions involving an alleged 'civil society', it appeared to be the most developed *and the least developed* nations which best approximated the American model.

the 'American economic model' might transform the world (either by example or by main economic force), was already losing at least its elements of distinction.

Free land had largely disappeared in the early twentieth century, and the consequentiality of federalism had declined sharply with the coming of the New Deal and the Second World War. Conversely, the American manufacturing system and the American corporate form were widely adopted in the resuscitating post-war economies, converting these factors into the 'developed'—not just the 'American'—model. Eventually, with the passage of further time, it would also become clear that what had been distinctive in the American economic miracle was not the rate of growth *per se*—this would be equalled by other nations as they experienced the same miracle—but rather the fact, possibly not to be equalled again, that this growth had been attained in tandem with huge immigration and native population increase. That accomplishment, while genuinely exceptional, was also, again, largely in the past. In its place was only the very tentative possibility that an exceptional economic *history* had produced a sufficiently different economic *mentality*, that the 'spirit' of free land and federalism would shift and find its focus in a more purely institutional, rather than geographic, marketplace.

When looking at American religious life, on the other hand, Andrew Greeley discovers a realm producing radically different answers to the main queries about American exceptionalism. In answer to the question about the impact of the last thirty years, for example, he notes, in striking contrast both to grand sociological arguments and to popular journalistic perceptions, that *almost nothing* has changed in the character and nature of American religious belief and experience during this entire period. Moreover, in further contravention of an apparent consensus among élite observers about American exceptionalism in the realm of religion (or at least, a greater willingness by scholars to grant an American exemption here), Greeley argues that world religious patterns suggest that it is not the United States which, in its beliefs and practices, is distinctive at all.

Thus on most available measures of mass belief and behaviour—from church attendance, through acceptance of Christ as saviour, to certainty about an after-life, to literal interpretations of the Bible—comparative percentages in the United States are nearly unchanged for the period in which survey items have existed, roughly forty years. There are, of course, smaller currents of change within this roughly constant stream.

Within Protestantism, the fundamentalist denominations have gained
somewhat, at the expense of the main-line liturgical churches. Within
Catholicism, there was a decline in church attendance and contributions
for a short period, in apparent protest at certain papal policies, most
especially on birth control. Nevertheless, the most dramatic apparent
changes in church behaviour are to be found principally at the élite
level. Moreover, these turn out either not to reach very far down into
ordinary religious life, or are actually far less inconsistent with mass
beliefs than is commonly supposed.

Even more strikingly, Greeley notes that none of these developments looks particularly deviant in world perspective—unless they
are observed narrowly from Western Europe, and especially from
the United Kingdom. Indeed, it is Western Europe generally, the state–
church societies more particularly, and Great Britain most especially,
which deviate from the world pattern—and whose scholars have been
most responsible for deeming the American experience 'exceptional'.
In actuality and by contrast, perceived American exceptionalism in the
realm of religious life is not in decline—but neither are the phenomena
which compose it particularly exceptional. If the entire world of
nations is the framework, the centrality of religion to American life is
hardly deviant. If the developed nations are the framework, the most
developed is—still—the most religious.[2]

Yet another, very different, set of answers to the main organizing
questions about American eceptionalism arise from an examination of
the realm of cultural life. In his aggressive and challenging look at
American culture—beginning with his title, 'Resolved, That Individualism and Egalitarianism Be Made Compatible in America'—Aaron
Wildavsky searches for the possibility of exceptionalism in a composite
political culture. In an initial argument roughly parallel to that of
Peter Temin, Wildavsky finds a historically distinctive American
pattern in the attempt to blend the cultural strands of individualism and
egalitarianism, as opposed to the blend of hierarchy and egalitarianism
which would come to characterize Western European life during much
of American history (and which might be argued to characterize newly
developed Asian nations like Japan as well). Yet where Temin finds the

[2] In leading off the discussion of this paper, Richard Carwardine attempted, among several
larger points, to resurrect a more specifically American exceptionalism in this area, based on
an argument about the centrality of religious life *when coupled with* the level of economic
development—the US being different from the actively religious nations by being much
more economically developed, while being different from the highly developed nations by
being much more actively religious.

old model of American economic exceptionalism fading gradually but ineluctably over the last thirty years, Wildavsky finds the old model of American *cultural* exceptionalism explicitly under assault from a new approach—purely egalitarian and aspiringly democratic—which, if it triumphed, might be *every bit as distinctive* in world perspective.

The argument begins by taking culture in its largest sense, as weaving together the values people hold, the social relations they prefer, and their beliefs about the world in general. The American cultural hybrid, in turn, present at the founding and reinforced at most subsequent historical stages, was distinguished by an alliance between those whose highest value was individualism and those whose highest value was equality. Equality of *opportunity* (or at least, lots of opportunity, coupled with an effort through public policy to prevent the introduction of artificial barriers to mobility and change) was the device for reconciling these two values. From the beginning, and continuing up to the challenge of the modern era, every explicit attack on this peculiar synthesis was met by a reformulation—and hence affirmation—appropriate to the conditions of its time.

Such a reconciliation found natural expression during the colonial and founding eras, in the view that state power was the main barrier to liberty and equality. It found natural expression again during the Jacksonian and later nineteenth-century eras, in the view that state power—in the service of big business, this time—was the main barrier to liberty with equality. This view achieved a further re-prieve during the New Deal and Second World War eras, through governmental efforts to shore up these (dual and joined) values, at home and abroad. Since that time, however, there has been a further profound challenge to this synthesis, from those who argue that equality of opportunity cannot exist before there is full equality of condition. Said differently, the old model is not so much implicitly fading as explicitly under attack. If it meets this challenge, the result will validate, once again, a peculiarly American cultural exceptional-ism. If it falls to that challenge, the result, if it can successfully guide government for any extended period, will be even more distinctive in world perspective.[3]

---

[3] In his opening commentary, Stephen Fender addressed culture in the other major sense, of the expressive artistic and, especially, literary products of a society. He noted that certain themes recur persistently in this—the unwillingness or inability to resolve tensions and contradictions, a perennial adolescence and the perpetual striving for some new world or condition, even emigration and/or reformation as individual decisions to abandon the old (and corrupted) and to seek the new (and better)—each and all cumulating in a larger social pattern.

A further twist on these arguments, about the current state of American exceptionalism in the large, is provided by Martin Trow in his overview of 'the American model' of higher education. That twist is embodied by the argument that the preconditions for a very distinctive evolution in educational practices were present in the United States almost from the beginning, but that these were activated considerably *later*— with the result that American educational patterns have been getting *increasingly* distinctive throughout American history. Indeed, even when taxed with the question of the last thirty years, this analysis suggests that for every degree of 'Americanization' in European educational practices, for example, there is equivalent evolution in the American model as well, so that the gap between systems does not appear to be narrowing.

Along the way to these conclusions, this essay provides a density of description and analysis which invites the more pointed testing of alternative grand interpretations. Moreover, Trow goes on to offer a proposed method of *hunting* for exceptionalism, involving study of the comparative 'period' and 'sequence' of educational developments. When this method is applied to the United States, a number of diagnostic characteristics of American higher education—and even of its links to preparatory, secondary education—stand revealed. Indeed, these actually begin outside the formal system, with a set of societal values in which college-level education gets a high priority, leading to a desire (and support) for permitting any individual to secure as much higher education as possible. Such distinctions then continue, and multiply, within the formal organization of higher education.

That organization features numerous and highly diverse institutions as its fundamental elements. These offer an early emphasis on general education, in part in response to the character of secondary schools but in any case, most critically, *by means of* an elective system, modular courses, and portable credits. And the resulting educational complex is governed directly by powerful administrators, secondarily by lay boards, and only tertiarily by a large professoriate with a relatively flat hierarchy. All this is integrated, finally, through an active concentration on direct links back to the larger society, including a view of students as a clientele capable of defining their needs, of alumni and the surrounding community as a potential repository of resources and hence as a demander of services in return, and of other educational institutions as potential competitors in terms of the character and quality of their product. The contrast with systems—almost all other systems— where the student population is small, national standards are crucial, the professoriate functions as a strong guild, and central government is the major funder as well as client, remains, accordingly, striking.

Trow thus attempts to systematize the historical method in order to address the issue of exceptionalism, specifically in education. Richard Rose adopts the alternative systematic approach, mobilizing aggregate measures of contemporary governmental activity for the full range of developed (of OECD) nations in his inquiry into the possible exceptionalism of American outputs in public policy more generally. What Rose learns is in many ways a recapitulation, statistically, of the evolution of the entire argument over 'American exceptionalism'. In this, he moves first to exceptionalism as simple similarity or difference; then to exceptionalism as deviation from (or conformity to) some larger, general pattern; and finally to exceptionalism as a comparison of composite approaches to larger social realms—in this case, the realm of public policy in general.[4]

Thus there were and are individual areas of public policy where the United States is the clear outlier, just as there were and are areas where this is evidently not so. When the focus shifts from individual peculiarities and distinctions to general patterns and their conformers or deviants, however, the United States, while clearly moving away from the generally hypothesized association between economic growth and governmental programmes, cannot be said to be exceptional, for other nations are moving that way too, and indeed, this conventionally hypothesized association is not even a reasonable summary of general *non-American* behaviour. Nevertheless and finally, the general *model* of development abstracted from Amercian national behaviour can be interpreted as one clear and distinct alternative, but an alternative which must be labelled the 'American Pacific model' if it is accurately to summarize current realities.

Rose begins at the level of individual distinctiveness by noting that in terms of public effort—the share of national resources devoted to governmental programmes—the United States is a clear outlier among OECD nations, falling at the low end of this continuum. On the other hand, in terms of actual benefits—the real economic level of those programmes—the United States remains deviant but in the *other* direction, falling at the high end of this particular continuum. Moreover, there are further American peculiarities within these aggregates, especially in an emphasis on defence and a de-emphasis on domestic welfare.

---

[4] See my preface for a short summary of that evolution.

Yet when these aggregates themselves are examined for the direction of their movement, it becomes clear that while the United States was, thirty-plus years ago, less of an outlier than it is today, this growing American divergence is only a particularly clear example of a general tendency for the OECD nations as a group to diverge among themselves on all of these measures. In fact, the larger and richer nations among this group are, if anything, more likely to adhere to the pattern characterizing the United States. In any case, it is dissimilarities, not similarities, which increasingly characterize the developed nations.

When these tendencies are reassembled into general categories, then, they imply that the old model of economic development and public policy, based upon Scandinavia and Britain—featuring greater governmental activity as overall economies grow—is now under challenge. Moreover, the challenging model is increasingly dominant, featuring greather concern with the sustained prerequisites of economic growth and greater provision of domestic welfare through the market, through not-for-profits, and through the household/family. The United States may have led the way—may still lead the way—within this model, but Japan is just as clearly a major exponent (hence the 'American Pacific model'), and the two nations have growing company within 'their' model. Accordingly, the next group of economically emergent nations, presumably in the Mediterranean and the Pacific Basin, will inevitably choose some version of these models, with no clear reason to suppose that a given nation will make a given choice.

Finally, in attempting to pull all these realms back together, Seymour Martin Lipset argues for yet another general interpretation. In this, the diagnostic characteristics of American life, properly understood, do acquire a new incarnation in each distinctive historical era. Yet while period details change, the essence embodied by them— that set of diagnostic characteristics—does not. Lipset uses the notion of 'Americanism', as ideology, to isolate this essence: a blend of egalitarianism and populism, voluntarism and anti-statism, individualism and moralism, which creates truly distinctive national patterns of behaviour. These are first addressed through the question originally associated with the coining of the term 'American exceptionalism', namely, why is socialism (which is to say, working-class consciousness) so weak in the United States? But the answer is then taken back to much earlier historical roots, and forward to an array of distinctive behaviours in the modern era.

Along the way, Lipset argues implicitly for an approach to the

question which does not disaggregate the phenomenon, either by
realms or through individual measures, but which instead seeks a
comprehensive national comparison. In attempting this comparison
with the United States at its centre, his essay begins by locating the
answer to the question 'Why no socialism?' in such basic background factors as a widespread suffrage, rapid economic growth, easy
geographic mobility, and the absence of social deference—summed up
in the notion of a country defined by ideology, by 'American*ism*', rather
than by history or geography *per se*. The more distant historical roots
of this ideology derived from a self-consciously new land and from an
anti-statist revolution, but by the time the question of *socialism* was an
intellectual issue, these had been buttressed by developments in
politics, in economics, in social relations, and even in religion.

Thus in politics, there was a divided and contentious system of checks
and balances, reinforced by a huge number of directly elected offices,
by such devices as the initiative and referendum, and by a voting system
which encouraged broad consensual alternatives. In economics, there
was the long-time *laissez-faire* attitude on the part of the nation (and its
government), followed by rapid economic growth and geographic mobility,
producing a low class-consciousness which was additionally augmented
by immigration and by an economic materialism which was not seen as
evil or sinful. In social relations more generally, there was not just
the absence of a feudal hierarchy/aristocracy, but a clear emphasis
on meritocracy. Even in religion, there was not just the inevitable
voluntarism of churches which had to be persistently created anew as
the nation expanded, but a history of self-conscious independence
(Burke's notion of Americans as 'the Protestants of Protestantism, the
dissenters of dissent') coupled with a constant resurgence of utopianism
and moralism, of efforts to reform evil and regenerate social life.

Lipset argues that the resulting national orientation can be observed
concretely in limited and distinctive realms, as with the realm of
philanthropy, just as it can be observed in the more consensually
negative products of the same society, as with crime and familial
instability. Indeed, one of the further advantages of this global view of
'Americanism' is that it explains how meritocracy and deviance, or
patriotism and war resistance, can coexist easily, almost necessarily.
Such a view does not deny either that there are certain inevitable
structural similarities in developed societies which bring the United
States closer to them or, since the United States achieved some of
these earlier, that other nations were necessarily 'Americanized' in

the process. Yet this overview, in Lipset's own concluding words, suggests that 'In line with Marx's anticipation, ... that "the more developed country shows the less developed the image of their future", the United States is less exceptional as nations develop and Americanize. But, given the structural convergences, the extent to which it is still unique is astonishing.'

Populism, Individualism, Democratization, and Market-Making

The variety of social phenomena covered in these essays, not to mention the variety of conclusions drawn by their authors about the history and fate of American exceptionalism, suggest that any further—putatively integrating—generalizations based upon them will testify more to imagination than to comprehension, more to impetuousness than to common sense. *One* such generalization does, it seems to me, follow safely enough from these essays as a group. A concept born in controversy and capable of sustaining debate among subsequent social thinkers has apparently not lost that potential. Said differently, one major continuity between these investigations and their historical predecessors is a continuing ability to generate analytical differences and stir argument.[5] This new look at American exceptionalism, accordingly, is not likely to be the last.

Yet to these eyes, there is also a set of themes, or at least recurrent concepts central to the analysis, which run additionally through each and all of these essays. Indeed, even as these essays were being presented and analysed, attacked and defended, this small set of themes—these conceptual continuities—surfaced repeatedly and linked them informally. These themes thus surfaced across a remarkable range of social sectors. They surfaced across the full range of national history. As a result, whether or not these sum up to an 'American exceptionalism,' they do appear to constitute 'the American model', and they are thus likely to be integral to the *next* incarnation of that model, if and when someone stops to enquire about the fate of American exceptionalism, another generation down the road.

[5] Here, the journalists present for the conference which produced these essays—John Grimond, American Editor for *The Economist*, and Leslie Stone, Chief Commentator for the BBC World Service—insisted that *part* of the data for any American exceptionalism consisted of a national belief in the concept. If the public believed in it generally, then the concept had some reality by virtue of that belief. If they acted to *sustain* (their view of) the essence of their exceptionalism, then that view attained a further, concrete reality.

Accordingly, the final sections of this concluding essay will focus directly on these four themes—on populism and individualism, on democratization and market-making—and on their interaction. Such themes (like everything else associated with the notion of American exceptionalism?) have the vices of their virtues. Any connecting concepts which span these realms and this time-period are necessarily (and perhaps dangerously) vague and general. Nevertheless, there did appear to be four such themes, two on the personal and two on the institutional level. Personally, explanations of the organization of American life in each of these realms appeared to be heavily dependent on the notions of 'populism' and 'individualism'. Institutionally, explanations of the outlines of American life in these realms appeared equally dependent on the notions of 'democratization' and 'market-making'.

At the start, then, it seems necessary to set these notions out, very concisely, in the abstract. It will then seem even more necessary, I fear, to plunge them back into specific social realms—into government, economics, religion, culture, education, and public policy, as these have been presented here. So, in the abstract, with numerous concrete referents to follow, four definitions must begin the analysis:

1. On the personal level, 'populism' is the doctrine that all members of society should be conceived as social equals, quite apart from any circumstances of birth or achievement. This implies that collective public life, including public activities in the widest sense and not just politics and government, should reflect the social *style*—the operational values—of modal members of society.

2. 'Individualism', in turn, is the doctrine that the single and independent members of that society ought to have a right to construct their personal lives according to their own (single and independent) preferences. This implies a collective social life which is effectively an aggregate of these preferences, or of accommodations among them.

3. On the institutional level, 'democratization' is the notion that major social institutions (again in the widest sense) should be run so as to be directly responsive to the wishes of their (often varied and various) publics. This ordinarily implies structural mechanisms for collective decision-making—ranging from an openness to participation through arrangements for majority voting—which aspire to *guarantee* such responsiveness.

4. Finally, 'market-making' is the notion that organized alternatives—in products and services, of course, but also in occupations,

entertainments, and even lifestyles—ought to appear or disappear as there is (or is not) sufficient demand to sustain them. This includes the further presumption that a constant change in the 'menu' of these available alternatives (by way of 'marketplaces', broadly conceived) is itself a further, desirable goal.

Before looking for the presence of these organizing notions in a variety of social realms, and thus defining them much more effectively in context, it is again worth noting that each of these pairs of concepts is usually treated, in the abstract, as comprising pairs of *opposites*. That is, it is more common to emphasize populism *versus* individualism, democratization *versus* market-making, and thus to portray these abstract descriptions as ends of a continuum, not as simultaneous characteristics. If there is something additionally distinctive about American life in these terms, then, it is that such apparently (or at least frequently) antithetical concepts can in practice (and to borrow Wildavsky's phrase) 'be made compatible'.

The most definitionally straightforward way to search for that compatibility might be to begin with the realms of government and economics, from which the basic *names* for the four key integrating concepts derive. On the other hand, for that very reason, it may be more convincing to use a quite other realm to inaugurate the survey—for example, the realm of religious life—since neither populism nor individualism, neither democratization nor market-making, are usually associated with it. Moreover, among these four concepts, market-making may provide the best introductory example, precisely because it is so apparently alien to sacred discourse. Yet it is surely convention and inertia which separate even this notion from the religious realm, at least in the United States—since there may be no more extended, no more varied nor more deliberately promotional, 'religious marketplace' anywhere in the world.

The fundamental variety essential to such a marketplace includes, of course, not just a major presence for the Protestant, Catholic, and Jewish faiths in the large. It extends, especially within the single largest category of these (Protestantism), to a multiplicity of denominations and sects as well. This variety is then effectively energized, made real, by the fact that these are real and *active*, not definitional, categories. The full dynamic of market-making is completed, finally, by multiple and recurring investments of conscious energy, both by the demoninations and by their individual churches, in seeking (active) members—that is, to continue the metaphor, in 'competing' for membership and support. This is perhaps most commonly (if a bit superficially) noted in the use of modern communications technology, especially television in our day, which provides everything from broadcasts of mainstream liturgical services through forums for self-conscious 'televangelists'. Yet these more dramatizable manifestations are really only, at bottom, further evidence of the general and continuing drive to survive and prosper in the 'religious marketplace'.

Here as elsewhere, however (in a general phenomenon to receive more attention below), the presence of extended 'market-making' does not imply the absence of institutionalized 'democratization'. Indeed, the latter is also evidently central—even diagnostic—in the specifically American incarnations of these various churches. Much of this institutionalized democratization was historically inherent, as a nation developing through immigration and through migration west-ward, through the settling of a huge geographic frontier, saw churches established as soon as there were communities large enough to people them. Such churches were inevitably free of much central (administrat-ive or theological) direction. Even more to the point, they had to be responsive to the needs and wishes of their prospective clienteles, rather than to any external hierarhy—which was largely non-existent, in any case. But, in fact, these historical patterns continue comfortably into the present, for different but clearly related reasons.

The *geographic* territory for church expansion, for example—the modern practical counterpart to 'the frontier'—may no longer be 'the West' as a physical region, but it just as clearly *is* 'the suburbs' as a territorial category. New communities in our time are generally sub-urban rather than specifically Western; new suburbs need new social institutions, including—early on—new churches; new churches need to attract members by providing desired services, by being res-ponsive (once again) to membership wishes. Moreover, while the self-consciously (and physically) *new* churches are appearing in the suburbs, older church districts are simultaneously acquiring a socially different—and in that sense, also 'new'—clientele, which recapitulates the process yet again, needing a different set of programmes and requiring a different set of concerns.

By the same token, the *governmental* aspect of these churches makes the theme of continuity even clearer. For in the modern world as in the nineteenth century, territorial expansion, congregational creation, and physical church construction have all been facilitated by the same democratizing mechanism, by the institutionalization of lay boards to manage most church activities. And while the practical reach of this device is most complete in the Protestant sects—with their emphasis on individual churches which form themselves and select their own preachers—its ability to penetrate the American *Catholic* Church may be its most impressive achievement. Operational rule by the laity, or operational decay if the laity withdraws its support, is by now a general, not a Protestant, American characteristic.

'Individualism', like 'market-making', is a notion not commonly encountered in the realm of religious life. Yet it does clearly apply, as Andrew Greeley effectively reminds us, in two distinct fashions. One stems from the variety of religious options which are practically available to the individual American. If most Americans nevertheless grow up within one denomination, having learnt its rituals and having become associated with its dominant clientele, there is a process of choice inherent even in that. There is also the minority which actually does choose an entirely different religious tradition, shifting most commonly in our time from high to low Protestant (from the liturgical to the pietist denominations within Protestantism) but accompanied by other eddies as well.

'Individualism' is even more relevent in a second sense, however, the sense in which, in the United States but surely not in all societies, the choice of a religious identity is a central part of self-definition. 'What are you?' is in part answered by 'a Lutheran', 'a Catholic', or 'a Southern Baptist'. It may well be that this answer gains consequence where religious identities are themselves highly diverse. It may be that it gains additional consequence where social roles, ordained or even achieved 'places', are ambiguous and fluid. In any case, this answer— Lutheran, Catholic, Baptist, or whatever—is important to establishing individual identity, to giving boundary and definition to the individual American.

Once again, however, that boundary is *not* the site of conflict between the abstractions of 'individualism' and 'populism', at least when made concrete in the realm of religion. For, in fact, the populist side of the American religious experience also has several distinctive facets, facets which not only reinforce each other but sit quite comfortably with religious individualism. The most evident and direct of these applies to internal church governance. This infusion of populism *within* religious life is exemplified in the view that not only church activities but even the identify and character of—(indeed, even the sermon from) the living local embodiment of church officialdom *should* accord with the social outlook of the congregation. Such an insistence on 'representation', in the sense of sharing modal premises about the world outside, is, of course, populism at its most pointed.

Yet there is a second, larger, but more amorphous aspect of populism which is intimately associated with the realm of religious life. This second aspect is concerned with guaranteeing that religious values shape a larger national—especially governmental—life. In other words, rather than being concerned with the central place of populist values within American religion, a full-blown populism is concerned with the central place of religion in American public life. This second, complementary aspect is perhaps best captured in the general view that public officials of all sorts ought to *have* a religion, and ought to value it. Support for self-consciously religious values, with their content deliberately left undefined, is in fact a central tenet of a distinctively American populism. If religious officials in one's own church ought to reflect congregational values, then public officials in larger national life ought also to reflect the centrality of religious values to community life more generally.

It is easy to see the historical roots of this peculiar pattern, this distinctive combination of four main themes. A country with a heavy leaven of religious dissenters from the start, who viewed religious life and religious freedom as essential, then grew through massive immigration and simultaneous migration westward, which added further national religious variety along with the multiplication of largely autonomous and self-governing, local congregations. Yet the extent to which the basic patterns underlying this development *remain* vital and central was dramatically demonstrated, yet again, in early 1989. Formally, the least yielding of the great faiths to all these notions is Catholicism. Neither democratization nor market-making, neither populism nor individualism, are supposed to be relevant to the organization tracing to St Peter.

Nevertheless, when Pope John Paul II, with his main doctrinal lieutenant, Cardinal Joseph Ratzinger, came to America in March 1989 to meet with the American Catholic bishops, it was hard not to hear echoes of an argument first mounted by Jay Lovestone, leader of the American Communist Party, to *his* international counterparts more than sixty years before—an argument about 'American exceptionalism'. For if the assertions of the bishops had to be summarized in one notion, it was that while they were indeed dedicated followers of Rome, their superiors also had to understand that given the inherent and extreme differences of American life, the bishops were *forced* to do things differently, in order to accomplish the same (mutually desired) results.[6]

Politics and Economics: Home Grounds

While the realm of religion shows these themes at their most stark, precisely because of their apparent terminological irrelevance, the realm of government has been intimately and inherently associated with two of the four, namely, populism and democratization. The very word 'populism' owes its existence to an explicitly political movement of the late nineteenth century, though the underlying impulse runs back nearly to the beginnings of a separable American politics and has continued, in easily recognizable form, down to the present. In the same way, the explicitly political, general notion of 'democratization' was inherent in the rationale for a separate American republic, though only later did self-conscious efforts at a particular kind of structural reform make that notion part of a recurring political movement, with a recurring and specific procedural agenda. If the realm of religion best attests to the societal reach of these general terms, then, the realm of government gives two of them their most pointed definition.

In the case of populism, this definition is still not without confusion or controversy. The various incidents associated with the populist impulse across history—from the original American Revolution, to the more metaphorical Jacksonian 'revolution' a half-century later, to the formation of an actual Populist Party a half-century after that, all the way up to the 'anti-Washington' electoral campaigns of the 1970s and 1980s—each contain elements peculiar to their own time and place. Nevertheless, a minimal definition, from elements found in all these incarnations, would emphasize social equality, the belief that all members of society have the same right to be treated as personal equals. Leaders, accordingly, in any walk of life, should have (and demonstrate) 'the common touch', operating on shared premises about appropriate behaviour.

At the aggregate level, such social equality implies that collective public life—again, not just in politics, but in religion and, as we shall

[6] See Peter Steinfels, 'U.S. Prelates Open Talks in Vatican', *New York Times* (3 March 1989), A9; Steinfels, 'Meeting with Vatican Soothes U.S. Archbishops', *New York Times* (12 March 1989), A22; and Steinfels, 'The Vatican and the American Ways', *New York Times* (19 Mar. 1989), IV. 9.

see, in economics or culture too—should reflect the dominant attitudes and values, the modal social style, of the populace. These propositions, fundamental planks in the platform of 'Americanism', have ordinarily implied certain further characteristics. They have, for example, produced a politics organized less in terms of left versus right and more in terms of 'the little man' versus 'the interests'. This particular (populist) orientation is essential to understanding, in turn, how a mass public can be anti-big-business at one point, anti-big-labour at another, and anti-big-government at yet a third—the wrath of 'the little man' merely shifting as the relevant, offending, 'big interest' shifts. Finally, the impulse also has its associated dark side. Social majoritarianism is not necessarily tolerant of deviant views and styles; an insistence on dominant cultural values can easily slide over into nativism or racism.

No less a source than the Constitution itself affirmed the abstract centrality of deliberate structural 'democratization', in its determination to have representative government and individual rights. Yet the Constitution actually offered as much a 'republican' as a 'democratic' institutional solution, providing for substantial indirect representation and decision-making. Across time, however, in an intermittent but apparently relentless trend, there has been an attempt to open the proceedings of that government to public intervention, most often by attempting to transfer key decisions directly into public hands. As a result, 'democratization' in the American context has come to imply a more specific procedural programme, involving a central place for citizen participants and, ultimately, some means for decision by majority vote.

Towards this end, the original non-party system favoured by the founding fathers was quickly converted into an internal two-party system and then into external mass parties—at a very early point by comparative international standards. What eventually stopped at that point in most other nations, however, continued in the United States with the introduction of the formal primary election into these parties, so that the mass public could choose not just ultimate office-holders but party nominees. Along with this came the more symbolic embodiments of structural democratization: the initiative, the referendum, and the recall. And lest these seem a unique but essentially historical development, two further facts should be noted. One is that most of these democratizing procedures, and most especially the primary, remain as the institutional framework for *current* American politics. The other is that one of the great rounds of self-conscious democratizing reforms in all of American history actually falls comfortably within our time, within the last thirty years, in fact.

The realm of politics, then, has explicitly contributed two of the main themes running through all of these essays, or at least the *terms* which are most often used to denote those themes. This does not mean, however, that the *other* pair of themes in this fourfold interpretation are in any sense absent from the governmental realm. Indeed, a comprehension of American politics and government would be impoverished—would be nearly impossible—without the notions of 'individualism' and 'market-making' or their equivalents. If the definitions of these notions are more commonly derived from economic life, and if they gain perhaps their most striking validation from their utility in understanding American religious life, they nevertheless claim a central place in American politics as well.

The standard interpretation of individualism in American life (defined more precisely in the economic realm and developed more richly in the realm of culture) crosses easily, with inescapable implications, into politics. Historical settlement through foreign immigration and internal migration, along with the resulting social diversity and emphasis on self-reliance, institutionalized in everything from a free-enterprise economy through a rights-based jurisprudence—these are the preconditions for a politics in which individuals (collected into individual electoral districts) demand that their particular and personal collection of wishes and values be represented in government, rather than some rationalized, even homogenized, national programme. Once again, such individualism coexists comfortably with (rather than standing in opposition to) populism. Indeed, it is precisely this combination which underlies the American preference for social equality but not material levelling.

If that could be described as 'individualism from below', however, it is in fact met equally by an 'individualism from above', in the behaviour of the public officials elected by these individual citizens. A federal system with single-member districts, whose members are chosen by plurality vote, surely encourages a decentralized, entrepreneurial, and locally adaptive politics from the élite side as well. The introduction of primary elections into such an arrangement then seals its inherent individualism, from both sides. Individual citizens acquire a means for ensuring that their representatives stand for district interests, not some national party platform; individual candidates acquire a means for securing a party nomination on their own initiative, quite apart from the wishes of any party apparatus. Structural democratization, in this way, actually increases the variety of options—the 'market', if you will—available to the general public.

Indeed, the presence of 'market-making' in a description of American politics hardly seems discordant, since (as both Daniel Bell and Richard Rose note from different but reinforcing perspectives) the historical preference in American society for a weak 'state' which leaves most activities outside the compass of government has long been accepted as a general characterization. Government has left most potential spheres of policy to the external (economic) market-place. When government *has* sought a policy-making role, even this has frequently involved a 'market-making' character—seeking not so much to set down a comprehensive bureaucratic programme as to manipulate incentives in order to elicit the desired outcome. These tendencies, in particular, have been grist for those who have argued that American politics is driven, not so much by classical ideologies, as by cycles of 'reform'.[7]

Yet in a more metaphorical sense, American government and politics *themselves* can be conceived as a huge 'marketplace', in which a variety of alternatives will always be competing and in which change in the menu of these alternatives, combinations and recombinations, is assumed to be both natural and desirable. This is true even of the fundamental organizing issues of politics. Socio-economic issues may dominate this marketplace at some times; foreign policy concerns may dominate it at others; social and cultural policy may dominate it at still others. Even then, this mix of central political concerns is still only half the picture. For at the same time, different mass constituencies and districts will *always* be mixing these basic concerns in different ways, just as different élite political actors will be seeking personal or group advantage through different coalitions—since all participants are theoretically entitled to pursue their own peculiar, individual, and idiosyncratic visions in this huge, metaphorical, and amorphous (political) marketplace.

If two of the terms for these main connecting threads in 'the American model' (populism and democratization) are originally and intimately associated with the realm of government, the remaining two (individual-

---

[7] This is most richly developed in Samuel P. Huntington, *American Politics: The Promise of Disharmony* (Cambridge, Mass.: Harvard University Press, 1981), but it is also implicit in (the otherwise very different) Richard Hofstadter, *The American Political Tradition and the Men Who Made It* (New York: Alfred A. Knopf, 1948). My own, more limited effort in this realm is Byron E. Shafer, ' "Reform" in the American Experience', *Corruption and Reform*, 6 (1991).

ism and market-making) are just as commonly and reliably associated with the realm of economics. Indeed, within economics, these
two are frequently treated as having a further, mutual, inherent
link: individualism conducing toward a market economy, the market
economy conducing toward individualism. But again, economics (like
government) provides major roles for their two apparent opposites as
well, so that practical links must evidently be found among *four*, not
two, connecting themes. Accordingly, another sketch of the place of
these four themes within American economic life, when added to
previous sketches from American religious and political life, sets the
stage for asking how two pairs of superficially antithetical concepts can
coexist comfortably, even symbiotically, within a society—and then
for asking why *four* themes should surface and be sustained in such
apparently disparate realms as religion, government, and economics.

While 'individualism' as a notion clearly encompasses more than
its place in the economic realm, that place is certainly central. In
most American approaches to thinking about economics, the individual
surfaces first as a key productive unit, and then again as an autonomous consumer. Yet the notion is not just stereotypical in economic
theorizing; it was also stereotypically connected with actual economic
development in the United States. Historically, the United States was
the ultimate *laissez-faire* society, as Seymour Martin Lipset correctly
notes, and 'rugged individualism' was long asserted to be at the heart
of this. The roots of this are painfully familiar. A nation peopled
originally by diverse groups, often of dissidents, was to grow by
internal migration and external immigration, making collectivism a
very difficult (and unlikely) personal orientation, and reinforcing
the   decentralized and autonomous economic activity which, in turn,
further reinforced individualism.

More critically, this same symbiotic relationship was to continue
over time. The individualism intrinsic to a mercantile and, especially, agricultural economy of the late eighteenth and early nineteenth centuries was thus to become the individualism intrinsic
to the emerging industrial economy of the late nineteenth and early
twentieth centuries, and ultimately the individualism intrinsic to the
increasingly post-industrial economy of the late twentieth and early
twenty-first centuries. At each point, the individual as a partially autonomous economic unit was necessarily central to an evolving economy,
just as that economy found ways of transferring this individual*ism*
into new economic (and social) contexts. The larger economic frame-

work and its main diagnostic elements might change dramatically from
era to era. The individualist impulse continued, and was easily recognizable within each.

Markets and market-making may be even more definitionally economic—and stereotypically American. Most concretely, as Peter Temin
notes, there was first 'the American System' of manufacture as the
United States began to take off economically, followed by American
pioneering of the modern corporate organizational form, the multi-
layered industrial corporation. Again, these were both cause and
effect of the emergence of a true mass market and (especially) mass
marketing, originally every bit as characteristic of what was then taken
to be a quintessentially American phenomenon. Moreover, these too
are hardly historical relics. They have been taken even further in the
last thirty years, producing a sense that one can 'market' nearly anything
in a self-conscious consumer society—not just goods and services, but
entertainment and leisure, and even (sub)cultures and lifestyles.

How did this apparent preference for market-making, even as buttressed by a continuing individualism, manage to persist? A nation of
dissenters, created through an essentially anti-statist revolution, might
suffice to explain its origins. But the changes from agricultural to
industrial to post-industrial economy were massive, and if market-
making and an associated individualism can be discerned within each,
that symbiosis only pushes the question one step further back. The
answer, in fact, appears to lie in marked and continuing *social diversity*,
as they played across governmental arrangements which were better at
responding to particularistic needs than at formulating national policies.

Said differently, a nation distinguished by an allegiance to an ideology of 'Americanism', and which needed constantly to reaffirm the place
of that ideology as a unifying factor, was a nation which was *not*
highly unified and integrated in most other realms. Not just ethnic and
cultural diversity, constantly reinforced, but geographic diversity, along
with extreme diversity in the character of local *economies* and in level
of *economic development*, continued to characterize the nation as a
whole. Government might well be open to the demands of the various
(and diverse) groups within it—might, indeed, be increasingly open by
virtue of increased structural democratization. But that did not mean
that those groups were increasingly unified around major public programmes to be managed by the government, nor that they were likely
to give up more narrowly targeted benefits in order to take a chance
on more nationally oriented policies, especially in a governmental

system which specialized in bringing in new demands and in constantly renegotiating earlier understandings.

Once more, however (and as oddly here as anywhere), the other main themes of 'the American model', populism and democratization, surface in the economic realm as well. Thus populism, that oft-alleged opposite to individualism, proves instead to be central to the operation of an evolving mass economy. In the simplest sense, this has to be so. Aggressive mass marketing cannot succeed without a popular desire to acquire the (ever-changing) products of an aspiring consumer society. Yet in a second sense, populism also shapes the *operation* of that society in crucial ways. At bottom, the popular desire for a particular product is, of course, what shapes the drive first to produce it, then to look for cheaper ways to produce it, and then to find ways to produce cheaper but acceptable substitutes.

At the same time, however, individuals left free to design their own lives, while they may insist on having an array of alternatives and on making their own choices among them, are nevertheless very likely to want, at most, some variant of what others have. Part of this, too, is inherent in market choice. Even 'free' markets do not provide unlimited alternatives, even in the 'home' of the *laissez-faire* economy. More to the point of populism, however, is that if markets are good at generating a changing range of options, people still tend to demand roughly similar things (or at least, *their version* of those things) as they learn about and experience emerging alternatives. One way to say this is to say that Americans, naturally, want the accoutrements of an 'American' lifestyle. Seen from the institutional side, conversely, gauging this economic populism is an important part of being successful in the mass (economic) marketplace.

Finally, democratization, perhaps the least traditional of these notions for classical economics, appears in one guise or another nearly everywhere one looks in the American economic realm, though there may be no other realm where the implications of this fact are so easily misperceived. Once, the corporate form itself might have been offered as evidence of an effective 'democratization', in the sense that it was a distinct move away from the dominance of economic activity by extended families and social élites, and towards responsiveness to an organized 'constituency'. Yet this development has not gone much further over time, and it has not reached nearly the level of structural democratization characteristic of government and politics, or even of organized religion.

More to the point, then, are aspects of society, essentially democrat-izing aspects—though none of them are unequivocally beneficial by virtue of that fact—which flow from the thorough *commercialization* of that society, from the injection of *economic criteria* into most aspects of American life. Here, as explicit and formalized economic transactions became part of the management of much of social life (not just employ-ment, but also housing, education, leisure, or even geographic mobility) they simultaneously replaced other central (and usually less democratic) criteria for decision in these realms. Such criteria included birth, manners, and connection; more ambivalently, they also included experience, training, and certification.

On the individual level, vigorous economic growth, thorough commercialization, and the attendant extension of the cash nexus to more and more realms of social life meant the abolition of the pos-siblity of any consensual sense of 'proper place' for individuals. This guaranteed them the ability to mix their resources differently, so as to construct a personal identity more on the basis of their own choice; more ambivalently, again, it implied that anyone who could pay the bill could have the item or experience in question. At the societal level, what this same composite pattern of economic development really implied was the dominance of a broad economic and social middle. It meant a broad range of essentially middle-class opportunities; it implied even broader middle-class *styles* for society as a whole, so that many of those who might not otherwise be categorized as 'middle-class' could aspire to have their version of these styles. All of this, of course, went a long way towards guaranteeing that developments, economic or otherwise, which did not please this broad middle stratum would not succeed.

The Persistence of Four Grand Cultural Themes

The realms of economics, government, and even religion thus attest to the fact that pairs of major *and allegedly antithetical* characteristics—populism *and* individualism on the personal level, democratization *and* market-making on the institutional level—can indeed coexist comfort-ably. This is hardly, of course, the first time that conditions which can be argued to be inconsistent in the abstract have been discovered together in concrete application. Yet not only can these grand character-istics evidently coexist; they can obviously function as central themes in describing major realms—the *same* major realms—in American society. Given that fact, it would be surprising if such large and apparently tension-filled conjuctions were not diagnostic characteristics of the society in which they actually appear. Nevertheless, when all this is recognized, the question remains: what is the explanation for the concrete coexistence of abstractly antithetical characteristics? How can this be?

The immediate (true but tricky) answer is that an explanation lies (and must lie) within the even-more-encompassing realm of American culture. In a sense, the appearance of these four grand characteristics in realm after realm of American society goes a long way towards suggesting the essence of that culture. On the other hand, an explanation rooted in American culture, so defined, need not be simply definitional. At a minimum, *socialization* into existing values and arrangements, values and arrangements embodying a prior coexistence of these four characteristics, surely does make their continued (co)existence more likely. Yet this is still not an explanation of how these four themes cohere. That requires some further elaboration of the means for the rise—and then the contemporary reach—of the elements which together comprise this culture, an elaboration buttressed by further, concrete examples.

How *do* populism and individualism, then—to take the first allegedly antithetical pair of cultural themes—coexist with (and even reinforce) each other? A quick review of their evolution in the realm of politics is highly suggestive. The American Revolution itself, the very beginning of a separate 'United States', combined the desire to affirm a recognizably different form of societal organization, much more self-consciously egalitarian in social terms, with an even more inescapable assertion of the right to be left alone, to do things according to autonomous local standards. By the same token, the first great upheaval in an independent American politics, the Jacksonian 'revolution' of the 1830s, combined these same values in the same way. The Jacksonians were more Western, more rural, more agricultural, less wealthy, and more occupationally autonomous than their political opponents. Given this social situation, they were able to assert simultaneously the virtues of 'the common man' and the right to manage their individual lives without co-ordination by some instrument of a single, national will—which in this case meant, most especially, a National Bank.

Both of these early (diagnostic and shaping) experiences showed a heavy strand of anti-statism, against the British government in the first case and against the new American government in the second. But if anti-statism was a frequent component of political upheavals in the

United States, it was not a necessary concomitant. In the late nineteenth century, the period which spawned a self-designated 'populist' movement, the popular complaint was principally against big business instead, against its stifling of individual preferences and individual opportunities. To the extent that this was intermittently a complaint against big (i.e. national) government as well, that was because government was seen as (illegitimately) in the thrall of business. Yet government was also viewed, potentially, as a tool for *disciplining* business on behalf of the public. What was not different, then—what was constant and continuing—was the joint impact of individualism and populism as a stimulus for fighting the perceivedly dominant institution(s).

Massive waves of immigration, coming at roughly the same time, only reinforced this synthesis. Thus waves of new immigrants, coming by definition from different nations and coming normally with different languages and even different cultural premises, inevitably reinforced the individualism of American society. Being different, they made the natives, too, additionally distinctive; lacking a shared tradition with those natives, they could not be relied upon for common, consensual, social responses. On the other hand, their very presence raised, most acutely, the need for—and needless to say, anxieties about—integrating them into American life, so that they *would* come to share the dominant social values characterizing their new society. 'Americanization' classes through the public schools were one product of this anxiety; intermittent nativist upsurges were a much less attractive variant.

Even more to this particular point, however, the period around the turn of the twentieth century may well have been critical to the 'fixing' of the link between populism and individualism within American culture. Or, at least, this period again affirmed the way in which an extended and continuing social diversity—an ethnic and subcultural diversity, of course, but also a geographic and regional diversity, an occupational and developmental diversity, and so on—was central to generating and sustaining this particular linkage. A society without this extended diversity might well not have produced such a linkage; the United States, however, was just such a society. Moreover, this was also the period when a joint mentality, sustained for over a century by a sequence of congruent but disparate historical events, was converted into an explicit ideology, into an 'Americanism', which could thereafter be consciously taught—and consciously learnt. Central to that ideology, of course, were both populism and individualism.

All this is evidence for the way in which these two themes came increasingly to be logically and intimately connected—or rather, to the way that, while they may be missing or antithetical in other societies, they *could* be logically and intimately connected (be 'made compatible') in the United States. For if citizens were to be free—indeed, to be encouraged—to pursue their individual preferences, opportunities, and lifestyles, with a minimum of intervention by ostensibly collective institutions, then some way had nevertheless to be found to permit effective social interaction among those citizens and to guarantee *some* consensual standards within which they could operate. Populism, as a demand for general observances of modal social styles, could—had to—provide this social lubricant. Seen from the other side, if social pressures rather than institutional co-ordination were to regulate society, then some reliable way had to be found to guarantee that *only* those social preferences which were widely shared were actually allowed to constrain personal behaviour. An aggressive, resistant individualism could—again, perhaps 'had to'—provide this check.

In any case, by now, the continuing conjunction of populism and individualism has not just roots in, but further consequences for, American culture. For example, this otherwise peculiar conjuction is itself a central explanation for the peculiarly American definition of 'equality', implying social but not material levelling. Such a definition is productive of continued misunderstandings with the non-American world. Thus Americans are forever discovering rampant 'inequality' in nations, even self-consciously 'social democratic' nations, which accept notions of deference associated with the holding of various positions, either ascribed or achieved. Conversely, non-Americans are forever discovering a United States characterized by rampant 'inequality' in material conditions. Yet a society which blends populism with individualism insists, quite logically, that no person is 'better' (intrinsically) than any other, but that each person must be permitted to construct his or her individual life as best (and as advantageously as) he or she can.

An inherent or at least 'explainable' consistency between populism and individualism on the personal level probably makes the linkage between democratization and market-making on the institutional level more plausible and easier to conceive as well. Again, there is nothing automatic about this linkage. But it surfaces in such an array of disparate realms as to suggest its centrality to American culture more generally. And again, given the evident coexistence of democratization and market-making as major institutional themes in the United States, along with the lack of any inherent need for them to coexist, some further general explanation for their linkage in American culture is required. For the sake of consistency, the realm of politics can be tapped once more to help explain why this coexistence can, in some circumstances, be entirely logical and natural. Yet this time, it is worth using instances from *contemporary* political life, to dismiss the possibility that some 'historical overhang' is actually the main explanatory force.

Fortunately, the tendency for democratization and market-making to exist side by side and to draw sustenance from each other is nowhere better illustrated than in the politics of our time. In fact, the period from the mid 1960s to the late 1970s was one of the great reform eras in American history—the founding, the Jacksonian era, and the progressive era at the turn of the 20th century are the others—when questions of structural democratization were explicitly at the centre of politics. Whether the product of this period came to countervail, to coexist with, or actually to expand the reach of market-making in American society can thus become a key test, not only of coherence between these two grand institutional themes, but of potential continuation in the modern world. Assuming that this institutional linkage, like the personal one between populism and individualism, *passes* that test, the details of its passage can be addressed for further, more general explanation of this practical compatibility among putatively incompatible concepts.

The modern reform era has certainly been characterized by multiple and extended, structurally democratizing initiatives. Thus it featured such self-conscious institutional adjustments as the extension of primary elections, at long last, to *presidential* selection, so that individual citizens could not just elect but nominate their presidents. The modern era featured a thorough reform of *congressional* procedures as well, changing the rules of operation for that last great bastion of intermediary élites in American politics by dispersing formal positions and resources more broadly and by opening legislative activity, even at the ultimate stage on the House and Senate floors, to a much broader array of participants. Such a list, however, hits only the high-points. The modern reform era actually went much further, to freedom-of-information and open-access rules inside the executive bureaucracy, for example, but really to almost any realm one could name.

Yet what it did *not* feature was equally important for this particular argument. For all these reforms, despite recasting not just the institutional structure of government but the practical politics occurring within it, did not produce more governmental programmes and thus an expanded role for the central 'state'. As a result, they did not produce a contraction in the use of market-making in pursuit of public preferences, even 'public policies'. In fact, most strikingly, this reform era was directly succeeded by a period when the increase of governmental programmes and the expansion of the state bureaucracy, proceeding more or less continually since the Great Depression and the New Deal, came to a halt. Some programmes were actually terminated; others were consciously moved out into the commercial marketplace.

In practical terms, then, the coincidence of major efforts at structural democratization with expansion in the scope of market-making re-affirmed the historical link between these two great institutional themes in American life, while bringing that link comfortably into the contemporary world. Moreover, the particular instance once again contains a potential key to explaining *why* this link can be (and is) inherent in the United States. Or at least, what happened in the late twentieth century to link democratization and market-making is already clear. The rise of new issues and new political coalitions, the central phenomenon behind all this, was not just a stimulus to structural reform, though it was certainly that; this rise was also an *explanation* of the preference for market-making within these newly democratized institutions.

By itself, the co-ordinated rise of new issues (and of the new political coalitions associated with them) comprised a perfectly simple and straightforward explanation for the coming of a reform drive. An older set of (in this case, social welfare) issues, mobilizing and supported by an older (class-based) coalition, came to stand in the way of newly significant divisions on cultural policy (abortion, permissiveness, crime) and foreign affairs (nationalism, interventionism, defence pre-paredness) which required very different social coalitions for their pursuit. Structurally democratizing reforms, to restore democratic responsiveness, were the nearly inevitable response—in the late eighteenth, early-to-middle nineteenth, late nineteenth/early twentieth, and now late twentieth centuries. Old issues and old coalitions clearly *were* in the way; democratization clearly appealed as the means to circumvent them.

These same new issues and new coalitions which were behind the democratizing drive, however, were also the reason that successful democratization produced the expansion, not the contraction, of market-making. Some of this was direct and intended, as with those issues (ranging from school prayer through economic deregulation) where a desire to get the national government out of local activity was inherent in the new issue itself. More of it was indirect and unintended, when a welter of cross-cutting issues and of shifting coalitions in effect prevented government from imposing any programmatic solution.

Increasing social (and hence political) diversity, when focused upon an increasingly democratized (and receptive) government, resulted, not in governmental growth, but either in stalemate or in an active preference for letting a decentralized 'market' actually provide the solution.

Yet seen in a more historical perspective, the specific example of the late twentieth century was only the latest incarnation of the generic American case. Impressive social diversity, along with a peculiar governmental structure, made democratization and market-making compatible, now as in the past. A society with numerous and diverse groups, holding amorphous and cross-cutting value preferences, would naturally acquire a politics featuring numerous and diverse social coalitions, around amorphous and cross-cutting policy issues. If its governmental structure was then continually reformed, seeking to *reflect* this diversity rather than to countervail it and produce some sort of programmatic response regardless, the result was likely to be a 'natural' compatibilty between such democratization and a tendency towards market-making.

Probably, the absence of uniform social experiences and of widespread interpersonal bonds in such a society made a turn to the market (rather than to government) a logical strategy for pursuing what would elsewhere be 'policy' wishes. Individual members of such a society were likely to prefer to be allowed to pursue their own preferences in a societal 'marketplace', rather than risk having too many (non)preferences imposed upon them by others, through government.

When their demands *were* pressed on government, however, especially if its structure was sufficiently democratized to provide some point which would register those demands, three general outcomes were surely likely. The first was stalemate; the second was a consciously narrow and localized policy resonse; and the third was some national response, followed shortly by reconsideration in all but the most consensual cases. When that is an accurate description, of course, then democratization and market-making should, naturally and logically, be linked.

Applications of 'the American Model'

Populism *and* individualism, democratization *and* market-making, these can be linked in practice, as they obviously are in American society; they can be linked in theory as well, through historical and contemporary explanations for their conjunction. Accordingly, they can plausibly serve as central themes—diagnostic themes—for American society, for an 'American model'. That being the case, they ought also to be reflected in the smaller and more focused, operational realms of that society. If these are the dominant themes characterizing the major realms of American society, and if they are united and sustained through a continuing American culture, then they ought to be applied and reflected—further 'operationalized'—in additional operating realms of that society.

Prime among these, both by virtue of its importance *and* of its frequently asserted role in reflecting (and sustaining) an 'American exceptionalism', is education. Education, especially higher education, can potentially play this role not so much because these other realms (politics, economics, religion, culture) are 'the shapers' and it is 'the shaped'. Obviously, once in place, an educational system plays a crucial role in *shaping* subsequent developments in many other realms. Rather, the educational realm can play this analytic role because it is less global than these others and its characteristics can thus be specified more concretely, and, in turn, because it *must* both reflect and transmit themes from these other realms—if they are indeed as dominant as they appear to be. As a major 'applied realm', education should thus reflect, operationalize, transmit, *and shape* the four grand themes of 'the American model'.

Distinctive elements in American higher education—sharply distinctive elements, as Martin Trow rightly points out—are not difficult to locate. The very size of the American effort at higher education remains unique among the developed nations; so does its internal variety. Its organizational structure is distinctive, with lay boards, strong presidents, and a flat faculty hierarchy. Its relationship to students is distinctive, both in what they can demand and in the services it aspires to provide. Its links to the society outside, finally, are distinctive as well, through fund-raising, research, and service provision. Cumulated, these elements only reinforce a sense of distinctiveness. Indeed, this is a realm where the United States remains noticeably different not just from Europe, but also from the emerging Asian states.

On the other hand, as Trow goes on to note, there are incipient signs of efforts at *convergence* among the developed nations. If this is a realm where Europe and Asia join in differing from the United States, it is also one where they appear to be 'Americanizing', through growth and diversification, through ties to other kinds of post-secondary education, through development of strong administrative leadership, and so forth. All of which only suggests, for higher education as for the other realms under investigation, that the key question remains the one 'in the middle', the question of whether there are larger clusters of traits which remain distinctive. Are the four major themes embodied within American higher education? Are they, indeed, central to its description—and comprehension? Can it, in turn, further validate them?

Evident incarnations of each of these four major themes are in fact not hard to find in the realm of higher education. Populism, for example, is immediately apparent in that most fundamental American proposition about higher education, the one which gives rise to much of the rest: that such education is a 'good thing', that as much as possible should be available, and that as *many* as possible should be encouraged to seek it. Yet populism is also inherent in the major concrete elements of the educational system. Thus it is present in the main educational programme itself, in an insistence on a 'liberal' or 'general' education for all undergraduates, an approach which seeks integration in a diverse educational population, of course, but also one which helps bring as many students as possible *into* college. Yet populism is also embodied in the very institutional structure of higher education, as with the generation of so-called 'community colleges', created to see that there is indeed wide access to higher education, in a setting which nevertheless reflects local values.

Not surprisingly, by now, an infusion of populism throughout the realm of higher education does not appear to be at the expense of individualism as a further characteristic. Thus within that huge educational establishment, there is also a huge variety of educational alternatives. Seen from one side, and despite a general commitment to a 'liberal education', colleges and universities manage to project strikingly diverse identities, differentiating themselves by academic stringency, substantive focus, career orientation, teaching or research emphasis, sacred or secular ties, and so on. Seen from the other side, despite a general quest for a 'college education', students are encouraged to 'shop'—the first of many market-making metaphors—for their individually preferred arrangements, including not just the main educational product but ancillary services and even recreational opportunities. In this interaction, colleges can maintain high individual autonomy in turn, subject to the ability to get various 'constituencies' (a democratizing metaphor) to respond to their offers.

Within American culture, the combination of populism and individualism was responsible for a peculiarly American definition of 'equality', implying social but not material levelling. Again, that definition, proceeding from that same combination, resurfaces in the realm of higher education. In the case of the leading clientele for colleges and universities, the students, the combination of the popular drive for a college education with individual autonomy in the choice of educational packages means that the widespread social categorization of 'college student' can coincide with a situation where some degrees will ultimately be much more facilitative of material attainments than others—but where the market, not the university system, will sort that out. In the case of the faculty, the result is even more stereotypical. Within individual institutions, the hierarchy of positions really is quite flat, and most individuals can expect to reach its top rung. At the same time, faculty members will be rewarded on the basis of their individual performance, though what this really means is that most will have to move *among institutions* in order to achieve material benefits from their formally similar status.

Incarnations of democratization are as easily located. In a summary sense, democratization is inherent in the need—and willingness—to be broadly linked to the larger society. The general means for this, the variety of sources of support for institutions of higher education (tuition, grants and gifts, public and private research support, subventions from several different levels of government) manages to keep these institutions simultaneously responsive to an array of constituencies and yet buffered from the wishes of any one. But the same situation is also recapitulated structurally. The simplest and most direct embodiment of this is the nearly ubiquitous 'lay board'. Even in the public (and more so in the private) institutions, such a board is charged, from one side, with linking the educational institution to its external constituencies. From the other side, a president actually manages his institution *if* he or she can maintain the support of a majority of the lay board.

Market-making, in some sense, also lies behind all of these, often quite explicitly. One of the obvious manifestations of being 'the first new nation' was that the commercial market actually predated the establishment of institutions of higher education in the United States. What resulted, for the composite sector of higher education, almost asks to be cast in market terms: competition, of course, for students, faculty, and financing; but also diversity of academic product; responsiveness to almost any organized interest which can conceivably pay the bill; institutional autonomy for decisions about placement in the larger market; and a mixed and shifting array of sources of external finance. Yet what resulted *inside* these institutions can perhaps best be portrayed in the same way. An elective system, modular courses, credit accumulation, and transfer based on a transcript—these really are, to borrow from Peter Temin on economic history, the 'American System' of higher education. They are the 'interchangeable parts' of a national system which is simultaneously autonomous and localized.

Again, the *link* between democratization and market-making is as direct and comfortable here as anywhere. Indeed, the single most distinguishing characteristic of American higher education, its massive size, is crucially underpinned by this particular link. The size of the American cohort seeking higher education is determined (and kept large) by a constant search for demands in society (in the form of potential students) and in the constant search for ways to meet those demands— the mass market producing democratic access. Unsurprisingly, once more, there is an accompanying attitude which is both product and encouragement of this tendency. For if Americans endorse the notion that higher education is a good thing *per se*, and if widespread college education thus meets a democratic standard, they also accept the view that *competition* is the best way to gain more of it, and more variety within it, thereby endorsing a crucial role for the 'educational marketplace'.

Higher education suggests, then, that the four main themes running implicitly through all these essays—the four continuing characteristics of American culture—can indeed be found, most concretely, in one of the major applied realms of American society. American higher education is certainly a concrete embodiment of populism, individualism, democratization, and market-making—and especially of the *conjoint* presence of those four grand characteristics. In turn, because they are so deeply embedded in the American system of higher education, that system must provide a further, powerful means of transmitting them from era to era.

In a different sense, of course, higher education is only one, albeit a major one, of the 'public policies' of the United States. In that light, higher education also emphasizes the way in which what is effectively a 'public policy' can result from a decision to leave one or another policy realm to the marketplace or, even more commonly in the American context, from a decision to *mix* attention to any given realm not just among various (sub) governments but *between* various governments and various private sectors. Indeed, the United States appears as leading evidence for the proposition that an inclination to have less of direct governmental provision is not necessarily an inclination to have less of the intended policy product—as, most dramatically, in the case of higher education.

It is difficult to move from these specific policy realms to a total picture—an aggregation—of public policies in a society, and not just because these policies can effectively be found in many (and mixed) locations. It is also nearly impossible to aggregate the amount of money spent on orthodox public works, for example, with the practical extent of various civil liberties. It is additionally difficult to construct relevant aggregates so that they can embody (and isolate) the influences of populism, individualism, and their institutional associates. Nevertheless, an attempt to operate even at this highly but still partially aggregated level, at least in the hands of a skilled practitioner like Richard Rose, manages to drive the analysis back to a middle level of abstraction— where the four central themes of these essays reside, and where arguments about American exceptionalism must be pitched in our time.

From one side, such policy aggregates, even when defined narrowly, in terms of governmental spending, highlight the problems with an approach to exceptionalism which focuses on the collection of idiosyncratic distinctions. American public policy *is* clearly distinctive on numerous such measures, just as it clearly is *not* distinctive on numerous others. From the other side, these policy aggregates are even more effective in highlighting the problems with an approach to exceptionalism which focuses instead on sole deviation from some otherwise universal process. Indeed, an investigation by way of the American case actually undermines the likelihood of finding *any* exceptionalism so defined—principally because the universe of nations is so dispersed as to undermine the possibility of any single, general, developmental model. Accordingly, if these policy aggregates move the focus 'up', away from mere idiosyncratic detail, they also move the focus 'down', away from deviations from a general pattern. The argument moves inevitably, then, towards a broad theoretical centre, towards a 'middle level' of abstraction where the concepts of populism, individualism, democratization, and market-making naturally reside.[8]

The Fortunes of American Exceptionalism

Approaching the notion of American exceptionalism through four main conceptual themes, of course, not only locates the analysis at a level where it would appear, theoretically, that it ought to be. This approach also appears to offer a sufficiently precise focus to prevent arguments

[8] A framework for thinking about 'middle-level theory' more generally is Robert K. Merton, 'On Sociological Theories of the Middle Range', in Merton, *Social Theory and Social Structure*, enl. edn. (New York: The Free Press, 1968), 39–72.

over the actuality of American exceptionalism from slipping away into ambiguity. Yet such an approach has three other, closing virtues— over and beyond the virtues inherent in validating these four grand characteristics as central, even diagnostic, features of a continuing American experience. First, this approach permits the addressing of American exceptionalism without having to resolve every associated substantive puzzle. Second, this approach still allows the analyst to drive back towards higher levels of abstraction. And third, such an approach establishes an initial focus for *subsequent* returns to the question of American exceptionalism.

In the first of these additional virtues, an approach to the American experience by way of these four organizing concepts allows substantial generalizations and arguments without having to resolve all the substantive questions which have become appended to the *issue* of American exceptionalism. For example, one of the persistently asserted peculiarities in the evolution of American society is the manner in which the United States appears as the model for development and modernity in some regards, while resembling consensually underdeveloped and unmodern societies in others. In religion, to take only one such instance, what has struck many observers as 'exceptional' is the fact that the most economically developed society has not been powerfully secularized in the process of development.

A whole series of hypotheses could follow from this perception alone. This might, of course, be what makes the United States truly exceptional, in the sense of defying the full 'normal' development curve. Alternatively, to echo both Andrew Greeley and Richard Rose, because the United States is *not* particularly distinctive from the world as a whole in many respects, the peculiarity may lie with the countries of Northern Europe and Scandinavia which, in *their* exceptional evolution, skewed the perceptions of scholars about a dominant model. Or perhaps again, all 'developing' societies adhere to one general model, all 'stabilized' societies to another, with the United States being exceptional only in the sense of being consistently misclassified into the second rather than the (appropriate) first category.

An approach to the question of American exceptionalism by way of this theoretical 'middle level'—by way of a small set of central concepts which gather numerous individual findings and span large societal realms at the same time—escapes the need to resolve that question. If what makes the United States distinctive is the central and continuing place of populism, individualism, democratization, and market-making—and especially of their conjoint and reinforcing character—then that *is* the basis for sustaining an argument about American exceptionalism. Moreover, it constitutes such a basis quite apart from any 'normal' developmental trajectory or 'Scandinavian model'. This is *not* to say that the question of the way these dominant empirical themes interact with (and support or challenge) these other hypotheses is uninteresting or unworthy of further investigation. Rather, this is merely to say that the essence of American exceptionalism does not require the resolving of this—related and interesting—set of arguments before it can be asserted.

A quite different virtue of this approach is that it not only escapes being trapped in certain prior, specific, substantive arguments; it also permits moving on to a considerably higher level of abstraction. Populism and individualism, democratization and market-making— these major themes do appear both to continue across American history and to cohere within the realms which they, in effect, link. Their mutual and continuing distinctiveness thus makes its bid as the central datum for arguments about 'American exceptionalism'. Yet it would certainly be possible to drive them further. For example, it is entirely reasonable to argue that what these themes really add up to, most fundamentally and at that higher level of abstraction, is one particular version of what has come to be known as 'the civil society'.

Such a society features substantial resources, along with substantial activities, which are not just outside the realm (and even the reach) of the state, but which can intermittently be turned to restraining or disciplining it. The notion itself emerged in a (European) context where it stood in obvious, theoretical contraposition to the notion of a self-conscious, national 'state'. American history, by contrast, unfolded in a context where the notion of 'the government' (effectively 'the government of the day') was common enough, but 'the state' was not; the nation thus developed for much of its history not just in general ignorance of, but without any felt need for, ◢ me further distinction between 'state' and 'society'. Indeed, if the nation was frequently anti-statist, and if governmental programmes moved back and forth between levels of government and even between government and the market-place, notions about 'the state' and its alternatives seemed largely beside the point.

Nevertheless, the United States is, at bottom, not just a generic 'civil society', but perhaps, as Daniel Bell notes, the archetypal one. At least, it is not just that the United States has tended to show a preference for anti-bureaucratic responses to those problems where government must inevitably provide the solution. Nor even that the United States has tended to show a preference for devolving 'policy solutions' onto the marketplace rather than government whenever possible. Rather, it is even the case that those who want to understand the 'latest developments' in American life are reliably well advised to look to the society, not the government, in seeking answers to their enquiry.

On the other hand, forcing a generalization to this level has costs as well as benefits. Classifying the United States as a civil society should not be a substitute for noting the central and continuing place of four other, somewhat less abstract themes. Calling the United States a civil society does not imply, either logically or empirically, that civil society in turn requires populism, individualism, democratization, and market-making, together, for its existence. In theoretical terms, that combination is so distinctive that its requirement would, in effect, radically devalue the notion of civil society as an analytic category. More concretely, it appears possible to retain—even to shift towards— far greater use of the market than of government, along with far more emphasis on society than on the state, without requiring the introduction of, for example, populism. Aggregate statistics on the changing relationship between nations and their public policies would also seem to affirm this concrete possibility, through what Rose describes as the (spreading) 'American Pacific model'.

In the end, the distinctive and organizing themes remain the 'big four'—populism, individualism, democratization, and market-making. Their historical persistence appears impressive; so does their contemporary reach, across societal sectors, 'back' to culture itself, and 'forward' to applied policy realms. An argument about 'American exceptionalism', then, can certainly be mounted around these— conjoint—themes, and *any* such argument is likely to partake (at least implicitly) of their substance. What remains is only the question of where these themes are likely to be in another generation or two. Hidden inside that question, of course, is the further issue of whether they will continue, by that time, to look as distinctive.

Where will the substance itself go? There seems to be no point in trying to answer in detail. The detailed worlds of the federal, the Jacksonian, the progressive, or the post-war eras—to skip across the surface of American history—were all noticeably different; so, presumably, will be the world of the twenty-first century. A major factor uniting these other periods, however, was the possibility of reinterpreting period details around four grand and continuing conceptual themes. That does mean, at a minimum, that these themes should still serve as an initial organizing framework, that the search for *their* detailed incarnation in a new historical era should serve as an initial, simplifying device. The four themes have arguably surfaced in every one of those preceding eras; their place in the twenty-first century will at least be the first analytic item for investigation.

But will these themes themselves—in their mutual presence, linkage, and reinforcement—seem as distinctive in another generation as they (still) do today? Again, if a detailed answer to the first question cannot reasonably be hazarded, a directly supportable answer to the second is literally impossible. Except, perhaps, for those who answer on the basis of extended historical continuities, of the continued resurfacing of major themes from particular (and otherwise strikingly varied) historical contexts—for whom the answer, or at least the hypothesis, is likely to be 'yes'. There are evident cautionary notes for such an affirmation in the essays of Bell, Temin, and Rose, to the effect that if larger differences fade, lesser ones are likely at least to blur. Yet there is a different kind of caution in the essays of Lipset, Wildavsky, and Trow, to the effect that even if other nations move towards this peculiar conjunction of traits, as observed in the world of the early 1990s—however unlikely that prospect itself may be—the United States will also surely continue to evolve. What these four grand themes implied, in their operational detail, was different in the late nineteenth century than in the late twentieth, even though thematic continuity was their most striking implication. Why should what they imply in the early twenty-first century not be different, at least in its details, as well—thereby sustaining, by reinventing, an 'American exceptionalism'?

Index